IS IT R

MERIDIAN

Crossing Aesthetics

Werner Hamacher
& David E. Wellbery

Editors

Stanford
University
Press

———————

Stanford
California

IS IT RIGHTEOUS TO BE?

Interviews with Emmanuel Levinas

Edited by Jill Robbins

Stanford University Press
Stanford, California

"Discussion Following 'Transcendence and Intelligibility'" was
originally published in French as "Entretien avec Emmanuel Levinas"
in *Transcendance et intelligibilité* ©1984, Labor et Fides.

Support for the translation was provided by the French Ministry
of Culture.

Printed in the United States of America
on acid-free, archival-quality paper

Library of Congress Cataloging-in-Publication Data
Levinas, Emmanuel.
    [Interviews. English. Selections]
    Is it righteous to be? : interviews with Emmanuel Levinas /
edited by Jill Robbins.
    p.   cm.   (Meridian)
    Includes bibliographical references.
    ISBN 0-8047-4308-8 (alk. paper)—ISBN 0-8047-4309-6 (pbk. :
alk. paper)
    1. Ontology. 2. Ethics. I. Robbins, Jill. II. Title.
III. Meridian (Stanford, Calif.)
  B2430.L484 A513 2001
  194—dc21   2001040030

Original Printing 2001

Last figure below indicates year of this printing:
10   09   08   07

Typeset by BookMatters in 11/13 Adobe Garamond

Contents

Acknowledgments

The completion of this book would have been impossible without the tireless labors of Andrew Schmitz and Benjamin Friedlander. They generously gave their time and expertise, reviewed with me the entire manuscript for consistency and readability, and helped with the scholarly apparatus. I am enormously grateful to them. In addition to the translators—Andrew Schmitz, Marcus Coelen, Thomas Loebel, Bettina Bergo, Alin Cristian, Michael Smith and Maureen Gedney—I would like to thank John Llewelyn, Kenneth Dauber, and Bronia Karst, who read portions of the manuscript and offered invaluable suggestions. Thanks to Nicole Martello for editorial assistance and to Aaron Alter for technical support.

IS IT RIGHTEOUS TO BE?

... s Vous, Monsieur!"

er the first place in everything. From the
en door right up to the disposition—hardly
ands it—to die for the other. In this attitude
sal of the normal order of things, the natural
ence in being.

view with François Poirié

nuel Levinas that follow, ceding one's place
f the kind of gesture that Levinas terms *eth*-
st yield" invariably denotes "my place in the
ing to the phrase of Pascal that Levinas
ion of the whole earth." *Place* also denotes
term for man insofar as he asks the ques-
ig of beings. Levinas asks: "Is not . . . the
rpation or violence with respect to the
iesy?"). To cede one's place to the other is,
a primordial level—the self's essential ten-
ere" in its being, it is also to assert the another to Heidegger's question of the being

... between Levinas's sense of ethics—as interruption on a
primordial level—and its usual sense as right conduct, a system of moral
precepts, or any particular morality, may be apparent. Levinas's descriptions of the encounter with the other take place on a level more originary
than the empirical. Jacques Derrida alludes to this transcendental motif in
Levinas's philosophy when, in his 1963 "Violence and Metaphysics," he
proposes that Levinas gives us not an ethics but "an Ethics of ethics."[1]
Levinas specifies that the proper form of the question is not "Is my life
righteous?" (a question that would belong in effect to the derivative sense
of ethics, insofar as it already presupposes the being of the questioner),
but rather, "Is it righteous to be?" ("Reality Has Weight"). "Do I have a
right to be?" he asks ("Who Shall Not Prophesy?"). "Does our very being

already legitimate our wish to be? It is . . . a matter of . . . finding reasons for being, for meriting being" ("The Philosopher and Death").

Within Levinas's description of positive responsibility, the apparent continuum between a simple act of courtesy and total self-sacrifice, or dying for the other, may be surprising. There is indeed something excessive about responsibility in Levinas's account, not just because he names it in extravagant fashion, using terms like *obsession, hostage, passivity, persecution,* and *trauma,* but because it is limitless: I am never done with my responsibilities. Yet a similar continuum can be found—in a negative fashion—in Levinas's interpretation of the interdiction that the face of the other (*le visage d'autrui*) addresses to me. Not primarily a thing seen or intended, the face in Levinas's descriptions is precisely that which divests itself of its plastic form. To encounter a face *as* a face is to encounter a nakedness, a mortality, a destitution, "a being face forward precisely as if it were exposed to some threat at point-blank range" ("The Philosopher and Death"). Exposed to death (and to murder as well), the face is defenselessness itself. But the face (and this is one of the paradoxical features of Levinas's account) commands me *in* its very defenselessness. It orders "thou shalt not kill." To encounter the other thus, by way of an interdiction, puts my spontaneity and my—ultimately murderous—freedom into question. This is accomplished as shame, a structure which Levinas likens to an "intentionality in reverse" (*Totality and Infinity,* 84).

Hence in addition to the biblical prohibition against murder, the phrase "thou shalt not kill" announces, in more general terms, the "arrest" of the self's habitual tendency, the cessation of all possibility and power (expressed in the single word *pouvoir*). "Thou shalt not kill" announces the im-possibility of murdering the other insofar as my freedom is converted to service, as Theo de Boer explains it.[2] Murder is also impossible because the other's ethical resistance is one "no finite power can restrict."[3] "Thou shalt not kill" has, arguably, in Levinas's account an enlarged sense: killing ultimately includes the omission of any act that could alleviate the other's distress. He elaborates: "There are a variety of ways to kill. It isn't always just a matter of killing, say, with a knife. The everyday killing with a good conscience, the killing in all innocence—there is such a thing as well!" ("Being-Toward-Death"). It is as if the habitual economy were all about killing, as if *not* to cede one's place to the other were to kill, "as if the very imposition of [a being's] existence were already to jeopardize someone's life" (Poirié). The prohibition, then, is not merely negative;

it is precisely the paradigm for positive responsibility. Levinas glosses it: "'Thou shalt not kill' signifies . . . 'thou shalt do *everything* in order that the other live'" ("Discussion"). "'Thou shalt not kill' signifies 'you shall defend the life of the other . . . you will answer for the other!'" ("In the Name of the Other"). Responsibility is thus an incessant *answer*ability for and response to the other.

The interviews with Levinas collected here, conducted by diverse interviewers in diverse contexts, took place between 1982 and 1992 (the final one three years before his death, on December 25, 1995). They are situated, then, at the close of a sixty-year career. While many of Levinas's themes, such as his analysis of murder, hearken back to the mature ethical philosophy of the 1961 *Totality and Infinity* and to key texts from the late 1940s, his formulations about responsibility are invariably marked by the distinctive idiom of the later work, represented by the 1974 *Otherwise than Being*. *Otherwise than Being* radicalizes and exceeds *Totality and Infinity*'s project. The ethics that *Totality and Infinity* defines as the putting into question of the self in the presence of the other becomes, in the later work, a putting into question of the very closure of the philosophical discourse itself. *Otherwise than Being* seeks to depart from an ontological language, to discursively pass over to what is other than being, even if such an effort always risks falling into a being otherwise, that is, into a modality of being.

The later work that sets itself this formidable task necessarily has a certain opacity—both of language and of the themes treated. It is also associated with a specific terminology, two examples of which are already in play. The often-iterated phrase, "perseverance in being," alludes to the *conatus essendi*, a term used by Spinoza in his *Ethics* (part 3, prop. 6), which may be rendered as "the essential tendency for a being to persist in its being." Levinas characteristically (and not unproblematically) applies the term to Heidegger, and transforms it into an anti-Heideggerian formula. Levinas even formulates his project as a whole as an effort "to imagine an anthropology different from that which starts from the *conatus essendi*" ("The Philosopher and Death"). The term *holiness* (*sainteté*) also punctuates these interviews. Used interchangeably with the term *sacrifice*, *holiness* refers to a being's withdrawal of its interestedness in being. Since, as Levinas puts it at the beginning of *Otherwise than Being*, "*esse* is *inter-esse*," holiness is its beyond-being or "otherwise than being" (*Otherwise than Being*, 4).

In spite of the differences between the later work and the mature philosophy—in which the normal order of things which needs to be challenged is now the *conatus* rather than the habitual economy—the common threads of ethics as interruption (*Otherwise than Being*, 43, 56, 89, 101) and the figure of reversal or inversion (*Otherwise than Being*, 12, 47, 70, 101, 107) are nonetheless apparent. So is the fact that ethics happens in and as language: "Après vous, Monsieur!" "This little effort of courtesy is also an access to the face! . . . Is not the first word *bonjour*? As simple as *bonjour*!" (Poirié). A "*bonjour* presupposed by every *cogito* and by all self-reflection" ("Proximity and the Other"). Here, as in the account that Levinas provides in *Totality and Infinity*, language (and generosity) are the sole exceptions to the self's habitual economy, in that they maintain and affirm asymmetry and separation.

What kind of language is this that accomplishes the nontotalizing relation to the other? The ethical language is primordial: it precedes and "underlies" all discourse and communication (Poirié). It has neither a semantic function (that is, it is not referential or denotative) nor can it be conceived as a semiosis, which as a system of referrals within immanence would destroy transcendence. Ethical language is interlocutionary; it never speaks about the other but only to him or her. Its essential feature is "interpellation" (*Totality and Infinity*, 69). "Language," asserts Levinas, "is always addressed to the other" ("The Usefulness of Insomnia"). In the later work, Levinas invariably calls ethical language the "saying." The saying is speech *before* it congeals in the said, which absorbs alterity into thematization; it is a mobile orientation toward the addressee.

The "interpellation of the I by the face" ("Discussion") inaugurates a "conversation" that is not a dialogue in any usual sense, as it is characterized by neither reciprocity nor recognition. Levinas calls it "a conversation [*entretien*] which proposes the world. This proposition is held over [*se tient entre*] two points which do not constitute a totality" (*Totality and Infinity*, 96). This conversation is not to be confused with the image of two already constituted poles between which speech appears (which would allow the relation to be viewed synoptically). As Maurice Blanchot elaborates it, this strange speech is "beyond the reach of the one who says it as much as of the one who hears it. It is between us [*entre nous*], it holds itself between us [*se tient entre*] and the conversation is the approach on the basis of this between."[4] Such is the interpellation, literally an interruption by speaking.

In this opening conversation, the *fact* of speaking is more important that any word or content. Ultimately, the primordial conversation is contentless, or prior to content (and for this reason, ethical language is not something that one can ever claim to be taking up). As the previous analysis of "thou shalt not kill" suggested, the other's command is not necessarily a categorial prescription. It is more like what Jean-François Lyotard calls "a prescription that there be prescriptions."[5] There is, in other words, something deliberately general and empty about the other's speaking command. The same observation can be made about the rare examples of ethical language that Levinas provides throughout his writings. The examples—which include "Bonjour" (Poirié; "Proximity"); "Shalom" ("Vocation"); "Après vous Monsieur" (Poirié; "Vocation"; "In The Name of the Other"; *Otherwise than Being*, 117); "Here I am" ("The Philosopher and Death"; "The Other, Utopia, Justice"; *Otherwise than Being*, 114)—are in fact empty bits of everyday language in which Levinas glimpses transcendence.

If the examples of ethical language that Levinas provides are few, one may observe, similarly, that Levinas gives us very few examples *for* the ethical in his work, as if it could not be translated into empiricism. Specific ethical prescriptions, all of which draw on the resources of the biblical diction, include turning one's cheek to the smiter (*Otherwise than Being*, 49, III; *Collected Philosophical Papers*, 146), tearing the bread from one's mouth and giving it to the other (*Otherwise than Being*, 55–56, 64, 72, 74, 77, 79), assuaging thirst or giving to drink, clothing the naked, feeding the hungry (Poirié). Like ceding one's place to the other, these examples would seem to be located at the intersection between the transcendental and the empirical. In Levinas's interpretation, "après vous, Monsieur" means "ontological courtesy, being-for-the-other!" ("Vocation"). He states specifically that the condition of saying "après vous, monsieur" is my being hostage to the other (*Otherwise than Being*, 117). In a manner comparable to the Heideggerian discovery of "finite transcendentals," exemplified in the Heideggerian analysis of moods, Levinas indeed locates a certain transcendence in the factical.

But Levinas also makes explicit precisely where he departs from *Being and Time*'s descriptions. In "Dying-for," a paper first delivered in 1987 at the Collège International de Philosophie [reprinted in *Entre Nous*], in an argument which is in the background of a number of these interviews, and which he revisits in detail in "The Other, Utopia, and Justice," Levinas formulates his reservations. At issue is Heidegger's association of *Eigent-lichkeit* (authenticity) with *Jemeinigkeit* (mineness) ("The Other, Utopia, and Justice"). This association is first apparent in section 4 of *Being and Time*, where, in Heidegger's formulation, "*Dasein* is a being that... in its very being that being is an issue for it," a formulation to which Levinas refers repeatedly. According to Heidegger, in *Dasein's* concern for its being, the structure of care (*Sorge*) comes into view, just as it does in *Dasein's* being "ahead-of-itself," its potentiality for an authentic standing before it-self in being-unto-death (section 41). When in section 47 of *Being and Time*, Heidegger treats the possibility of experiencing the death of others, he asserts that the death of the other in no way gives access to an authen-tic being-unto-death: "Death is in every case mine." He discounts the au-thentic possibility of *Dasein's* going beyond its own being-unto-death, of *dying-for* the other: "No one can take the other's dying away from him. But that always means to sacrifice oneself for the other in some definite affair. Such dying-for can never signify that the other has thus had his death taken away from him in even the slightest degree."⁶

Contra Heidegger, who emphasizes that everyone dies for himself, Levinas asserts: "I am responsible for the death of the other" (Poirié); "Dying for the other can concern me more than my own death" ("The Other, Utopia, Justice"); "The human consists precisely in opening itself to the death of the other, in being preoccupied with his death" ("The Philosopher and Death"). For Levinas, concern over the death of the other *precedes* the concern over authentic death and the concern for being. Thus while Heidegger does indeed broach, in section 26 of *Being and Time*, the possibility of solicitude (*Fürsorge*) as an expression of being with others, such solicitude must always, in his account, first come up against a stumbling block, which is the inauthenticity of the "They" (*das Man*). However, solicitude in Levinas's new understanding of it is not merely to be grafted onto being-with (*Mitsein*). It is not conditioned by being. At stake is not a being-with (*avec*) but a for-the-other (*pour-l'autre*). Every-thing that in Levinas's later work falls under the name *substitution* is at work in this "for-the-other." Levinas formulates the difference between solicitude in Heidegger's and his own sense as an alternative between (1) *Eigentlichkeit*, thought in terms of "the unalterable 'mine' of the human," of *Jemeinigkeit*, of everything proper, in its own right, and (2) the human devotion to the other, "the excessiveness of sacrifice" (*Entre Nous*, 211–12). In short, the relation to the other in sacrifice may not have an authentic ontological significance, but it has an ethical one. It is "a breakthrough of the human putting into question the ontological necessities and the persistence of a being that perseveres in its being" ("The Philosopher and Death"); it "indicates precisely a beyond-ontology or before-ontology" (*Entre Nous*, 217). Like ceding one's place to the other, dying-for is "the very miracle of the human in being," when "the human overwhelms the inhuman in being, always preoccupied with itself" ("Vocation").

Ceding one's place to the other is, for Levinas, an "extraordinary" event ("Vocation"), by which he means that it is an exception to the natural order of things: "We are all enchained to ourselves, in the grips of our concern to be, which Heidegger summarized by saying, at issue for a being—*Dasein*—is this being itself. . . . Within this tension lies the source of egoism. . . . And yet it does happen that a man dies for another, that the being of the other is dearer to him than his own. This is only possible within the order of the human, and it is found nowhere else. 'Après vous, Monsieur,' as it is said in French manners" ("In the Name of the Other"). In short, ethics hardly ever happens, but if it does happen, the human is the only possible site for it. The "extraordinary and everyday event of my responsibility"(*Otherwise than Being*, 10) is at once exceptional and ubiquitous in factical speech.

To be the other's *hostage*, in Levinas's terminology, is to be obligated to an immemorial debt that I do not remember contracting. This obligation, which is not voluntary, holds me to a condition of passivity, like that of creation, where I am neither the author of myself nor self-contemporaneous. Moreover, I am obligated, in Levinas's frequent phrase, "straightaway" (*d'emblée*). This is to say that the obligation is immediate and does not go by way of the theoretical. Responsibility as Levinas conceives it does not begin in freedom, and this is one of the ways in which Levinas's account goes against the grain of the traditional philosophemes of ethics. He explains: "Heteronomy is somehow stronger than autonomy here, except that this heteronomy is not servitude or bondage" ("Philosophy, Justice, and Love"). He also characterizes his ethical thought as "a rehabilitation of heteronomy" ("Discussion"). Levinas's 1968 text, "The Temptation of Temptation" (from *Nine Talmudic Readings*) had already underscored that the constative origin of freedom cannot be thought in terms of freedom.

In addition to a critique of freedom, Levinas's ethical thought contains a critique of identity as well. For the responsibility which Levinas describes as so imperiously incumbent upon me is not necessarily something that a self or a subject can do. Turning one's cheek to the smiter is not an act that one performs, Levinas explains (*Otherwise than Being*, 111). Sacrifice is not a will for sacrifice (*Otherwise than Being*, 55). Since the encounter with the other puts the self and its *pouvoir* radically into question, the ethical response to the other who puts me in question is not a response-ability at all; there is *in*ability there. How, then, can this responsibility be? Levinas describes it in paradoxical terms: it draws from "the resources—or the poverty—of my uniqueness as an I" ("Being-for-the-Other"). To respond to the other is, as it were, to dig deep into one's poverty, in a hollowing out that allows for neither the self nor its initiative. Levinas's ethics become legible only within a certain experience of impossibility.

This impossibility is only underscored by the ontological insecurity of the ethical event. Recall Levinas's assertions: yielding to the other is "hardly possible [*à peine possible*], yet holiness demands it" (Poirié). "This [dying for] is only possible within the order of the human [*Cela se peut dans l'humain*]" ("In the Name of the Other"). In his 1980 "At This Very Moment in This Work Here I Am" Derrida draws attention to the doubleness of Levinas's syntax at such textual junctures, a syntax which seems to introduce deliberately a precariousness into his ethical discourse. "This is only possible within the human" seems to adhere to the classical form of a statement on the condition of possibility ("it has not been rendered possible except by way of the human"), but it also allows for a second, other sense ("it has been rendered only possible, that is, probable"). The ethical event is, in Derrida's words, "menaced by its very rigor."[7] But this is one of the risks that Levinas's quasi-transcendental philosophy deliberately runs. As an "Ethics of ethics," Levinas's philosophy seeks not to issue particular ethical directives, but to change the way in which philosophy is written. He willingly characterizes his ethics as "utopic" ("the ideal of holiness utopically commands our being") (Poirié), which he means in the more literal sense of the word. Without place, not in the world, holiness is "a no-place prior to the there of being-there, prior to the *Da* of *Dasein*, prior to that place in the sun that Pascal feared was the prototype and beginning of the usurpation of the whole world" (*Entre Nous*, 216).

⌒

Due to the range of topics covered in these interviews, I have divided the volume into three parts. Part 2 is concerned with the ethical philosophy and is largely continuous with Levinas's formal philosophical publications. As in those works, Levinas tends to assume the reader's familiarity with the history of philosophy. He engages frequently not only texts of Heidegger, but those of Husserl (his studies with these two giants in Freiburg in 1923–24 are a frequent point of reference in the interviews). There are condensed comments on Plato, Pascal, Hobbes, Kant, Bergson, and Merleau-Ponty which are of interest. Although nowhere do we find in Levinas a systematic destruction in the Heideggerian style of the history of philosophy from the vantage point of the forgetting of the ethical, we can perhaps begin to envision—especially with regard to Hobbes and Kant—what a "Levinasian" critical retrieval would look like. The decisive place granted to Franz Rosenzweig continues a meditation Levinas began thirty-five years earlier at the Colloques des Intellectuels Juifs de Langue Française. At that time Levinas credited Rosenzweig with discovering the ontological structures of Jewish ritual life and marked his debt to this "father" of Jewish philosophy. At several junctures, Levinas also differentiates his philosophy from that of Martin Buber, whose I-Thou relation Levinas sees as too formal and reciprocal. Parts 1 and 3 of this volume are devoted respectively to biographical—personal and intellectual—and theological questions. This not to say that the interviews that fall under these rubrics are devoid of philosophical interest. Nearly half of the long interview with François Poirié with which the volume commences is concerned with philosophical matters. "On Jewish Philosophy" does not even assume that religion *has* a relation to philosophy, although it finds resources in its heterogeneity to philosophy.

The interviews as a whole help to clarify Levinas's place in French thought. While Levinas has been known to serious philosophers in the European tradition for a long time, he has come to the attention of literary critics more recently, primarily through the writings of Derrida and Blanchot. The outstanding feature of Levinas's intellectual life was his sixty-year friendship with Maurice Blanchot, which became a "friendship" between their two oeuvres as well. Levinas wrote four essays on Blanchot, collected in *Proper Names/On Maurice Blanchot*. Two of Blanchot's books, *The Infinite Conversation* and *The Writing of the Disaster*, are written as it were under the sign of Levinas. In conversation with Poirié, Levinas recollects his initial meeting with Blanchot at university and the nature of the man. Georges Bataille, himself a central interlocutor in Blanchot's meditations on friendship, wrote an engaged review of

Levinas's early work. However, despite the "communication" which may ensue between their philosophies, Levinas and Bataille seem to have held each other at arm's length. Levinas did meet Sartre a few times after the war; his comments about him here are largely anecdotal. When an interviewer asks about structuralism, Levinas avers that he is not "tempted" by it (Poirié). Of Lévi-Strauss, apart from saying that "no norms for thinking followed" from him ("Being-Toward-Death"), he confines himself to polemical references,. A contrast with the genealogy of Derridean deconstruction—which also began in phenomenology—is pertinent here: unlike Derrida, whose critique of structuralism is the result of a sustained confrontation with and reading of Lévi-Strauss and Saussure, Levinas's encounter with structuralism is neither deep nor decisive. The most serious discussion in which he positions himself in relation to structuralism and poststructuralism is found in the 1970 "No Identity." Even there, Levinas's encounter with texts by Michel Foucault and Michel Serres is indirect, based largely on Blanchot's discussion of them in "Atheism and the Cry." Nonetheless, Levinas's critique of structure, echoed in these interviews, has certain similarities to Derrida's. Structuralism, Levinas says, is too formal: "In certain trends in structuralist research, rules, pure forms, universal structures, ensembles which have a legality as cold as mathematical laws are isolated" ("Philosophy, Justice, and Love"). Whereas in thinking the ethical, or in thinking the reinscribed heteronomy, "you do not remain in the formal; you think starting from a content" ("Philosophy, Justice, and Love").

In Part 2, Levinas exposits the central features of his ethical thought and, in the process, often deepens certain emphases. For example, Levinas is often at pains to point out that *face* is "the concrete figure" in which the notion of alterity acquires its meaning ("Being-for-the-Other"). Readers of *Totality and Infinity* may recall that Levinas first introduces the face there as a "deformalization" of the apparently empty idea of infinity. In conversation, Levinas spells out the precise necessity for this phenomenological deformalization and why the face should not be confused with that which has only a formal signification. "Logically, within all multiplicity, *a* is the other of *b* and *b* is the other of *a*, but each remains what it is in the ensemble formed by the multiplicity of *terms* which are formally united" ("Being-for-the-Other"). Certainly this is why the relation to the face is hard to think; even "'relation' rests on the ground of the ensemble," he observes ("Intention, Event, and the Other"). But the other presents himself *as* an other "as it were torn up from the common genus which unites us" (Poirié), excluded or excluding himself from the extension of genus ("Being-for-the-Other"). Individuals within a genus are merely "anonymous points within the logical extension of the concept" ("Responsibility and Substitution"). That is why to the term *individuality* Levinas opposes *uniqueness*, or "uniqueness without genus" ("On Jewish Philosophy"). This is the kind of reasoning which leads Levinas to assert: "The other is not other because he would have other attributes. . . . The other is other because of me: unique and in some manner different than the individual belonging to a genus. It is not difference which makes alterity: alterity makes difference" ("Vocation"). In other words, insofar the other is other *before* any attribute, other kinds of difference are derivative upon ethical alterity. Within the biblical diction that Levinas often deploys, "the stranger, the widow, the orphan" are not categorial determinations of the other. They refer to the other's defenselessness, to the other as someone about whom one worries.

In these interviews, Levinas explains what he was working on during the last years of his career, namely, "a deformalization of the notion of time" ("The Other, Utopia, Justice"), "diachrony . . . the very articulation, the very concreteness of the temporality that signifies through the other" ("On Jewish Philosophy"). He clarifies and elaborates issues that do not receive extensive treatment in the main philosophical works. These include the question of pre-philosophical experiences and their relation to philosophy ("Reality Has Weight"; "On Jewish Philosophy"); the ethical signification of money ("Awakening"; "In the Name of the Other"). But most notably, questions about the third party, justice, and the State receive significant elaboration here.

Levinas began his thinking about justice and the third in the 1954 "The Ego and the Totality," a concern he registers briefly in *Totality and Infinity*. At the time of these interviews, Levinas has just written "Sociality and Money" (1985–86), and is preoccupied with what it means not only to respond to the demands of the face-to-face situation, but also to approach the third party.[8] With the third, the necessity for justice and the State comes into view: "The work of the State, while denying it in some manner, comes to supplement this work of interpersonal responsibility which touches the individual in his uniqueness and which is the work of the individual in his uniqueness as the one responsible" (Poirié). Without justice and the State, *goodness*—or what he elsewhere in the interviews calls *mercy, charity, hesed,* and *love*—runs the risk of being wrong. But justice (like the State), effects a modification, even a violence, with regard to face: "Justice is already the first violence," says Levinas ("Being-Toward-Death"). For justice entails "a comparison of what is in principle incomparable" ("Philosophy, Justice, and Love"). Indeed, in justice, "the unique incomparables *must* be compared," as Levinas asserts repeatedly ("On Jewish Philosophy"; Poirié; "Being-Toward-Death"; "Philosophy, Justice, Love"; "The Other, Utopia, and Justice"; "Responsibility and Substitution"). Such a comparison amounts to the "return of the unique to the community of genus" ("Vocation"). "This is the Greek moment, the entire political thinking of Greece" comments Levinas (Poirié; "Being-Toward-Death"). Does this mean that in justice the relation to the face—goodness—is lost? This is a question which Levinas poses in a talmudic register as the difference between *hesed* and *tzedakah* (Malka). Insofar as justice is incompletely just, and has to be made better ("Being-Toward-Death"; "In the Name of the Other"), justice requires, in its turn, the intervention of goodness.

"Greek," in Levinas's usage, is a language, the language of philosophy, a way of making explicit, the way of speaking in the university. "When we think, we speak Greek, even if we do not know this language" Levinas asserts ("Reality Has Weight"). Not just one language among others, "Greek" is the possibility of intelligibility: "To speak in a Greek way means, as in Plato, that there is a reply to every objection, that . . . what one said yesterday must be true and important today as well. One must use words whose deeper sense is not simply presupposed" ("Being-Toward-Death"). The Bible may be essential to thinking (Poirié), but "everything must be spoken in Greek" ("Reality Has Weight")—even, presumably, "thou shalt not kill," the Saying of intrahuman responsibility. Not only must everything be spoken in Greek, "Everything must be able to be translated into Greek!" ("Who Shall Not Prophesy?"). To the extent that philosophy does make use of religious experiences, it is already a Septuagint (Malka), a translation of the Bible into Greek. When an interviewer suggests that given Levinas's criticisms of the "Greek" language—a language that privileges the Said, comparison, knowledge—his insights could in fact have been derived solely from Hebrew sources, he protests: "I'm all for the Greek tradition!" ("Who Shall Not Prophesy?"). At the limit, one doesn't even gain access to the Hebrew "original" without a necessary relay through the Greek language. "Knowledge is necessary to the ethical signification of transcendence as proximity, which precedes the discourse of knowledge" ("On Jewish Philosophy"). In this context Levinas speaks of Europe as the "convergence" between the biblical and Greek traditions (Poirié; "Reality Has Weight"; "Being-Toward-Death").

Levinas's usage of the terms *Greek* and *Hebrew* is not primarily historicist: "It is . . . a matter of indicating the great directions, not a precise designation of historical wholes," he explains ("Awakening"). However, there are places in these interviews (which are, admittedly, "outside" the philosophical works proper) where, in speaking about the convergence of the Bible and Greece, Levinas does seem to refer to particular historical traditions, and these references are exclusionary and ethnocentric. A content erupts in which "Greek" becomes precisely a dismissal or omission of other traditions. Suffice it to say that, as in the case of other suppressed alterities within Levinas's discourse—such as the feminine—we are obligated, especially to Levinas, thinker of excluded alterity, to bring to bear upon his thought a corrective. Speaking of the feminine, which Levinas would not claim to be excluding from the primordial "après vous, Monsieur," insofar as ethical difference is prior to sexual difference, Levinas's response to one interviewer's question about the daughter reinstantiates the very problem he is being asked about.

Part 1 of this volume contains, in the long interview with Poirié, the most detailed and the sole extended biographical discussion Levinas has had with an interviewer. Going beyond his usual biographical points of reference (his years of study in Strasbourg and Freiburg; the teachers who were important to him; his attendance at the famous Heidegger-Cassirer debate at Davos, his naturalization as a French citizen), he gives a picture of prewar Jewish life in Kovno, Lithuania, and recounts his own wartime ordeal. For four years he was incarcerated as a French prisoner of war in a labor camp in Hanover, Germany. There, segregated from non-Jewish prisoners, he worked in a labor commando in the forest. During this time his wife and daughter were in hiding in Paris, his wife's mother having been deported. After the war he learned of the murder of his family—two younger brothers, and his maternal and paternal grandparents—noncombatants in Nazi-occupied Soviet territory. (In Lithuania, there had been no pogrom for seven hundred years. But 150,000 Jews were murdered between June and December 1941. Eventually, 95 percent of the Jewish population was annihilated.)[9]

"For the Jews of Lithuania, what was life like?" asks Myriam Anissimov. Levinas responds: "To understand this universe, you should read Vassily Grossman." Levinas refers to Vassily Grossman's *Life and Fate* a dozen times in these interviews. The book, completed in 1960, was suppressed for twenty years; the Russian text was not published until 1980, in Lausanne by Editions l'Age d'Homme. Grossman (along with Dostoevsky) provides in these interviews Levinas's preferred literary examples of "goodness." In Grossman, he finds in the exceptions of goodness "an ethics without system." But to actually follow Levinas's suggestion to Anissimov, namely, to read *Life and Fate*, produces a peculiar effect. No doubt in his answer Levinas wished to evoke a certain intellectual ambiance within a socialist and Jewish milieu, that of the Bund. But what sticks out in Grossman's thousand-page book is its depiction of a mass execution and its showing—deploying the author's technical expertise as a chemical engineer in the Donbass mines—of what it is like to die inside of a gas chamber. For the contemporary reader, the (impossible) perspective that Grossman shows amounts to the breaking of a representational taboo within Holocaust literature, never to show the inside of a gas chamber. Of course, Grossman was the journalist who first brought to the world's attention the extermination of the Jews in the Soviet Union, publishing "The Hell of Treblinka" in 1944. He was co-editor, with Ilya Ehrenbourg, of *The Black Book*, eyewitness accounts of the murder of Jews in Nazi-occupied Soviet territory. To a certain extent, Grossman's works have to be understood in the context of an official "forgetting" of the Holocaust in Soviet history at the time.[10]

In the interviews Levinas also recalls the extraordinary talmudic teacher he met in Paris after the war, who went only by the name Shoshani. Grungy, "dressed like a hobo," Shoshani would, at random, suddenly appear and, after conducting marathon study sessions, disappear. As Levinas puts it, Shoshani, on account of his great learning, was "dispensed from the yoke of civility" (Poirié), a fact which, in Salomon Malka's research on this enigmatic figure, did not endear him to everybody.[11] Levinas characterizes his teacher as "a terrifying dialectician—he could defend one day to the same students almost the contrary of what he had taught the day before" ("Discussion"). What he taught, moreover, was not a content but the manner in which the Talmud was to be approached (Poirié). According to Malka, the master to whom Levinas refers here and elsewhere as "pitiless" more often than not wore a sardonic smile. Elie Wiesel had the same teacher, and Wiesel's recollections of the man with a "harsh, disagreeable voice" and an aggressive pedagogical style register his ambivalent admiration.[12] But somehow, in Levinas's case, Wiesel remarks: "Shoshani was able to give and Levinas to receive."[13]

This no doubt asymmetrical giving resulted in Levinas's publication of at least five books of talmudic readings. These readings of haggadic texts from the Talmud are a record of Levinas's thirty-year involvement with the Colloques. In them Levinas makes explicit the alternative intelligibility—going against the grain of the Greco-Christian conceptuality—that the Talmud dissimulates. In interviews, Levinas's own midrashic modality, which he characterizes as an interpretive relation to the gaps between (scriptural) utterances ("On Jewish Philosophy"), is often in evidence. He has a habit of responding to questions as if all answers were to be sought and found in the Hebrew Bible. When asked, "How, concretely, is responsibility for the other translated?" he replies: "The other concerns me in all his material misery. It is a matter eventually of nourishing him, of clothing him. It is *exactly* the biblical assertion: clothe the naked, feed the hungry, give shelter to the shelterless. The material side of man, the material life of man concerns me and, in the other, takes on for me an elevated signification and concerns my holiness. . . . As if with regard to the other I had responsibilities starting from eating and drinking" (Poirié). Here, in fact, Levinas is not citing, but rather using an idiom which *sounds* biblical. He proffers a narrative expansion of a given biblical verse. His topic recalls *Difficult Freedom*'s emphasis that the highest spiritual is the material. Elsewhere, he glosses "feeding the hungry" and "clothing the naked" as *giving*, namely, a nontotalizing approach to the other equiprimordial with language ("Philosophy, Justice, and Love"). The interviews also contain references to extremely condensed talmudic passages and a plethora of biblical citations—usually from the prophets and Psalms. "No doubt I cite the Bible too much," he acknowledges with mock ruefulness (Poirié). There, too, the interrogative way in which Levinas makes use of biblical verses implies the legacy of Shoshani. And, since the Jewish reading of the Bible never goes without reference to the rabbinic commentaries that precede it, this reading is a relation to a word "always already past," within an atmosphere in which "transmission and renewal go hand in hand" ("Discussion").

Levinas does not mind being called a Jewish thinker. But he does mind "when by it one understands something that dares to establish between concepts relations which are based uniquely in religious traditions and texts, without bothering to pass through the philosophical critique" (Poirié). To overemphasize the Jewish "key" to Levinas's work is to risk overlooking the distinction he maintains, invariably in the extraphilosophical medium of the interview, between his philosophical writings and what he calls his "non-philosophical" or "confessional" writings. While arguably this distinction between his two types of writings is ultimately not absolute, one should understand why, for good philosophical reasons, he insists on it. As a phenomenologist, he does not presuppose any exegetical or doctrinal adhesion to the text. That is the meaning of his frequent assertion that he doesn't prove by means of the verse; he illustrates (*Collected Philosophical Papers*, 148). "A philosophical truth cannot be based on the authority of a verse. The verse must be phenomenologically justified. But the verse can allow for the search for a reason" (Poirié). Here Levinas's very assertion of the distinction between the two kinds of writings does not go without acknowledging a certain interplay between them. The search, or midrash, the starting point of which is the biblical verse, may "motivate" the ethical thought which in turn "must" receive a philosophical description. The statement serves more generally to indicate the way in which Levinas's philosophical works can indeed be said to be inflected by Judaism.

Part 3 is organized around theological issues. "Judaism and Christianity after Franz Rosenzweig" and the "Discussion Following 'Transcendence and Intelligibility'" are interfaith conversations in an ecumenical spirit. There Levinas's interviewers confront within Levinas's ethico-religious language what are historically sedimented terms. For example, *diaconate*, the (Greek) term which Levinas has, since the 1963 "Trace of the Other," used to characterize a subjectivity entirely given over to service, is one which he recovers from Isaiah 53 (one of the suffering servant songs). "Would it then be possible to find ourselves in Isaiah 53 . . . as the lamb of God?" asks a German cleric. "Isaiah is full of chapters in which one can find oneself," Levinas replies diplomatically ("Judaism and Christianity"), nonetheless clearly resisting the Christian typological reading of the suffering servant. On the other hand, he reports that Jewish readers have found suspicious his use of the term *kenosis* to denote responsible subjectivity ("Discussion"). For Levinas himself, along with the word *love*—rejected and then taken up again in the course of the interviews, a vexed term is *passion*. Although in a few places Levinas does use a formulation like "the passion of the Jews under Hitler" ("Being-Toward-Death"), "the passion of Israel at Auschwitz" ("Who Shall Not Prophesy?"), "the passion that one calls Holocaust" ("Necessitating Judaism" [1980] in *Beyond the Verse*), perhaps when he is trying to promote understanding and analogy, this naming is for him ambivalent. This has been apparent since the late fifties, when Levinas said of this "passion," "it drained out all the meaning of Isaiah 53" (*Difficult Freedom*, 12). To the extent that both terms, *passion* and *Holocaust*, tend to reinforce a sacrificial and sacramental interpretation of the event, Levinas prefers the term *shoah* (the Hebrew word for "annihilation, widespread catastrophe") to name what is for him "Nameless."

Many of the theological issues which come up in this volume are pragmatic: the relationship between Judaism and Christianity after the Holocaust, Levinas's positive response to the 1964 papal encyclical, "Nostra Aetate" ("Declaration on the Relationship of the Church to Non-Christian Religions"). The declaration, an ecumenical document par excellence, emphasizes the spiritual patrimony common to Christians and Jews. While affirming the unity of the two religions implied in the typological relationship between the two testaments, the declaration de-emphasizes the supersessionary relationship of New to Old implied, and repudiates specifically the thesis, based on the Gospels, that the Jews are guilty of deicide.

The abstract question of theodicy—the philosophical justification of suffering—is broached in "Being-Toward-Death" (from Part 2) and in "Judaism and Christianity after Franz Rosenzweig," in a manner that follows the line Levinas takes in an essay written in 1982, "Useless Suffering." The essay opposes two points of view on suffering: the phenomenological, in which suffering is intrinsically for nothing and admits of no meaning, and the theological, which interprets suffering as a consequence of sin, that is, as having a meaning. Levinas sides with the phenomenological point of view, noting that "after a century of nameless suffering," the always problematic question of unmerited suffering (which finds its classic formulation in the book of Job) changes direction, rendering "impossible and odious any thinking that would explicate this useless suffering by the sins of those who have suffered" ("Useless Suffering," 163). Auschwitz (as he phrases it here) is associated with the end of theodicy. Yet still, after Auschwitz, even if it doesn't "pay" to be good, one cannot deduce from this the absence of the good ("Being-Toward-Death"), an argument

Levinas had advanced in the 1955 "To Love the Torah More than God" (*Difficult Freedom*, 142–45). If, after Auschwitz, suffering again takes on a meaning, this would not be the restitution of its former theological meaning. The meaning is ethical, "the sole principle which it is not possible to contest," namely: "the suffering of suffering, the suffering for the useless suffering of the other, the just suffering in me for the unjustifiable suffering of the other" ("Useless Suffering," 159). Spiritually closer to God than confidence in some theodicy, this ethical principle is "so imperiously incumbent" upon man that it presupposes a certain atheism. In short, after Auschwitz, one still has an obligation to say the good, but not in the form of an "edifying discourse," not in the form of preaching (which, he explains, always implies a "happy end" ["Being-Toward-Death"]). If this is still religion, it is a religion without promise.

But the question remains, Is what Levinas calls dying-for sufficiently distantiated from its expiatory associations? That Levinas speaks of suffering as "the suffering *of* suffering" suggests that the term, like *sacrifice* (the withdrawal of being's interestedness), has primarily a technical sense. One could make a similar argument for the term *expiation*, which Levinas seems to avoid in his postwar work through *Totality and Infinity*, but begins using in the 1970s. There, and throughout the later work, the term is recontextualized to describe responsible subjectivity. No more than the terms *suffering* or *sacrifice*, he cautions, is this term to be understood in a mystical manner. Ethical conduct, he asserts, "is not a manifestation of the sacred" (Malka).

What is Levinas's reader to make of his increasing post-1975 tendency to drop the word *God* into an otherwise philosophical discourse? The collection *Of God Who Comes to Mind* appeared in 1982, and in these interviews one gets a sense of Levinas's complex and idiosyncratic usages. For example, in the citation with which I began concerning the holiness which cedes its place to the other, he goes on to say: "For me this is the moment where, through the human, the beyond being—God—comes to mind" (Poirié). "My attempt consists in saying that the relation with the other, with the face . . . is the very place where God comes to mind" ("Discussion"). "In my relation to the other, I hear the word of God" ("Philosophy, Justice, and Love"). These locutions assert that the face is the site of the word of God, that the word of God is the very obligation or commandment that the face addresses to me. That the relation to God never accomplishes itself in the absence of the relation to man is a familiar enough emphasis within Levinas's hermeneutic of Judaism: "God . . . approaches precisely through this relay through the neighbor" ("On Jewish Philosophy"). In other usages, the word *God* is intertwined with the technical vocabulary of the later work, as when Levinas refers to "the original goodness of man toward the other in which, in an ethical dis-inter-estedness—word of God—the inter-ested effort of brute being per-severing in its being is interrupted" ("The Other, Utopia, and Justice"), or when he asks, "If God is not this other—or His excluded middle—who breaks with the alternative freedom/nonfreedom?" (Malka). Ultimately it can be argued that the term *God* is something of a placeholder, the name for responsibility within the interhuman. That God is a preeminently empty notion, that to subject God to thematization entails a destruction of transcendence, Levinas had established in the 1975 essay "God and Philosophy," which forms the core of *Of God Who Comes to Mind.*

~

The interview texts cannot be considered "binding," as Levinas did not have final say over the redaction of each interview. Moreover, there is on the part of interviewers a wide range of closeness or lack thereof to his thinking. Three of the interviews were originally conducted in German. This makes certain problems in translation as well as transcription in-evitable. A few inadvertencies have been corrected. Only a few trivial rep-etitions have been deleted.

PART I

Intellectual and Personal Biography

Interview with François Poirié

Q.: You were born in 1906 in Lithuania. What sort of childhood did you have?

E.L.: It was, one might say, a very short childhood that lasted until the beginning of the war. I have few memories; things come back to the mind in a disordered way: the festivals of the third centenary of the house of Romanov with all the commotion abruptly overwhelmed this provincial city. I also remember—but that was earlier—the news of the death of Tolstoy. Then my family's departure away from the border zone that Lithuania was; the beginning of the war; the migration across diverse regions in Russia while waiting for the end of the conflict. Images become foggy in the change of locale and memories risk being known rather than remembered. In 1916, Kharkov in the Ukraine is where the refugees resided. The war of 1914 never really finished; the revolution and the postrevolutionary troubles, the civil war, all that fuses with the war of 1914.

Q.: What social milieu did your family belong to?

E.L.: My father had a bookstore in Kovno. It was the main city of the district, the center of government such as it was in Russia. There were gymnasia or *lycées*. My father's customers were government officials and those from the *lycée*. It was a bookstore with a stationery section, but it was the bookstore that was essential. The feverish period of book orders, at the beginning of the school year probably, comes back to me.

Q.: What were people reading?

E.L.: I have no recollection. But I can envisage the whole thing somewhat. This provincial city was, all the same, a central city. Germany—Europe, as one used to say there respectfully—was altogether close; the principal road was called Nicholas-Prospect, which became, in the independent Lithuania that we got to know later, Freedom Way, for the freedom which came to pass after the end of Russian domination.

Q.: It's hard to imagine what the climate was for a family like yours.

E.L.: It was a little bit reflected in the structure of the city. There was the old city and the new city. The old city was inhabited in large part by Jews. It wasn't a ghetto, there was no ghetto in that area, but Jews were the old citizens of Kovno, and they had acquired their houses and remained neighbors there. There were many synagogues and places of study. The new city was not really newer. When one pronounces the word Lithuania, perhaps one does not know that it designates one of the parts of this Eastern Europe in which Judaism knew its highest spiritual development; the level of talmudic study was very high, and there was a whole life based on this study and experienced as study.

The intellect was on the alert; it wasn't a mystical Judaism at all. On the contrary, it was attached to the dialectic of rabbinic thinking across the commentaries upon commentaries that are unfolded around the Talmud and in the Talmud. It's the country of the famous Gaon of Vilna of the eighteenth century, the last great Talmudist of genius. Intellectual modalities more open to the general culture and modern civilization, already imposed on my time, could not have effaced the prestige of this past. The generation of my parents, while having received this culture and all the while continuing to initiate youth into Hebrew, saw the future of young people in the Russian language and culture. That was the future, however uncertain it might have been. In my father's home, and in those of all the families of his generation, Russian was spoken with the children, and the importance of Russian culture in my eyes remains great; it goes a long way back. Russian authors like Pushkin, Gogol, Dostoevsky, Tolstoy retain all their prestige in my mind, in spite of everything dazzling in my Western life. An anecdote: several years ago I received a visit from an Israeli originally from Eastern Europe. Walking into my home, he saw the complete works of Pushkin on the bookshelves: "One can see right away," he said, "that one is in a Jewish house!" This was a sure and objectively valid index.

Q.: And the relations between the Russian state and this Jewish community—were they easy and uneventful?

E.L.: You know, this took place, all the same, under a regime in which Jews were not citizens or were second-class citizens, in which their stay in Russia was limited to the provinces at the border of the empire. In order to live in Moscow in those days you had to have special rank, whether that be graduation from a university or belonging to a leading trade guild. The dividing line had to do with the possibilities of development and emancipation.[1] But at that time, at least there, and compared to all the postwar chaos in the Ukraine, where my family lived until 1920 (where sometimes the White Russians came, sometimes the Reds, sometimes the Whites once again, sometimes the Ukrainian nationalists), my childhood under czarism was, and remains in memory, happy and harmonious.

Q.: You give the impression of an extraordinarily peaceful life. Was it not so simple for the Jewish community?

E.L.: There one could maintain an element of peace, and childhood could be preserved from shocks. Of course, you have documentation of the life and the social condition of Jews in Eastern Europe. All the same, it is different from the trouble which began at the end of August 1914 and never ended, as if the order had been forever disturbed.

Q.: You knew that there were pogroms there?

E.L.: Yes I knew, but that happened "elsewhere" in this vast Russia. Lithuania was spared. There was no memory of a pogrom in Lithuania itself. The Lithuanian population was very peaceful. And in spite of the anti-Semitic horrors that were played out there after the National-Socialist occupation in 1941, the Lithuanian intelligentsia often demonstrated itself to be courageous.

Polish Judaism has retained less peaceful memories. But all these countries on the Baltic coast—which became after 1919 three independent states: Estonia, Latvia, and Lithuania—enjoyed a certain peace and a certain order, a certain regularity to which my account perhaps testifies. Unless this be but the testimony, in spite of his innocence, of a "bourgeois" child. I know how much the word is often or naturally monstrous.

Q.: To come back to your family, were your parents very religious?

E.L.: When one was Jewish in that country, the rhythm of Jewish life dominated the rhythm of public life, without it having been necessary to make a special decision. A world in which religion in its essential manifestations was present as a collective form. No properly interconfessional social life in spite of the absence of any ghetto. I forgot to mention: Zionist tendencies were also perfectly natural. The Jewish state was still an insistent dream, not merely a fleeting reverie. Within this state of mind and—above all—during this epoch, religion couldn't be challenged. We didn't think about the extreme forms of religion much. At the home of my grandparents in the old city, religion exalted daily life, but in its invariable forms. I often think that Christianity, which appeared to us only in its exterior forms, must have been lived in the same manner. The church had a central place in public daily life but also belonged, in our eyes, to the quotidian, with neither solicitation nor temptation, without liturgical enthusiasms. What was essential in the spiritual—and this remains a very "Lithuanian" Judaism—did not reside for me in mystical modalities, but in a very great curiosity for books. I often say that books are more interior than interiority, which is not a paradox at all, but supposes a perception of degrees in interiority, and a distrust of untutored fabrications.

Q.: Was the Bible essential reading?

E.L.: I learned to read Russian all by myself from the label on the cocoa served in the morning, "kakao," the two *k*'s facilitating things. From the age of six, I regularly received courses in Hebrew, but already as for a modern language, with a reader and workbook: a Hebrew which already believed itself to be freed from the "empire" of religious texts; modern Hebrew, the same as biblical Hebrew but presented in a book with illustrations. Biblical texts would come soon afterward. And equally extraordinary, during the entire time of my family's migration, at every step, from Kovno in Lithuania to Kharkov in the Ukraine, the Hebrew teacher, engaged immediately, was, according to my father's wishes—how would I say it?—the first source of comfort. Then I entered the *lycée* in Kharkov at age eleven, having been prepared by private lessons. It was still under the czarist regime; I was admitted to this *lycée* of Kharkov with four other little Jews for the entire class: the *numerus clausus*! And the acceptance into the *lycée* was celebrated at home like a true family holiday, a promotion! A doctorate! But I already knew the Bible which had been taught to me since Kovno: Hebrew texts that I knew how to translate, texts taught without the famous commentaries which later seemed to me essential. No mention was made of the marvelous rabbinic commentaries; that was yet another homage to modernity!

Q.: How did you experience the Russian revolution?

E.L.: I was, after all, very young in February 1917 when the czar abdicated. It was during the year which followed my entrance into the *lycée*, and that remained for a long time the principal event. I did one year in the *lycée* under the czarist regime and under the regime of the February revolution. Without understanding anything about the October revolution. I didn't know how to situate exactly the first Bolshevism, the constitution of the White armies in the south, the civil war period. These events were very troubling for my parents. They were Jews and they were bourgeois. They were frightened by what the Russian revolution represented and in the family there was the old view of things; what counts above all in life is education! But all around me, there were great youth movements. I didn't remain indifferent to the temptations of the Leninist revolution, to the new world which was about to come. But without the engagement of a militant.

My parents took care of us without harshness, without violence, and wished to preserve us from political participations. In July 1920 the family benefited from the first possibility which was offered of leaving Russia to return to Lithuania. From 1920 to 1923 I lived in Lithuania again. The Lithuanian state was constituted according to all the bourgeois rules and guarantees. The return to normality gave me the impression that something important had been missed, that history was continuing without me in Russia. This is an impression which stayed with me for a very long time. It required an immersion in the true West and perhaps in its philosophy for me to situate Russia in terms of Europe. I can't make these memories any more precise than this: there was not yet Stalinism in the country we had just left and which was already so incomprehensible to my family. The country conserved in my mind something mysterious and privileged. It was like a messianic era which had been opened and closed. It was in this undecided state—despite what seemed to me to be the unshakable evidence of Zionism—that I found myself until the end of my secondary education and until my arrival in France.

Q.: In 1923 you left for France. Why France?

E.L.: Because it is Europe! I chose France on account of the prestige of the French. In France, I chose the city closest to Lithuania, Strasbourg. And I went to Strasbourg—not because this city had been reconquered by its country—but because it was the closest. And there must have been already something of an antipathy toward Germany during that epoch, perhaps owing to the disorder of inflation, a foreseeable threat, a presentiment perhaps.

Q.: When you arrived in Strasbourg you began philosophical studies.

E.L.: I did a year of Latin first and then I started studying philosophy.

Q.: What led you to philosophy?

E.L.: I think that it was first of all my readings in Russian, specifically Pushkin, Lermontov, and Dostoevsky, above all Dostoevsky. The Russian novel, the novel of Dostoevsky and Tolstoy, seemed to me very preoccupied with fundamental things. Books shot through with anxiety—with an essential, religious anxiety—but readable as a search for the meaning of life. The meaning of life was a phrase often spoken in the *lycée* with reference to Turgenev's heros. Quite essential that. These are novels in which love's dimensions of transcendence are already revealed in its modesties, before the appearance of anything erotic; in which an expression like "make love" becomes a scandalous profanation, not merely an indecency. The feelings of love as portrayed in books, these, certainly, were the source of my philosophical attempts. In the *lycées* in Lithuania, according to the Russian tradition, no philosophy, no course in philosophy, but if you will, an abundance of metaphysical anxiety. And then, in my case, solicitation of Jewish texts which, since my first readings in philosophy, were already present to my thinking, and which seemed to lead me to what I call philosophy. I'm not sure that this was a preparation for Plato and Aristotle, but in any case, it is what corresponds to my tastes for general philosophy.

I also remember one of the very important things from the time of my first studies which I continue to emphasize: I went to Maurice Pradines's course on the relations between ethics and politics. And he offered the

Dreyfus Affair as an example of the ethical overcoming the political. It was a very strong impression you know, Jews everywhere in Eastern Europe knew the name of Dreyfus. Old Jews with beards who'd never seen a letter in the Roman alphabet in their lives spoke of Zola as if he were a saint! And then all of a sudden, before me, a professor actually chose that as an example. What an extraordinary world! The four persons whom I encountered at Strasbourg as philosophy professors, teachers uniting, in my naive or perspicacious eyes, all the virtues of the university, remain for me true men, who are unforgettable! I remember that at the Sorbonne, in the closing seminar in 1976, in my remarks upon taking my retirement, I remembered them publicly, saying, "Now those are men!" Here are their names: Maurice Pradines, professor of general philosophy; Charles Blondel, a psychology professor who was very anti-Freudian; Maurice Halbwachs, a sociologist, killed during the war, assassinated as a martyr; Henri Carteron, who was professor of ancient philosophy and who died prematurely; Martial Gueroult succeeding him—he was very remarkable, but not one of the four of my first thinking. Charles Blondel very quickly became a man to whom I could say everything; Pradines, admirable teacher, much colder, but who spoke so well of Dreyfus.

Q.: In Strasbourg you met Maurice Blanchot. What kind of man was he? He has written about you; you yourself wrote about him later. Does your thinking have something in common?

E.L.: We were together during nearly my whole stay at Strasbourg; maybe he arrived two or three years after me. I can't describe him. Straightaway, I had the impression of an extreme intelligence, of an aristocratic cast of mind. Very distanced politically from me during that epoch, he was monarchist, but we very soon got to understand each other. He mentions me sometimes in his books, and I feel honored when, in his writings, our thoughts are alike. We think alike on many matters. He underwent an altogether interior evolution without the least concession, even with regard to himself. The impression of a man without opportunism. He experienced the occupation in an extremely heightened and painful way; I must mention especially that he saved my wife during the war while I was in captivity; he also experienced 1968 in an extraordinary manner. He always chose the least expected, most noble and difficult path. This moral elevation, this fundamentally aristocratic nature of thinking, is what counts the most and edifies.

Q.: What would these two young students at Strasbourg have talked to each other about?

E.L.: Philosophical things, literary things. Early on he introduced me to Proust and Valéry; we hadn't, if I remember correctly, spoken much about surrealism. We conversed about the phenomenological questions with which I was preoccupied. With him, very abstract notions opened up unexpected vistas, and things took on new life. He was always of delicate health and those around him wondered how, with all his tablets, he managed to survive. For me he stood for the very epitome of French excellence; not so much on account of his ideas, but on account of a certain possibility of saying things which is very difficult to imitate, appearing like a force from on high. Yes, it is always in terms of height that I speak of him.

Q.: Did you know French when you arrived in Strasbourg?

E.L.: Very little!

Q.: How did you manage?

E.L.: Languages are never an obstacle! The first year, I read Corneille— in an edition with notes—continually consulting a dictionary. Also, I remember a novel by Georges Sand which I read with a dictionary too. But when I arrived I still pronounced the *u* in the word *guerre*.

For me, you understand, the soil of that language is the French soil. I still speak Russian very well, German and Hebrew well enough; I read English, but I often thought, at the beginning of the war of 1939, that one waged war in order to defend the French language. It may sound like a whim, but I seriously believed it! It is in that language that I feel the living nature of the soil.

Q.: In relation to France, a source of great admiration for you is Bergson.

E.L.: I think he is absolutely and scandalously forgotten nowadays, in a universal ingratitude. He is still waiting to get out of Purgatory. But I think that everything new about the modern and postmodern philosophy of time, and in particular the venerable newness of Heidegger, would not have been possible without Bergson.

Q.: What was your relation to Bergson?

E.L.: You must realize, at the time of which I am speaking, that is to say, from 1924 to 1930, during the first years of my studies in France, that that *was* philosophy, taught as the new philosophy, and I remained very faithful to this sensation of novelty: in the notion of duration, in the notion of invention, in all the putting into question of substantiality and of solidity; in the putting into question of the notion of being, a little bit beyond being and otherwise than being, the whole marvel of diachrony; in the manner in which, for the man of our time, time is no longer simply a broken eternity or the missed eternal that always refers to something solid, but on the contrary, the very event of infinity in us, the very excellence of the good. Plenty of technical moments in the Bergsonian discourse. His quarrel with associationism or with mechanistic biology concerns me less than temporality, its superiority over the "absolute" of the eternal. The humanity of man is not just the contingent product of temporality but its original effectuation or the initial articulation.

Q.: In 1928–29 you went to Freiburg to take classes with Husserl. What interested you in his thought?

E.L.: The whole adventure of phenomenology that opened a path which seems to me, as one says today, *incontournable*, necessary, that which one cannot get around. (I don't know why this word is not liked. In Russian the simple word "necessary" means precisely that which one cannot get around.) Well this is what I couldn't get around: I was at the end of my *licence* without any clear decision about the future, and I took a look around and a young person, Gabrielle Peiffer, was reading Husserl at the Institute of Philosophy at Strasbourg. She recommended that I read this difficult author. I read the *Logical Investigations* very closely and I had the impression of gaining access not to yet another speculative construction but to a new possibility of thinking, to a new possibility of moving from one idea to another, different from deduction, induction, and dialectic, a new way of unfolding "concepts" beyond the Bergsonian appeal to the inspiration in intuition. I had the impression of gaining access to the fact that the gaze directed to a thing is also a gaze which is covered up by that thing; that the object is a blinding abstraction if it is taken by itself; that it gives you less to see than it shows, creating an ambiguous discourse; that in turning back to consciousness, to the forgotten experience which is intentional—that is, which is animated by an intention intending something else than this mimed experience—and which, always the idea *of* something, opens a horizon of meanings, one discovers the concreteness or the truth where the abstract object is situated. The passage from the object to the intention and from the intention and to all that it carries with it as a horizon of intentions would be the true thinking and the thinking of the true, or, if you will, the world of what is given to you in purely objective knowledge. Sometimes I formulate this by saying that one must move from the object to its mise-en-scène, from the object to all of the phenomena that its appearing implies. To illuminate objectivity by its phenomenology, like a director who passes from the text to the concrete event and who is obliged to add the plenitude of appearances in which this event will appear or in which it will become truly visible. Thus to prevent the seeing being blinded by what is seen. There the essential thing amounts to understanding and describing the secret intentions of intentionality.

What seemed to me rich in possibilities was this new attention to the secrets, or to the forgotten facts of consciousness, which, outside of psychology or objectivity, revealed the sense of objectivity or of being. Of course, I went to see Husserl in complete agreement with his definition of the philosopher as the one who is an eternal beginner in philosophy, but who is at the same time firmly entrenched in a certain way of formulating his uncertainties. It was as if understanding the entry into philosophy by a young person who approaches a great master were important, even outside the eternal debates. As if one had first of all to find again one's very first beginnings, one's original hesitations.

I must have been rather childish or ungrateful. The great thing that I found was the way in which the direction given by Husserl was continued and transfigured by Heidegger. It was as if, to use the language of tourists, I went to see Husserl and I found Heidegger. Of course, I will never forget Heidegger's relation to Hitler. Even if this relation was only of a very short duration, it will be forever. But the works of Heidegger, the way in which he practiced phenomenology in *Being and Time*—I knew immediately that this was one of the greatest philosophers in history, comparable to Plato, Kant, Hegel, Bergson. I have named five crossroads of philosophy: onto-theology, transcendental philosophy, reason as history, pure duration, and phenomenology of being distinguished from beings. Not that I take very seriously this way of orienting oneself in the space of thinking. But whatever a serious orientation might be, Heidegger would not be absent from it.

Q.: You met Husserl. What kind of man was he?

E.L.: He gave the impression of being somewhat pat, despite his emphasis on research. He had finished the research of his research, this would be much more exact to say.

Certainly he believed that phenomenological research had just begun and that every discovered domain gave way to group work which would have to continue the investigation. But as to the methodology of the open horizons, there was no longer any surprise. The manuscripts piling up— and they are admirable in their precision and testify to an ingenious acuity of observation—were confirmations of earlier suggestions. These suggestions received considerable developments, fruitful enough, but the suggestions themselves were no longer unexpected. Sometimes one could guess them from the already published work. There was also something pat about his oral teaching. It was difficult to enter into a dialogue. When you asked him something, there was always evocation of the famous manuscripts where this theme had already been treated. Your question was always answered by an elaborate development, a lecture, but perhaps this line no longer struck you. You often had the impression, perhaps wrongly, that you knew the order of development and that you guessed the secret. On the contrary, with Heidegger—especially in *Being and Time*, which was still phenomenology—every page was absolutely new. I'm telling you impressions now; I am not sure whether they were as true as they were sincere. Husserl seemed less convincing to me because he seemed less unexpected: that's paradoxical or childish. With Heidegger, everything seemed unexpected: the marvels of his analysis of affectivity, the new access to the everyday, the difference between being and being*s*, the famous ontico-ontological difference. The rigor with which all that was thought in the brilliance of the formulations, absolutely impressive. Still today all this is more precious to me than the last speculative consequences of his project, the end of metaphysics, the themes of *Ereignis*, the *es gibt* in its mysterious generosity. What remains is Heidegger's ingenious application of phenomenological analysis discovered by Husserl and, alas, the horror of 1933.

Q.: I'm curious to know: what kind of rapport would you, as a student, have had with teachers like Husserl and Heidegger?

E.L.: I knew Husserl when he was very old, I went to his house, I gave

French classes to Mme Husserl who had very graciously and generously asked for them. I felt a very great respect—despite the disappointment which I did not always admit—a sense of being present at a very important moment—at the last judgment—of thinking.

Q.: And what are your memories of Heidegger?

E.L.: No personal rapport outside of classes and seminar discussions. I was able to attend the famous encounter in Davos in 1929, where Heidegger spoke of Kant and Cassirer spoke of Heidegger. Cassirer, the neo-Kantian, spoke of *Being and Time* and of Heidegger interpreting Kant. Here was a chance to see Heidegger outside the academic setting. An encounter which remains memorable. I also remember a show put on by the students in which I got to play the role of Cassirer; that of Heidegger was conferred upon the future Professor Bolnow. At that time I had an abundance of very black hair; we put a lot of white powder on my hair in order to evoke the noble gray head of the master. As for Bolnow, who must also be retired now, I furnished him with the reply which to me seemed to caricature the etymological findings of Heidegger: "Because interpreting means to put a thing upside down (*Weil interpretari heisst eine Sache auf den Kopf stellen*)."

Q.: From a philosophical point of view, what did this encounter between Heidegger and Cassirer represent?

E.L.: At the time, it probably represented the end of a certain humanism, but perhaps today a fundamental antinomy and profound antiquity, of our civilization and of philosophy. And the eternal reply of Cassirer, a humanist of refined and patrician manner, neo-Kantian, glorious disciple of Hermann Cohen, modern interpreter of Kant, taking the intelligibility of the sciences as his point of departure, very similar to our master Léon Brunschvicg; and like him, in the continuity of rationalism, the aesthetic and the political ideas of the nineteenth century. Very removed from positivism and banal scientism, of course, but who was perhaps persuaded, like Brunschvicg, that mathematical invention was the inner life itself and that the thinking about an inevitable death is not a philosopher's first thought. But maybe today in minds like Blanchot's—in a mind like Blanchot's—two souls coexist and converse which anywhere else do not understand each other or hardly listen to each other.

On the other hand, there was Heidegger, the philosopher who did not take exact science as his point of departure, physico-mathematical science, taken for the source of intelligibility and for the meaning of that which is thought. But the Heidegger of Davos comes back to me across the Heidegger of Freiburg, the one of being understood starting from its verbal form as the event of being and as that which is an issue for men. A necessary meaning to the understanding of all beings. For Heidegger, science is certainly one of the modalities of the intelligible, but a modality that is already derivative. He sought the origin in the human being, whose being consists precisely in understanding being and thus the point where the being of beings acquires a meaning. There was a new way, a radicalization of philosophical interrogation, a priority with respect to reflections on physico-mathematical sciences. A thinking whose hold on the entire philosophy of our century is well known. A new outcome of Greek thinking which no longer appeared uniquely as the dawn of modern science but as the awakening of the question of being, but perhaps also as the place of its first covering up. But these deviations also always attest to itineraries in their necessary ways, in their ambiguity, in their necessary and dramatic erring. Never simple errors or detours, a new pathos of thinking. A passion for the origin of meaning in a direction different from the Cartesian and Kantian orientation which finds again in these orientations relays of ontology. Problems which were more important and more fundamental than that of the foundations of the sciences.

Q.: And all this took place in the form of dialogue?

E.L.: At Davos, in the form of dialogues and in the form of a series of lectures or simple verbal exchanges. Each one spoke in turn, there were some questions, discussion sessions, I believe. For a young student, the impression was of being present at the creation and the end of the world.

Q.: People felt a great trembling?

E.L.: Certainly! Cassirer presented an order which was going to be undone. Now one has a slanted perspective which perhaps falsifies memories. I think that Heidegger announced a world that was going to be turned over. You know who he would join three years later: one would have to have had the gift of prophecy to sense this already at Davos. I have thought for a long time—in the course of terrible years—that I had felt it then, in spite of my enthusiasms. The value judgments made about each of them have necessarily changed over time. And during the Hitler years I reproached myself for having preferred Heidegger at Davos.

Q.: This may seem anecdotal, but what kind of person was Heidegger?

E.L.: It's hard to respond. Everything he said to me was hidden by his grandeur. He seemed very authoritarian, his word was very measured, knowing that it was measured—not dogmatic, certainly, but enunciating his truth in a strong manner. What did he not turn upside down! But he always turned something upside down! Not very tall, walking around in a skiing outfit.

Q.: How do you explain Heidegger's attitude in relation to National Socialism?

E.L.: I don't know; it's the blackest of my thoughts about Heidegger and no forgetting is possible. Maybe Heidegger had the feeling of a world that was decomposing, but he believed in Hitler for a moment in any case. How is this possible? To read Löwith's memoirs, it was a long moment. His firm and categorical voice came back to me when I used to hear Hitler on the radio. Maybe there was a familial determinism also; Mrs. Heidegger was very early Hitlerian.

Q.: I get the impression of a division between your Strasbourg period and that which you were before Strasbourg, someone who learned Hebrew and read the Bible.

E.L.: During my years at Strasbourg I did not further my readings in Hebrew, I read much less in it. It was a bit later that I went back to it. But there was no rupture, I never abandoned it. There was no crisis. I was simply very taken by the new things I had to learn; a lot of French, don't forget. At Strasbourg I was led—still, it is very curious—to the importance of the Holy Scriptures by a passion brought to medieval studies which had developed in my Catholic friends from contact with Henri Carteron, the teacher of whom I have already spoken. Henri Carteron was prematurely deceased and I dedicated my first book on Husserl to his memory. Around Carteron, Saint Thomas in particular had taken on great importance. And I said to myself: all the same I should not forget my own texts; my interest in Jewish studies was revived in the course of my research plan, which was, in fact, altogether exterior to Judaism properly speaking. Later, returning to Lithuania on vacation, I made contact again with the traditional library, with Jewish studies. I had never completely abandoned them, but they did not have in the beginning a consciously acknowledged influence on my philosophical studies.

I would say to myself: there is something to explore, some corners more mysterious than I had previously believed when the reading of the prophets with my regular professors seemed to me a bit scholastic. But these were not true ruptures, nor true recoveries. It was much later, in the course of meeting some exceptional persons endowed with a very high Hebraic culture when I began to consecrate more time and to interest myself in it in a more direct manner. Never like in relation to an object, but rather like to my own substance.

Q.: What were the relations between Husserl and Heidegger?

E.L.: Husserl was convinced that Heidegger remained his disciple, and he discovered slowly, I think, that Heidegger was not teaching the "transcendental reduction." There is a letter by Husserl to one of his students where this disenchantment is recounted.[2] And even the distanced character of the meetings between Husserl and Heidegger in Freiburg was noticeable. It must have been quite dramatic.

Q.: But the rest of you who were students...

E.L.: We knew it very well. But on the basis of texts that were read and compared. Not on the basis of facts.

Q.: You realized it?

E.L.: We compared theses and divergent orientations, but we also looked for signs of continuity. In my first book, which appeared over fifty years ago, I made an effort to present Husserl's doctrine while finding Heideggerian elements in it. As if Husserl's philosophy already stated the Heideggerian problems of being and beings. I don't think, by the way, today, that I was completely wrong.

Q.: Would you say that you were a disciple of Heidegger?

E.L.: I think neither that I have arrived at this point nor that I have the right to it, but I cannot deny a part of my life nor the astonishment with which I still today read a Heideggerian text, especially *Being and Time*, where I am taken by the power of the analysis.

Q.: How did your itinerary continue in the years preceding the war?

E.L.: After my dissertation I asked for French citizenship and received it; I married, did my military service in Paris (in the 46 R.I. de
la Tour D'Auvergne, experienced like a historic time), and I entered the
administration of the pedagogical section of the Alliance Israélite
Universelle. I have to say a couple of words about this institution. The
Alliance Israélite Universelle was constituted in 1860 in an effort to
work for the emancipation of Jews in those countries where they still
did not have the right to citizenship. The first Israélite institution with
an international vocation founded according to the French ideas of the
rights of man. In this inspiration there was no Zionist intention. What
was at stake was the emancipation of Jews in the countries where they
lived without being recognized as citizens. The action was in the beginning turned toward the non-European countries, to the zones of the
Mediterranean basin; toward North Africa; toward regions of Europe,
Turkey, and Asia, some of which have since become Syria, Iraq, and
Iran. Very soon this activity became educational work. The foundation
of French schools of the first order, which meant also and especially for
the idealists of the nineteenth century, who were contemporaries of the
great revolution of 1848, the elevation of humans to universal culture,
the affirmation of the glorious idea of 1789. These schools had an extraordinary development. I'm telling you a bit about the old history. All
the Jews of the Mediterranean area educated in these French schools of
the Alliance—even sometimes to the detriment of their own traditions,
traditions which were later rediscovered in new syntheses—esteemed
France as their homeland through the French language and through
French ideas. This educational work has certainly been reoriented since
the end of the war.

Q.: What function did you have in that educational work?

E.L.: It was very late, during the last years preceding the local nation-
alisms before the war. I took care of these schools here in Paris. There was
an entire correspondence attached to problems of administration, of ped-
agogy and of conscience. This was prolonged after the war by my ap-
pointment as director of the Ecole Normale Israélite Orientale in Paris,
which for a hundred years educated the teachers for these distant schools.
I was drafted in 1939. I left the office on 45 rue de la Bruyère at the head-

quarters of the Alliance, and I returned to it after my return from captivity, when I became director.

Q.: And intellectually?

E.L.: During these years before the war I wrote philosophical texts which had no especially Jewish thematic to them but which probably stemmed from that which the Judaic classifies or suggests as the human. One of these texts, *De l'évasion*, was republished a short while ago. My young friend Jacques Rolland wrote an introduction and notes for it and turned it into a book of a hundred pages. In the original text, written in 1935, one can distinguish the anxieties of the war to come. And the whole fatigue of being, the condition of that period. Distrust in relation to being (which, in another form, continued in what I was able to do after this date) arose at a time in which the presentiment of the imminent Hitlerism was everywhere. Will my life have been spent between the incessant presentiment of Hitlerism and the Hitlerism that refuses itself to any forgetting? Not everything was related in my thoughts to the destiny of Judaism, but my activity at the Alliance kept me in contact with the Jewish ordeal, bringing me ceaselessly back to the concrete social and political problems which concerned it everywhere. In Europe, outside of the Mediterranean region of the schools of the Alliance: notably in Poland, where the proximity of a hostile Germany nevertheless reanimated anti-Semitic instincts barely put to sleep. Concrete problems with spiritual repercussions. Facts that are always enormous. Thoughts coming back to ancient and venerable texts, always enigmatic, already disproportionate to the exegeses of a school. Here you have, in administrative and pedagogical problems, invitations to a deepening, to a becoming conscience, that is, to Scripture. That is at least what I have always felt approaching texts. *De l'évasion*, which Jacques Rolland commented on so well, signified— beyond the Jewish condition—the human.

Q.: History was very oppressive for you at that time?

E.L.: Yes. But, you know, it is very difficult to communicate this, this kind of uninterrupted despair which was the Hitlerian period in Europe, rising out of the depths of this Germany which was so fundamental, this Germany of Leibniz, Kant, Goethe, and Hegel.

Q.: And of Nietzsche.

E.L.: Nietzsche was himself brought to the point of despair. I myself link what Nietzsche wrote always to the presentiment of a time in which all the values would dishonor themselves; he denounces the values which will become confused and contradict themselves some decades later. And still, today, I tell myself that Auschwitz was committed by the civilization of transcendental idealism. And Hitler himself will be found again in Nietzsche.

Q.: What were you doing during World War II?

E.L.: I was taken prisoner of war very early. I had been certified military interpreter several years before 1939 and was drafted as an interpreter of Russian and German. I was taken prisoner in Rennes with the Tenth Army on its retreat. After several months' internment in France, I was transported to Germany. Here I was directly restrained to a special status: registered as a Jew but spared by my uniform the destiny of those who were deported, grouped together with other Jews in a special commando. Working separated from all the other Frenchmen in the forest, but apparently benefiting from the dispositions of the Geneva convention protecting prisoners of war.

Q.: How did your incarceration go?

E.L.: When we were transported into Germany to a stalag near Hanover the newcomers were separated: the Jews on one side and the non-Jews on the other. The Jews destined for a special commando. During this period, I greatly appreciated—it's one of my very important experiences of Christianity—the fraternal humanity of a man of the stalag in whom I could trust, who with each of his gestures restored our consciousness of the dignity within us. The man was called Abbé Pierre. I never knew his family name. There have been many citations of Abbé Pierre since then, in the chronicles of charity in France. I often think of this person who helped us, comforted us, as if the bad dream had disappeared, as if language itself had found again its lost accents and returned to a nobility before corruption. Later, for every problem that came up in the Jewish commando, we wanted to go back to the camp to talk to Abbé Pierre again.

In a general manner, I think that Christian charity did not appear to many of us except during the Hitlerian persecutions. Paradox of the experience. I always said to myself that the executioners of Auschwitz—

Protestants or Catholics—had all probably done their catechism. Nevertheless, what we experienced within the civilian population—simple believers and members of the hierarchy who welcomed, helped, and often saved many of us—is absolutely unforgettable, and I have never stopped reminding others of the role played—with a lot of ruses and risks—in the rescue of my wife and daughter, by the monastery of St. Vincent de Paul near Orléans. We admired this devotion also in the prisoner camps in the person of chaplains, even if they did not succeed in suppressing the racial discrimination which was the rule in prisoner camps.

Here I was in a Jewish commando. It was not a period of torture. We went to work in the forest; we spent the day in the forest. Materially supported by care packages, morally by letters, like all the French prisoners. The light one extracted from the spare time spent reading. Fraternal contacts between very different social and cultural groups. Books would arrive; one didn't know from where. Manual workers would read Anatole France and Proust. And this form of cultivating discussions during work hours was very beautiful. Now I am coming to the story of the friendly dog. A little dog associated himself with us prisoners one day as we were going to the workplace; the guard did not protest; the dog would install himself in the commando and let us go to work alone. But when we used to come back from work, very relieved, he welcomed us, jumping up and down. In this corner of Germany, where walking through the village we would be looked at by the villagers as *Juden*, this dog evidently took us for human beings. The villagers certainly did not injure us or do us any harm, but their expressions were clear. We were the condemned and the contaminated carriers of germs. And this little dog welcomed us at the entrance of the camp, barking happily and jumping up and down amicably around us.

Q.: What did you read during your captivity?

E.L.: I read Hegel, of course, but many philosophical texts of all types. Plenty of things I had not had the time to read before: more Proust than ever, the authors of the eighteenth century, Diderot, Rousseau, and then random authors. And all of a sudden I would ask myself, "What good is all this?" But in this life of daily physical work in the forest—under the surveillance of guards who were without brutality—from the point of view of culture, the time was not wasted.

It was paradoxical, everything was provisional in some manner. We asked ourselves what the purpose of all this was, and if we would get out of it. But this relative immunity of prisoners of war in a commando lost in the forest created a balanced universe: very few cultivated people, but everybody read and everybody was also posing questions. We didn't know what was happening on the outside. The minor pieces of information we received from German radios, carefully interpreted and reinterpreted in our own way, concerned only military operations. That was our contact with the exterior world. We knew the positions of the enemy at Stalingrad and elsewhere much better than we knew what was happening with our own families, who didn't wish to alarm us in their letters. From time to time, news would filter through: such and such a family had lost one of its members; another didn't answer anymore. New atrocities, coded formulas that one sought to interpret in hope and in consolation.

Q.: No rumor reached you about the exterminations?

E.L.: No. Later, a bit of that filtered in very slowly. All that our families had experienced was not known; all the horrors of the camps, unimaginable. In the reasoned consciousness of a destiny without pity or exception, a consciousness without illusions—the provisional everydayness and forgetfulness in books or in derisory lucidity with or without degradation.

Q.: It was also in captivity you began your first book, *Existence and Existents*.

E.L.: Yes, I started to write, but the book was not ready when I came back.

Q.: When you returned to France, what did you do?

E.L.: I found again the office on the rue de la Bruyère and it was there that I was entrusted with this school where I lived for many years. I directed it from 1946 until entering the academy in 1961.

Q.: The intellectual scene of the time was busy with people like Sartre, Camus, Merleau-Ponty. What were your relations with them?

E.L.: I had already seen Sartre before the war. After *Nausea* I met him at Gabriel Marcel's house. I had been invited in the period preceding the war to the sessions at Gabriel Marcel's house. They took place on Saturday night once a month for philosophers, and there I attended a presentation given by Sartre. At Gabriel Marcel's, during that time, the future

readership of Sartre was forming, the readers of all the philosophical per-
colating set in motion by Sartre's *Being and Nothingness*, which appeared
during the war. I found Sartre again in the full bloom of his popularity directly after the war.

Q.: You never met him afterwards?

E.L.: In total I met him three times. The year preceding his death I
went to him: he wanted me to participate in a special issue of *Les Temps
Modernes* relating to the Palestinian problem. I met him also when he received an honorary degree from the Hebrew University of Jerusalem. I
even have a very beautiful photograph where I'm congratulating him.
They were occasional contacts. I also wrote to Sartre when he refused the
Nobel prize. In the letter, which I consider important, I told him that in
having refused this prestigious prize, he perhaps was the only man who
had the right to speak and maybe this was the moment where he had to
speak: to go to Nasser in Egypt to propose peace with Israel. Crazy idea!
But I told him, "You're the only man Nasser will listen to." I was told
that, receiving this letter, he asked, "Who is this Levinas anyway?" Had
he forgotten? Had he forgotten *The Theory of Intuition in Husserl's
Phenomenology*, which, according to Mme de Beauvoir, had known a glorious moment? In *The Coming of Age*, Simone de Beauvoir recounts how,
at the Picard bookstore on the boulevard Saint-Michel, the book was dis-
played after its publication. Sartre flipped through it and said: "All this I
wanted to say myself, but Husserl has already said it."

Q.: And now his work?

E.L.: Early on I read *Nausea*, which appeared after my text, *De l'évasion*, and expressed the ontology of this horrible time before the war; I
cited *Nausea* in my later texts; I only knew *Being and Nothingness* from
the part I read upon my return from captivity. But I have for Sartre—although this will not please ingrates who permit themselves to judge
him—a very great admiration for his obvious genius, but also his vivacity,
his presence, his acts of imprudence.

The dynamism of Paris, or simply this extraordinary Parisian or French
way of being awake after all that had happened, for me this is greatness.
Sartre is being reproached, for lack of anything else to fault him with, for
having mounted a production during the occupation, an anti-German
play amid the German presence in Paris. He did not fear scandal. And

when someone recently told me about his inattention to the financial conditions of his own life, the way he spent money on others, his manner of giving—that is the measure of the human!

Q.: Having attended the courses of Husserl and Heidegger, do you find a newness in the philosophical work of Sartre, Camus, and Merleau-Ponty?

E.L.: In both Merleau-Ponty and Sartre, there was a new tone but also a speculative power, as neither could just receive something without recreating it. Minds too big to repeat.

Q.: At which moment did the desire and the need to publish come to you?

E.L.: Very early! I published my first essay on Husserl at age twenty-two in the *Revue Philosophique*, which at that time was edited by Lévy-Bruhl: "On the Ideas of Edmund Husserl."[3] I always had communication rather than publishing in itself as my vocation.

Q.: Also the vocation to make an oeuvre perhaps?

E.L.: A vocation perhaps secret to itself. I don't know if one ever makes an oeuvre, if one does not start from certain ideas which grip the heart. In the fatigue of being, of which I spoke to you earlier, in the account I gave in *De l'évasion*, I had perhaps the feeling of being tormented by something unique, and which still torments me.

Q.: What was the reception of your first book, *Existence and Existents*, which seems very distant from the social preoccupations which then dominated?

E.L.: My first book was *Theory of Intuition*.

Q.: That was your thesis!

E.L.: Yes, my doctoral thesis, written at age twenty-four and defended at the University at Strasbourg. I have already told you that the book had, notably, Sartre as a early reader; now it's in its fourth edition. It received a Prix de l'Institut. I mention this fact because I owed this distinction certainly to Léon Brunschvicg and it is very important to mention this very great mind among my teachers. In the Husserl book, I had to speak of his phenomenology within a philosophical ambiance which is difficult to imagine today. This movement of ideas which is, today, familiar to everyone in France was at the time almost entirely unknown.

As to the social preoccupations which dominated at the moment of my return, and which did not correspond to the themes of my writings, I don't consider my reflections to have been removed from the essentially human and, though written in a different vocabulary, to have treated anything but the social. So much for the journalistic reception of my work. But people always remembered my phenomenological specialty, attested to by my book, *The Theory of Intuition in Husserl's Phenomenology*. I had some favorable reviews, but in the end, nothing important.

As to *Existence and Existents*, what is important in that book is the description of being in its anonymity, a description very close to the themes of Blanchot. A convergence, a parallelism, what I call the *il y a* (there is). Whatever be my projects, my movements, my rest, *there is* being. *Il y a* is anonymous, *"il* y a" like *"il* pleut" ("it" is raining). *There is* not only something that is but *there is*, above and through these somethings, an anonymous process of being. Without a bearer, without a subject. As in insomnia, it doesn't stop being—*there is*.

Q.: Is this concept of the *il y a* close to the Heideggerian *es gibt*?

E.L.: Oh no, it is not the Heideggerian *es gibt*. The Heideggerian *es gibt* is a generosity. That is the great theme of the later Heidegger: being gives itself anonymously. But like an abundance, like a diffuse goodness. On the contrary, the *there is* is unbearable in its indifference. Not anguish but horror, the horror of the unceasing, of a monotony deprived of meaning. Horrible insomnia. When you were a child and someone tore you away from the life of the adults and put you to bed a bit too early, isolated in the silence, you heard the absurd time in its monotony as if the curtains rustled without moving. My effort in *Existence and Existents* consists in investigating the experience of the exit from this anonymous "nonsense."

An exit starting from something in itself and which I call in the book *hypostasis*. Getting out of the anonymousness of being—of the *there is*—by being*s*, by the subject who is bearer and master of being, of his being. In *Existence and Existents*, the *there is* first proceeds from a phenomenology of fatigue, of laziness; then the search for being, hypostasis. Nevertheless, at the end of the book, the essential idea that the true bearer of being, the true exit from the *there is* is in obligation, in the "for-the-other," which introduces a meaning into the nonsense of the *there is*. The I subordinated to the other. In the ethical event, someone appears who is the subject par excellence. That is the kernel of all I would say later. The first half of the book turns around the subject, and toward the end, the other appears: I am always I, preoccupied with my-self, the famous "being persevering in being." Eating, to take pleasure in eating, to take pleasure in oneself, that is disgusting; but the hunger of the other, that is sacred. Am I unjust with regard to the I? I am told that I reason in a masochistic way. We are in masochism, and already a bit in the ethical.

This theme is already formulated in *Existence and Existents*. It is my first book, a taking up in another form of *De l'évasion*. This horror of anony-mous being, obsession with this anonymity, this unceasingness; a bit like the nothing which annihilates (why does it not stay calm?). And already the radical difference is outlined, that which I will later call the funda-mental dissymmetry between me and the other.

Q.: You asked for a band around the book *Existence and Existents* with the inscription: "Where it is no longer a question of anguish." Was that irony?

E.L.: In my book, it is being that weighs…

Q.: Not the anguish of nothing?

E.L.: It is not the anguish of nothing, it is the horror of the *there is*, of existence. It is not the fear of death; it is the "too much" of oneself. It's true, since Heidegger and even since Kierkegaard, anguish is analyzed as the emotion of not being, as the anguish before [the] nothing, whereas the horror of the *there is* is close to disgust for oneself, close to the weari-ness of oneself.

Q.: So what is at stake is to leave oneself. But how to leave oneself?

E.L.: Now we are getting to the fundamental themes. Leaving oneself, that is, being occupied with the other, that is, with his suffering and death, before being occupied with one's own death. I'm not saying at all that this is done with cheerfulness, that it's no problem, nor above all, that this would be a cure from the horror of the weariness of being or from the effort of being, a way of distracting oneself. I think it is the discovery of the foundation of our humanity, the very discovery of the good in the meeting of the other. I'm not afraid of the word *good*; the responsibility for the other is the good. It's not pleasant, it is good.

Q.: You write that the rapport of the same and the other, that is to say of the I and the other, is language.

E.L.: Should language be thought uniquely as the communication of an idea or as information, and not also—and perhaps above all—as the fact of encountering the other as other, that is to say, already as response to him? Is not the first word *bonjour*? As simple as *bonjour*. *Bonjour* as benediction and my being available for the other man. It doesn't mean: what a beautiful day. Rather: I wish you peace, I wish you a good day, expression of one who worries for the other. It underlies all the rest of communication, underlies all discourse.

Q.: What project drove you at the beginning of your philosophical research? Does your work correspond to what you wanted to do?

E.L.: I started from the reservation with regard to being that I mentioned to you earlier. Not always in the form of dramatic thoughts. It wasn't very original at all: to start to understand the everyday as a monotony of instants which fall, the coming and going of existence in nonsense and boredom, through the gravity of the everyday, through the anguish of the political situation, the proximity of war and the triumph of Hitlerism.

In the *there is*, one finds all the gravity, all the seriousness of a lived adventure. It is this feeling which is reflected in my text, *De l'évasion*, and in the appearance of the *there is*. Then the consciousness of the ridiculousness of all these personal problems, when it is a matter of the other and his needs, of his presence and his life. I don't know whether this was my initial project or if it is my final project. I don't know anything about it; I am not able to say. I never thought about these things in terms of the pathos of a well-written biography. But in sum, the true, the incontestable value, about which it is not ridiculous to think, is holiness. This is not a matter of privations, but it is in the certitude that one must yield to the other the first place in everything, from the *après vous* before an open door right up to the disposition—hardly possible, but holiness demands it—to die for the other. In this attitude of holiness, there is a reversal of the normal order of things, the natural order of things, the persistence in being of the ontology of things and of the living. For me that

is the moment where, through the human, the beyond being—God—
comes to mind. I have spoken of this in my book of that title. If you will,
the situation in which God comes to mind would be neither miracle nor
the concern to understand the mystery of creation. Is the idea of creation
primary? The shock of the divine, the rupture of the immanent order, of
the order that I can embrace, of the order which I can hold in my
thought, of the order which can become mine, that is the face of the
other.

Q.: You say that the relation to the face of the other is straightaway
ethical.

E.L.: Ethics: a comportment in which the other, who is strange and
indifferent to you, who belongs neither to the order of your interest nor
to your affections, at the same time matters to you. His alterity concerns
you. A relation of another order than that of knowledge, in which the object is given value by knowing it, which passes for the only relation with
beings. Can one be for an I without being reduced to an object of pure
knowledge? Placed in an ethical relation, the other man remains other.
Here it is precisely the strangeness of the other and, if one can say so, his
"stranger-ness" which links him to you ethically. It is a banality, but one
has to be surprised by it. The idea of transcendence arises perhaps at this
point.

Q.: And the face?

E.L.: The face is not of the order of the seen, it is not an object, but it
is he whose appearing preserves an exteriority which is also an appeal or
an imperative given to your responsibility: to encounter a face is straightaway to hear a demand and an order. I define the face precisely by these
traits beyond vision or confusion with the vision of the face. One can say
once more: the face, behind the countenance that it gives itself, is like a
being's exposure unto death; the without-defense, the nudity and the misery of the other. It is also the commandment to take the other upon oneself, not to let him alone; you hear the word of God. If you conceive of
the face as the object of a photographer, of course you are dealing with an
object like any other object. But if you *encounter* the face, responsibility
arises in the strangeness of the other and in his misery. The face offers itself to your compassion and to your obligation. Of course I can look at
the face while defacing it, like any other plastic form, eliminating the

signification of the responsibility with which its nudity and strangeness encumbers me.

Q.: So it is a question of facing the other rather than defacing him?

E.L.: Yes, facing, except that very often one faces while defacing. Looking at you like at an image, one knows the color of your eyes, the form of your nose, etc. But, when I say to you, *bonjour,* I have blessed you before knowing you; I am concerned with your days, I enter into your life beyond the order of simple knowledge.

Q.: So it is ethics before everything else?

E.L.: The word ethics is Greek. More often, especially now, I think about holiness, about the holiness of the face of the other or the holiness of my obligation as such. So be it! There is a holiness in the face but above all there is holiness or the ethical in relation to oneself in a comportment which encounters the face as face, where the obligation with respect to the other is imposed before all obligation: to respect the other, to take the other into account, to let him pass before oneself. And courtesy! Yes, that is very good, to let the other pass before I do; this little effort of courtesy is also an access to the face. Why should you pass before me? That is very difficult, because you, too, encounter my face. But courtesy or ethics consists in not thinking that reciprocity.

Q.: Alterity is a theme that comes up very often in your work.

E.L.: Yes, an alterity which cannot be summarized in the fact that the other who resembles me has, in his characteristics, another attribute. Normally we say that a thing is other because it has other properties. There you have a piece of white paper, next to it a piece of black paper—alterity? They are other also by the fact that the one is in one place in space and the other is at another place in space; this is not the alterity that distinguishes you from me. It is not because your hair is unlike mine or because you occupy another place than me—this would only be a difference of properties or of dispositions in space, a difference of attributes. But before any attribute, you are other than I, other otherwise, absolutely other! And it is this alterity, different from the one which is linked to attributes, that is your alterity. This alterity is not justifiable logically; it is logically indiscernible. The identity of the I is not the result of any knowledge whatsoever: I find myself without looking for myself. You are you and I am I. This cannot be reduced to the fact that we differ because of our bodies or because of the color of our hair, or by the place we occupy in space. Don't you think that one is not surprised enough by this identity distinct from *a* is *a*?

Q.: How to encounter the other?

E.L.: To encounter, what does that mean? From the very start you are not indifferent to the other. From the very start you are not alone! Even if you adopt an attitude of indifference you are obliged to adopt it! The other counts for you; you answer him as much as he addresses himself to you; he concerns you!

Q.: How to go toward the other? Is it love that brings me to him?

E.L.: If you wish, without putting into this word all the literature that it evokes. If you take up again the term *nonindifference*, love then is perhaps an affective engagement where an intention of love is felt, the responsibility in being about which I spoke—all that spreads out in love. Responsibility makes precise something grave in the consciousness of alterity. Love goes farther; it is the relation to the unique. It is proper to the principle of love that the other, loved, is for me unique in the world. Not because in being in love I have the illusion that the other is unique. It is because there is the possibility of thinking someone as unique that there is love.

Q.: But every other is unique. And we do not love everyone.

E.L.: That is where we leave what I call the ethical order, or the order of holiness, or the order of compassion, or the order of love, or the order of charity, where the other man concerns me—independently of the place that is given to him in the multiplicity of humans and even beyond our appurtenance as individuals to the human genus. He concerns me as neighbor, as the first one to come along. He was the unique. In his face, despite the countenance he gave to himself, I have read an appeal addressed to me, God's order not to leave him. The interhuman relation in the gratuitousness or the holiness of being-for-the-other.

Q.: I'll ask my question again. We don't love everyone; we prefer, we judge.

E.L.: Everything is modified once the "everyone" is affirmed. There the other is not unique. This value of holiness—and this upsurge of compassion—cannot exclude or ignore the relation with others in the simultaneity of everyone. There is the problem of choice. Do I not have to discover, in my disinterestedness, the one who is other par excellence? Here is the problem of ratio. Exigency of a judgment but, from there on, exigency of a comparison between uniques and their return to the common genus. First violence, contestation of uniqueness. A violence nevertheless led by the initial for-the-other which is contested by the appearing of a third, fourth, fifth human being—all of whom are my "others." The necessity of separating, a separating precisely justified. Perhaps the very birth of an ideal of objectivity and of the social order (with its disorders), birth of institutions and the State, of the authority which is necessary to the very institutions of justice, even by this limitation of the initial charity out of which justice came. Solution of this internal contradiction in the liberal State which, behind all justice established as regime, anticipates a justice which is more just, and also leaves a place for the individual—next to and after the respect for justice—and for each individual's resources of charity and compassion. Justice does not give itself as definitive in a liberal State. We live in a society in which an even better justice would be necessary. I don't know whether you allow this somewhat complex system which consists in judging *according to truth* and in sentencing *in love* him who has been judged. The suppression of the death penalty seems to me an essential thing for the coexistence of charity with justice. This idea of a progression of justice and its openness is important for the very wisdom of its ameliorations. To search for a society which is straightaway charitable, a regime which is straightaway charitable, is to run the risk of Stalinism. I don't know if you see what I want to say...

Q.: Yes, goodness for all, regulated, obligatory...

E.L.: It is to think that one can circumvent charity—and the invention necessary to it—by installing laws which once and for all produce what can each time only be a personal act of compassion and love. Stalinism starts out with excellent intentions and drowns itself in administration. Oh, the violence of administration! It is important for me that the other be recognized, but since the unique ones are a multiplicity, calculations, comparisons—which cause the unique to disappear—are necessary. It is necessary that I rediscover the unique, once I have judged the thing; each time anew, and each time as a living individual and as a unique individual who can find, in his very uniqueness, what a general consideration cannot find.

Q.: What do you think of movements in favor of the rights of man?

E.L.: Movements with regard to the rights of man proceed from what I call the consciousness that justice is not yet just enough. In thinking the rights of man and in concerns for the rights of men in liberal societies the distance between justice and charity seeks to reduce itself. Movements reinvented ceaselessly and which, at the same time, can never leave the order of solutions and general formulas. They never fulfill that which compassion, the concern for the individual, alone can give. Beyond justice and law, this remains a call to individuals in their singularity that they always remain citizens trusting in justice. Remember what we have said concerning interdiction and the obligation to have regard for the face of the other. Justice is awakened by charity, but the charity which is before justice is also after. There you have it. Now one should laugh a bit, having the impression that I am delivering a sermon.

Q.: Concretely, how is the responsibility for the other translated?

E.L.: The other concerns me in all his material misery. It is a matter, eventually, of nourishing him, of clothing him. It is exactly the biblical assertion: Feed the hungry, clothe the naked, give drink to the thirsty, give shelter to the shelterless. The material side of man, the material life of the other, concerns me and, in the other, takes on for me an elevated signification and concerns my holiness. Recall in Matthew 25, Jesus' "You have hunted me, you have pursued me." "*When* have we hunted you, *when* have we pursued you?" the virtuous ask Jesus. Reply: when you "refused to feed the poor," when you hunted down the poor, when you were indifferent to him! As if, with regard to the other, I had responsibilities starting from eating and drinking. And as if the other whom I hunted were equivalent to a hunted God. This holiness is perhaps but the holiness of a social problem. All the problems of eating and drinking, insofar as they concern the other, become sacred. What is important is the notion of a responsibility preceding a notion of a guilty initiative.

Guilt without fault, as if I had to do with the other before knowing him, in a past that has never taken place. Very important, this responsibility without guilt. As if the other were always something to me, as if his condition of being a stranger concerned me precisely. Ethically I cannot say that the other does not concern me. The political order—institutions and justice—relieve this incessant responsibility, but for the political order, for the good political order, we are still responsible. If one thinks this to the limit, one can say that I am responsible for the death of the other. I cannot leave him alone to die, even if I cannot stop it. This is how I have always interpreted the "Thou shalt not kill." "Thou shalt not kill" does not signify merely the interdiction against plunging a knife into the breast of the neighbor. Of course, it signifies that, too. But so many ways of being comport a way of crushing the other. No doubt I cite the Bible too much. Let us cite Pascal's admirable formula: "This is my place in the sun, the usurpation of the whole earth begins here."[4] In this sentence of Pascal, by the simple claiming of a place in the sun, I have already usurped the earth.

Q.: You say that I am responsible for the death of the other. Isn't that too much to ask?

E.L.: Attention brought to the death of the other! Heidegger defined my finitude of human subjectivity by the fact that I am destined to die, that "I am unto death" where no one can replace me. I raise this to the notion that I am responsible for the death of the other, and even to the point of thinking: being affected by the death of the other is the remarkable and essential event of my psychism as human psychism. We are used to a philosophy where the confirmation of self is the principle of subjectivity and where spirit is equivalent to knowing, that is to say, to the gaze which takes in things, to the hand which takes and possesses them, to the domination of beings. In man, the contention of being, the effort of being, and the universal perseverance of being in its being are repeated and confirmed. I think, on the contrary, that in man this ontology is interrupted or can be interrupted. Within the vision I am developing, human emotion and its spirituality begin in the for-the-other, in being affected by the other. The great event and the very source of its affectivity is in the other! In all feeling my relation to the other intervenes. Here is my response to your questions about responsibility: "In this case life is impossible," you will say. I will say to you that the ideal of holiness utopically commands our being and explicates our very justice and the whole importance that we attribute to it. The entire detour of justice is necessary so that I can be concerned with myself. Here is the second sermon! [*Laughter.*] All this reflection is an attempt to think the ultimate structures of the human.

Q.: In the face to face between the "I" and the "you," between me and the other, there is a fundamental asymmetry.

E.L.: Yes! The other passes before I do; I am for the other. That which the other has as duties with respect to me, that's his business, not mine!

Q.: But it is a crazy demand!

E.L.: It is crazy, yes, and it cannot dispense with justice because my relation with other men is not a relation with a single man. There is always a third, a fourth, because in fact we are in a multiple society where, on the fundamental relation to the other the whole knowing of justice, which is indispensable, is superimposed. In pure charity, I know what I owe the other. What the other owes me, that's his business! It is in the face to face that I try to capture the human, the I as a "for-the-other." The notion of justice is deduced from it. The I is not uniquely that which returns to itself. It is he who has to do with the other. Traditional philosophy has habituated us to the punctuality of an I always itself, always reflecting on itself, and the reflexivity in this tradition is considered an essential interiority. I ask myself if interiority is the ultimate structure of the spiritual. All the same, you see that my language is not simply a sermon; it is also an attempt to philosophize.

Q.: Would you still say today, as you do in *Existence and Existents*, that the relation with the other is a movement toward the good?

E.L.: This formula seems to abuse the term *good* or use it too lightly. On the contrary, I want to take it seriously. I think it is at the center of the philosophical problematic. In all my effort there is as if a devalorization of the notion of being, which, in its obstinacy in persevering in being, conceals violence and evil, ego and egoism. It is the notion of the good which seems to me to correspond to my analysis of the for-the-other, conducted from the starting point of the phenomenology of the face. The good is the passage to the other, that is to say, a manner of relaxing my tension over existing in the guise of a concern for oneself, where the existing of the other is more important to me than my own. The good is the excessive importance of the other over me, whose possibility in reality is the rupture of being by the human or the good in the ethical sense of the term.

Certainly there is holiness, in being occupied with someone other before being occupied with oneself, in watching over someone other, in responding to someone other before responding to oneself. The human is the possibility of holiness. The patronizing slogans "being good," "being nice," which one smiles about, I take seriously. They must be thought to the limit, with rigor and acuity. To be for the other, to respond to the other, to love!

Q.: To be for the other, to be responsible for the other person, to want the good of the other, does not that go together with the interest that one has for him, even with love? Can one really be responsible for an other whom one considers an enemy?

E.L.: That one considers the other an enemy can happen and happens very often! I talked about holiness only as a possibility. But the human in being is that possibility. The possibility of hearkening to the original language of the face of the other in his misery and in his ethical command, this way of surmounting in one's own being one's effort to be, interests me. I even think that the good is older than evil. But the I is not necessarily up to that responsibility. Evil is the refusal of that responsibility, the fact of letting this prior attention turn itself away from the face of the other man. Evil is possible, but so is holiness. It does not have any meaning before the human, in the being where only this very being is at issue.

Q.: Am I responsible for the evil that the other commits?

E.L.: Up to which point does my responsibility extend? I think that in a certain way I am responsible for the evil in the other—for the evil that torments him as well as the evil he commits. Humanly, I am never in the clear toward the other man; I wouldn't be content with my happy perfection if I let evil continue or simply thought about punishing it. Concretely the situation is much more complex, because I never deal with only one person; I am always dealing with a multitude of persons, and consequently, these relations between persons and the context of the situation have to be taken into account. That is what limits, not my responsibility, but my action, modifying the modalities of my obligations. What I evoked as the problematic of justice, which seemed to deny, at first glance, this natural goodness, this simple and direct responsibility with respect to the other, which is at the same time the foundation and the demand of all justice. In the face of the other, I hear my responsibility for him. In the encounter I am concerned. He is nonindifferent to me. Nonindifference—already responsibility. But along comes a third party:

new responsibility. Unless one is able to decide by a clear and just judgment which one of the two concerns me first. I must compare them, render an account. It is the entire problematic of justice. I have called it the first violence: in the concern not to misrecognize the face of the other man is the refusal to see only the face.

Q.: It would seem that there is a great demand with regard to oneself, and you require that everyone meet this demand. Can one demand this of everyone?

E.L.: You know, as concerns the relation with the other, I always come back to my phrase from Dostoevsky. It is a central sentence in *The Brothers Karamazov*: "Each of us is guilty before everyone and for everything, and I more than all the others."[5] As if I were in the situation of the guilty one in the obligation toward others. The attitude of the other in no way intervenes in my responsibility a priori, in my initial responsibility with respect to the other who regards me. Moreover, without that initial guilt, almost nothing would remain of one's responsibility, due to a dividing of one's attentions. One sneaks out of it!

Q.: But this theme of responsibility, is it a metaphysical or a moral theme?

E.L.: I don't know the difference to which you are referring.

Q.: Let me ask it this way: Often, in reading you, one has the impression that metaphysics, understood as a science of the original or the absolute, is very close to the ethical.

E.L.: I am not at all frightened by the critique of the metaphysical world in the philosophy of today. But the term, in spite of everything, is traditionally loaded, and if I understand well, by metaphysics you understand a radical reflection which is perhaps also an initial and a final reflection. My response would consist in saying that the prior reflection of the human is precisely in a spirit which has been altered by the ideal of holiness; that the meaningful appears and signifies and has its importance above all in my relation with another person. To say it otherwise, the first act, the first intellectual act is peace. Peace, understanding by that my solicitation for the other person. Peace precedes my manner of thinking; it precedes the desire to know, properly speaking; it precedes objective thematization. There is reason when there is peace, when there is a pacific rapport from one person to another.

Q.: Peace with the other precedes knowledge, and the interpersonal relation is primordial. But how is this relation established?

E.L.: Listen, if this relation had to be established, that would mean we begin in solitude. On the contrary, the first shock of human psychism, its first pulsation, is precisely a search for alterity. Recently [in "Useless Suffering"] I had the occasion to reflect on pain; suffering is experienced par excellence as a being closed up within oneself, this superlatively passive suffering is like the impossibility of "getting out of it." At the same time there is, in this being closed up in oneself of suffering, the sigh or the cry which is already a search for alterity: I would even say, but many precautions would be necessary here, that it is the first prayer. It is in this first prayer that the spiritual really begins. And by saying prayer, evidently I anticipate the word *God*. But I think that this exteriority of which I speak, this intending of the face, or this approach of the face—"approach" is a good term, better than "relation"—this proximity, along with all that it implies of love and responsibility, is always at once the approach of the face and a hearkening to the voice of God. To the face of the other man, the alterity of the other, I connect the idea of a first shock where God comes to mind. It is in this sense that there is not a period of pure interiority. On the contrary, it is in the adventure or intrigue that is developed in relation to the other that, at certain moments, there is, separately, a kind of return to this pain preceding the first cry.

Q.: The theme of solitude is very present in your books; at the same time one has the impression that it is not a sad theme for you.

E.L.: Sad?

Q.: Yes, often solitude is thought about as something sad, but not in your work. After all, you have this formulation: "It is a matter of departing not from solitude but from being." How do you understand the word *solitude*?

E.L.: I do not have any sympathy for solitude. There is something good, something relatively good in solitude. It is perhaps better than the dispersion in the anonymity of insignificant relations but, in principle, solitude is a lack. My whole effort consists in thinking sociality not as a dispersion but as an exit from the solitude one takes sometimes for sovereignty, in which man is "master of himself as he is of the universe," in which domination is experienced as the supreme perfection of the human. I would contest this excellence. I understand sociality, peace, love of the other as the good, better than domination, better even than coincidence with the other. One speaks sometimes of coincidence with God, but there is no coincidence with God. This mystical event is always very suspect to me, unless it is a metaphor of something else, of a perfect accord with Him. Coincidence is fusion. For me, on the contrary, sociality is excellence, and one should never think sociality as a missed coincidence, as it is in a certain literature: in love, the lovers do not succeed in coinciding with each other, so to speak. Fashionable sadness! Love, however, is the proximity of the other—where the other remains other. I think that when the other is "always other," there is the essence of love. There was a famous discussion between Proust and Emmanuel Berl, in which Proust maintained that in love one never rejoined the other. Perhaps he deplored it, but he also maintained in a certain way that the more other the other is, the more he is loved, or rather, the more he is loved, the more he is other. I don't even know whether he thought that voluptuousness is the moment in which the other is the most other, that is to say, the most foreign, in which sociality, this nonindifference to alterity, is at its peak. And in this sense, love is not at all an eternal thirst. Love is an excellence, that is to say, the good itself.

Q.: You have written the extraordinary sentence, "The absence of the other in love is precisely his presence *as* other." But how to make this understood when, in love, one searches always to rejoin the other, to feel him as close to oneself?

E.L.: That's what I call nonindifference. This nonindifference can—in its double negation—be thought as a difference, as alterity. Here in language there is the possibility of expressing in a didactic manner this paradoxical relation of love, which is not simply the fact that I know someone—it is not a knowing—but the sociality irreducible to knowledge which is the essential moment of love. Practically, this goodness, this nonindifference to the death of the other, this kindness, is precisely the very perfection of love.

Q.: Close to love, there is another theme, that of filiality, which also has a relation to solitude. You say often that the son is that which is most close to me and at the same time is another, totally other.

E.L.: The big problem would consist in developing the theme of filiality in conjunction with the theme of love, which is a little bit the reality of things. In any case, in love there is, in my opinion, a new perspective. The very analysis of filiality is what one must insist on first, the fact that the son, and the daughter too, is other and is still, but only still, me. It is a relation which is not reducible to the possession of an object. Not solely because he or she is a living being but because the relation is different, as if in a certain sense—which is precisely filiality—here the other were I and I, an other.

Q.: When we hear the words "the father" and "the son," do we not enter directly into the religious sphere?

E.L.: They are, rather, terms which evoke the family. Is the initial relation to God familial? Certainly in religion we constantly evoke familial metaphors. But I think that the relation from stranger to stranger, becoming love and sacrifice, attests to the order of God even more. I have always admired the biblical formula, "Thou shalt love the stranger."

This relation can be prolonged in fraternal relations, but it is certainly in the relation to the other man, in my duties, in my obligations with regard to him, that the word of God exists for me. It is there that a considerable overthrowing of the natural order is produced: someone for whom I do not have regard regards me; that is the very paradox of the law of the stranger. Being, initially, that is to persist in one's being. It is in these terms that Spinoza understands existence. Being is the effort to be, the fact of persevering in one's being. And all of a sudden a rupture of that effort is produced in my responsibility with respect to the other, who logically is nothing, who is other, who is separated, who is stranger. I have this responsibility as soon as I approach the other man. It is in this sense that I speak of the word of God which overturns my perseverance in being into a solicitude for the other.

Miracle, first miracle. The first miracle, as I said, is in the fact that I say *bonjour!* I see a religious moment there. You just spoke of filiality, which I tried to describe in its originality as that which interrupts the persistence of the identical in its identity. That the identical par excellence, the I, has a son separated from him, an other, who is, nevertheless, as it were not completely other. It is as if in the son's alterity I could be affected; that is, after all, paradoxical. And in that sense it is, if you will, miraculous or religious. I think that the thematic of my relation to the son has a relation to the problem of death, as if his death concerned me more than my own, as if I went toward him, beyond the attachment to my own being. I have thought about this theme a lot. I don't take refuge in things not written; they are problems which have to be thought out; I am alluding to it right now. It is in this direction that I will look for the signification of the son, of genealogy... a way for me to have possibilities which, in a certain way, are beyond my possibilities. From a logical or ontological point of view, that is a great paradox, given that my possibilities are always contained in my being. One cannot have possibilities outside of one's being. The son does things, has another destiny than my own, and at the same time (there it is!) my destiny and not my destiny. In the same way there is in me responsibility with respect to my son, and there is in his alterity something which overflows my very finitude. This is how I will answer without making definitive statements. That is a direction in which one can look.

q.: In a parallel fashion, to create a work, is that not also a relation to the overflowing of the self?

e.l.: Yes, one can think that there is filiality in the work. Any instrument, any tool you make, will have a "destiny" through those other than myself who will use it; but it is, nevertheless, a signification where alienation is much more radical than in that of a written work, or a work of art. The others who enter by reading and by interpretation will participate more in my destiny than by using a machine which I might have constructed. A great text, a great work, participates in that essence of writing, in the religious sense of the term, and calls for an interpretation. There is a whole new destiny through interpretation. There is also filiality in relation to this future reader who is me, who has a relation of filiality to me, and who, at the same time, will freely read the work which is from me and will interpret it according to his very own being.

One should not think that there is here a multiplication of the miracle of filiality, but simply that the miracle of filiality is more complex, and that having a son is not only to leave him to his destiny. It is, on the contrary, his whole life, everything that he will read, everything that he will write, that belongs to me in a certain way through this son and through this work.

q.: And can one think of filialities which would not be of a biological order, which would be spiritual, like from master to disciple?

e.l.: You mean like fraternity? I don't know if every being, every man, can feel himself to be my son, but there can be fraternity between us. The real fraternity is fraternity by the fact that the other concerns me; inasmuch as he is stranger, he is my brother.

You will not understand fraternity except by declaring it nonbiological. Cain is not the brother of Abel! True "fraternity" has to be founded after the scandal of this murder, which is the murder of a stranger. But I want to say that the relation between father and son is a modality of that different strangeness; there is certainly a receptivity possible in respect to someone other who becomes central, in the same way that there are certainly, in the position of the master to the disciple, situations in which the disciple becomes the son. In Jewish thought, the relation of the master to the disciple is more paternal than the relation of the father to the son. This is an absolutely extraordinary thing. The son has more duties in respect to the master than he has in respect to his father. And when the father is master...

Q.: Very often you are presented as a Jewish thinker. Does that have any meaning for you?

E.L.: Well, listen, I am very happy that you ask me that question. To be considered a Jewish thinker is not in itself something that shocks me. I am Jewish and certainly I have readings, contacts, and traditions which are specifically Jewish and which I do not deny. But I protest against this formula when by it one understands something that dares to establish between concepts relations which are based uniquely in religious traditions and texts, without bothering to pass through the philosophical critique. There are two ways of reading a biblical verse. One consists in appealing to the tradition, in giving it the value of the premise in one's conclusions, without distrusting and without even taking account of the presuppositions of that tradition, and without even transposing its modes of expression, with all the particularisms which can be produced in that language. The second reading consists not in contesting straightaway, philosophically, but rather in translating and accepting the suggestions of a thinking which, once translated, can be justified by what manifests itself. For me, the relation to phenomenology has been extremely important: to say for every suggestive meaning the context of that meaning and what it presupposes as intellectual act and as spiritual atmosphere. Of course, I try to enter first into the language of the nonphilosophical tradition which is attached to the religious understanding of Jewish writings; I adopt it, but this adoption is not the philosophical moment of my effort. There I am simply a believer. A believer can search out, behind the adopted intelligibility, an intelligibility which is objectively communicable. A philosophical truth cannot be based on the authority of a verse. The verse must be phenomenologically justified. But the verse can allow for the search for a reason. This is the sense in which the words "you are a Jewish philosopher" are acceptable for me. It irritates me when one insinuates that I prove by means of the verse, when sometimes I search by way of the old ancient wisdom. I illustrate with the verse, yes, but I do not prove by means of the verse.

Q.: It is, by the way, for that reason that someone like myself, who is completely foreign to the Jewish tradition, can very well read you as a philosopher.

E.L.: Yes, I separate very clearly these two types of work. I even have two publishers; the one publishes my confessional texts, the other my texts which are called purely philosophical. I keep the two orders separate. In my commentaries—not only the philosophical ones, but the traditional ones—I refer very often to certain things which are understandable between persons of different beliefs. The verse always initially plays the role of illustration or suggestion—but there are situations in which an idea arises which takes on a certain force by the fact that this religious context brings with it a philosophical accent. The idea is then welcomed into the philosophical text and receives all the expression that it merits, while guarding the formulation which it had in the verse. To the notion "Thou shalt not kill," I give a signification which is not the simple prohibition of murder. It becomes a fundamental definition or description of the human event of being, a permanent prudence with respect to the violent and murderous acts against the other which are perhaps the very assertion of a being, as if the very imposition of a being's existence were already to jeopardize someone's life. And here, I link up with a text which I also consider a philosophical text, although it is by a religious and Christian philosopher. I quoted it a minute ago: "My place in the sun may be the image or the beginning of all usurpations." Of course, that is a vision of things where the idea of a nurturing earth to which one has absolute right is put into question. But this putting into question is philosophical; it is a not a simple reference, as one likes to say, to the migratory condition of the eternal Jew.

Q.: Yes because, when one says Jewish thinker, immediately…

E.L.: Right, one thinks of that. It is very important that it be Pascal who said it. It is enormous: "my place in the sun," but that is the first evidence; "there, already, is the usurpation of the entire earth," that is to say, the fact of depriving all the others of their place. Here I have given you an example. All the same, "Thou shalt love the stranger," which is found in the Bible thirty-six times, exclusively in the Pentateuch—thirty-six times, according to a talmudic text which adds, "and maybe even forty-six." When it says "thirty-six and maybe forty-six," this is to say, maybe fifty-six, maybe sixty-six. This is a manner of saying that it is important to feel it, outside of any statistical interest in the tradition. And one ends up understanding this formula, "Thou shalt love the stranger," not as an anti–Le Pen politics, but as the audacious and true affirmation that love itself, affectivity itself, and feeling itself have their initial place in the relation with the other, with the stranger which every man is for every other man. After all, everyone is a stranger. "I am a stranger on earth," says a verse of the Psalms, "Give me your law" (Ps. 119:19). There too is a verse that is philosophical from the start. Not only the avowal of a people without soil, but the signification of that presence on earth, of an exile behind the autochthonous, which is the definition of the pure transcendental subject and the primordial necessity of a moral law in that exile.

Q.: Would you say that you are a religious thinker?

E.L.: Here again, that can mean: are you a believer? do you practice a religion? But this is not as thinker in any case. Because your question asks: in your thinking, do the truths acquired once and for all by revelation intervene as the truths which constitute the basis of your philosophical life? I don't think so. But "religious" can also mean—I am repeating myself—suggestions, calls to analysis or research in religious texts, that is to say, in the Bible. But if you asked me the question differently: do you think that the Bible is essential to thinking? I would answer: yes!

Next to Greek philosophy, which promotes the act of knowing as a spiritual act par excellence, man is he who seeks truth. The Bible teaches us that man is he who loves his neighbor, and that the fact of loving his neighbor is a modality of meaningful life, of a thinking as fundamental—I would say more fundamental—than the knowledge of an object, than truth as knowledge of objects. In this sense, if one estimates that this second manner of being religious engenders thinking, I am a religious thinker! I think that Europe is the Bible and the Greeks, but it is also the Bible which renders the Greeks necessary.

Q.: That is to say religion and Greek philosophy?

E.L.: Yes, finally, religion, such as the Bible recounts it, promises it, because the human begins or, if you will, the subject begins, starting from its relation, its obligation with regard to the other. Certainly there is in the Bible an entire ritual life; it is probably essential too, and one must interpret it. But the fundamental thing traced in the Bible is a placing of the other as if in relation with me or, rather, the affirmation of my being as devoted to the other. "Thou shalt not kill" or "Thou shalt love the stranger" or "Thou shalt love thy neighbor as thyself": "as thyself" is very important and is added to "Thou shalt love the stranger," because "Thou shalt love thy neighbor as thyself" would signify rigorously that the attachment to the I is the fundamental attachment and that it must be projected from time to time unto the other, and that is why, "Thou shalt love the stranger"—whether it is said thirty-six or forty-six times—is as important as "Thou shalt love thy neighbor as thyself." All the rest is an ethics of comportment with regard to the other, in diverse degrees, at diverse heights. The whole characterization of man throughout the Pentateuch and Prophets is of man as independent subject and as responsible for the other. The Bible is also important in that sense. The great problem would consist in asking, what is the relation between the two traditions? Is it simply the convergence of two influences that constitute the European? I don't know if it is very popular to say this, but for me European man is central, in spite of all that has happened to us during this century, in spite of "the savage mind." The savage mind is a thinking that a European knew to discover, it was not the savage thinkers who discovered our thinking. There is a kind of envelopment of all thinking by the European subject. Europe has many things to be reproached for, its history has been a history of blood and war, but it is also the place where this blood and war have been regretted and constitute a bad conscience, a bad conscience of Europe which is also the return of Europe, not toward Greece, but toward the Bible. Old or New Testament—but it is in the Old Testament that everything, in my opinion, is borne. This is the sense in which I will answer your question: am I a religious thinker? I say sometimes: man is Europe and the Bible, and all the rest can be translated from there.

Q.: In your thinking, it would seem that you give a new sense to certain words; I am thinking notably of the word *God* or *chosen*. The chosenness of the Jewish people is often misunderstood, but you made its sense more precise.

E.L.: The chosenness of the Jewish people is a religious belief, but even on the traditional level, nonphilosophical, one has to make clear it is always considered as a surplus of responsibility, and as a surplus of responsibility demanded of oneself rather than others. Of course, very often it takes on an attitude of excellence, a pretension to aristocracy in the bad sense of the term, the right to privileges. In authentic thinking, however, it means a surplus of obligations. That this supplementary consideration, this supplementary precaution with regard to oneself, appears in the guise of ritual is perhaps the meaning of ritual and observance in Judaism, a chosenness in a sense independent of privilege, as if the Israelites felt more obligations and were held to more duties than others, which by the way, has caused them much trouble. I am coming back to my theme of responsibility. I have described in responsibility the relation of the I to the other, to the other as unique, inasmuch as responsibility for the other is already nonindifference and love. It's not love as amusement; it is the extreme importance of the other as unique, uniqueness by which the neighbor is to me precisely an other, that is to say, as it were, torn up from the common genus that unites us; the responsibility for the other is precisely not a simple kinship. The other man is other as unique in his genus and, as loved, unique to the world. Once you perceive him as an individual in his genus, he is already for you a "species of..." But to encounter him in his human uniqueness is not to abandon him: that is responsibility and nonindifference for the other. One is responsible for the person met on the street, and this responsibility is nontransferable. It is in this uniqueness of indeclinable responsibility that my own uniqueness resides in the end. I am responsible immediately, I and not another, and this "I and not another" is the world in which I am unique, in which the other man for whom I am responsible is unique. I am substituted for him in this responsibility, I am his hostage, responsible without having perpetrated anything against him, and responsible although he isn't anything to me or because he is nothing to me.

Q.: The other man is unique. But I, too...

E.L.: Where is my uniqueness? At the moment when I am responsible for the other I am unique. I am unique inasmuch as I am irreplaceable, inasmuch as I am chosen to answer to him. Responsibility lived as chosenness. The person responsible is able to avoid neither the appeal received nor his role in respect to someone else; ethically, responsibility is indeclinable. The responsible I is irreplaceable, noninterchangeable, commanded to uniqueness. Of course, in truth responsibility *can* be replaced, but then the relations between persons are established at the heart of a multiplicity and are regulated; not from one to the other in the uprightness of the face to face, but across a human multiplicity. This multiplicity of human beings must be organized, calculated. I can cede my responsibility within a society organized in a State, in justice. But even then, that which founds this demand for justice, that which obligates me to find justice, is the fact that I am responsible for the other man. I have called this uniqueness of the I in responsibility its chosenness. To a great extent, of course, this makes reference to the chosenness at issue in the Bible. It is thought as the ultimate secret of my subjectivity. I am I, not as master who takes in and dominates the world, but as called, in an indeclinable manner, in the impossibility of *refusing* this chosenness (to refuse it would be to accomplish evil). Freedom is here a necessity, but this necessity is also a freedom. This is how I will respond to your question concerning chosenness. The notion of chosenness as I present it is not an already religious category; it has an ethical origin, of course, and signifies a surplus of obligations. Do not think that the good God is mean by electing you in your uniqueness because, evidently, this causes you trouble; chosenness, rather, is the good. I come back to your earlier question about the notion of the good. It is not a happiness, this position of being responsible, but it is a dignity and a chosenness, and one owes gratitude for having been chosen. And even, this will be a reference to religion, one must be grateful for owing God gratitude. "We are grateful for having gratitude" is a liturgical phrase which always appeared to me as either bizarre or extraordinary. It doesn't signify "I owe you gratitude for having received something," it signifies that one owes gratitude precisely for having gratitude, gratitude for being in this apparently inferior situation of the one who renders thanks—when the superior one is God.

Q.: One thanks for giving instead of receiving?

E.L.: Yes, of course! And one even thanks for being in the position of owing gratitude for a situation which is no doubt inferior, a situation of infancy—which is supreme grace!

Q.: To consider the other not in his uniqueness but as the individual of a genus—I'm thinking notably of political discourse—is that not finally to avoid the encounter with the other, because it will always be of a group and not of an individual that one will speak?

E.L.: No, there is a justifiable motivation in considering the other as a genus in this appearance of the political, and I have given you the reason for that. We live within a human multiplicity. Outside of the other, there is always a third, and a fourth, a fifth, a sixth. In my responsibility I am exclusively responsible toward one even while thinking with regard to the others, but I cannot neglect anyone. Here I am obliged to think the other as under a genus or within the State. It is the fact of being a citizen and not simply a soul. A citizen is the gentleman who has been put under a genus; it is a gentleman who is given a genus, or a gentleman to whom I have given a genus. One must judge, one must know, one must do justice. This is the moment where all the Greek wisdom is essential. I said earlier: the Bible *and* Greece. This is perhaps the Greek moment, the entire political thinking of Greece, not simply this initial act of taking individuals in under a genus, of making them enter into a logic. Everything that I was developing until now on the subject of uniqueness, that was pre-logical. Not the savage mind, rest assured! Pre-logic. Only now one must pass by way of logic, one must make comparisons, one must say which of the two is guilty—and this is only possible in the State. Institutions and juridical procedures are necessary. You find again the necessity of the State. Violence, of course, in relation to the charity rendered necessary precisely by the charity inspired by the face of the neighbor. If the face had not appeared, one would have a purely violent multiplicity.

Q.: The State considers the individual in his genus.

E.L.: In his genus, and through institutions. Consequently, the work of the State, while denying it in some manner, comes to supplement this work of interpersonal responsibility which touches the individual in his uniqueness and which is the work of the individual in his uniqueness as the one responsible. Responsible according to a condition of hostage, because he responds to that which he has never committed, because he does not respond from any act of freedom committed beforehand, because he responds to a past which is not his own and which was never present to him. Philosophically, a remarkable situation in this responsibility of a hostage! Idea of a past which has never been my present, immemorial past, a past probably absolute, a past in its very own category. And then, there is this entering into the genus, the question we spoke about earlier: if, ultimately, the unique ones have to enter the genus, why then insist so much on the uniqueness? Isn't that a useless construction we set up? Since one has to go through the idea of the State, can one not reach it starting from the Hobbesian principle of "man as wolf to the other man"? One arrives at the State with a little bit of reason, a little bit of Greek spirit: this war of all against all leads man to construct a legal State where general principles are established, to which one submits oneself because the principles guarantee that the others will also submit themselves. Everything holds together because of the menacing return of the situation where man is wolf to the other man. Why, then, should one insist on the notion of the man who is *not* wolf to the other man, of the man who is responsible for the other man who always encumbers him? I think that the universality of the law in the State—all this violence done to the particular—is not license pure and simple, because as long as the State remains liberal its law is not yet completed and can always be more just than its actual justice. Hence a consciousness, if you will, that the justice on which the State is founded is, at this moment, still an imperfect justice.

One has to think it in an even more concrete manner, with a preoccupation with the rights of man which is not coincident, in my opinion, with the presence of the government. The concern for the rights of man is not a function of the State; it is in the State an institution which is not of the State; it is the call of humanity, which is not yet accomplished in the State. So one comes back to this surplus of charity or of mercy from which the State would issue—the first important thing. The second important thing: in the State where laws function in their generality, where verdicts are pronounced out of a concern for universality, once justice is said there is still, for the person as unique and responsible one, the possibility of or appeal to something that will reconsider the rigor of always rigorous justice. To soften this justice, to listen to this personal appeal, is each person's role. It is in that sense that one has to speak of a return to charity and mercy. *Charity* is a Christian term, but it is also a general biblical term: the word *hesed* signifies precisely charity or mercy. There is this appeal to mercy behind justice: this is how the necessity of the State is able not to exclude charity. I will give you, if you wish, an illustration, not with an example but with a text of Jewish origin. There is, say the rabbis (who are considered terrible people asking minute and ridiculous questions—their manner of treating the most important questions), a scriptural problem. One verse says: "The judge does not look at the face of everyone" (Deut. 11:7), that is to say: he does not look at the man who is in front of him nor does he consider this man's particular situation. For the judge, the man is simply someone who has to answer to the accusation. And there is another verse, a verse of benediction of the priests, which says: "May the Eternal turn His face toward you" (Num. 6:26). The rabbis answer in their manner: "Before the verdict, no face; but once the judgment is pronounced, He looks at the face." I am very happy to have been able to give you an example of what an illustration by the verse can be. I did not start from this text; I discovered it after the fact. This is altogether strange…

Q.: This presence of the singular in the universal, in the State, can one not rediscover it in the condition of the Jewish people? The testimony that the Jewish people have brought to humanity, is it not precisely of a singularity in and for the universal?

E.L.: I will accept the idea that the singular contributes to the universal because that doesn't harm anyone. The pope himself, in his declarations after the Council in the famous "Nostra Aetate," has recognized in the existence of the Jewish people almost a character of necessity. I cannot restate his exact formula, but he said that one has to listen to what the Jews say, that one has to listen to their readings; he didn't wish to say simply that one has to be courteous with respect to them. It is as if there were still, despite the "all has been consummated," a permanent signification of religious Judaism in the Christian perspective. I mean: a concrete signification of the persistence of the Jewish people, their readings, what they say and what they interpret.

Q.: I would like to come back to this necessity of the Jewish people.

E.L.: Listen, I'm not certain whether "necessity" was the right word. But in any case, the word pronounced by the pope was a positive one, which gave a value to the survival of Judaism, other certainly than the value one owes to every life. He even used, during his visit to a synagogue of Rome, the term *elder brothers*, speaking of the Jews. Of course in the Bible the elder brothers are often those who turn out badly, but the expression wanted to suggest: those of whom one can expect something because of their experience, precious experience which can be useful for the younger ones. If you want me to deal with the problem of Judeo-Christian relations today, I have to pose the problem in a more general manner. The great difficulty or the great misunderstanding is linked certainly to the history of Christianity. With books which, in their totality, do not have an exclusively dogmatic signification, but which speak of charity and the love of the other—the Sermon on the Mount is an admirable text for every reader. In the history of the Church there have been terrible years. For us, the memories of the Inquisition and the Crusades retain an anti-Jewish signification, the atmosphere of which spreads itself out over centuries, a very cruel atmosphere, very harsh. The hard task for the Jews throughout history has been to think that the tender figure of the Crucified accommodated itself to these cruelties. It was the fundamental contradiction of the charity of the new message. All this is today sometimes only memory, but sometimes still recent memory. The other day I was asking a religious German who was extremely open and pious why Jesus during the Crusades remained immobile on his cross. He answered: "You understand, Christ went to the end of his ordeal. There, if you will, was the peak of his humiliation. To support cruel acts by Christians was the ultimate humiliation of his Passion." To this I responded, "We will not agree on this. The suffering inflicted here was not uniquely his own; it was also the suffering of the victims."[6] For me, the very important moment of the Judeo-Christian drama is the Hitlerian drama, where Jews, certainly, knew Christian charity, for which I will never able to render enough thanks, but they also knew that the executioners of Auschwitz must have all done their catechism, and that that did not prevent them from committing their crimes.

But perhaps I am wrong to insist: everything that we knew in France, and even in Poland, and even in Lithuania, as Christian charity must be recalled before everything. Unforgettable things. I think that finally there was in the Church, in face of this torture, this misery, this abyss of Hitlerism, a comprehension directly evidenced toward the Jewish population. There begins, in my opinion, a new period in Judeo-Christian relations. From my perspective, a very large role was played—from 1935, when I got to know it—by the philosophy of Franz Rosenzweig. I will tell you two words about this philosophy, which is too complex to be exposited here, all the positions, journeys, and developments of which one could not enumerate with a single feature. I don't follow Rosenzweig all the time, by the way, although I have adopted certain of the fundamental positions of his purely theoretical thinking. This philosopher maintains that truth by itself—not due to the accidents of its history—is manifested in two forms, Jewish and Christian, and that these two forms are irreplaceable; the one cannot be converted into the other, but the one is indispensable to the other, without it being possible to say that the one is better than the other. Rosenzweig was born into an extremely assimilated family and was close to conversion to Christianity. Many members of his family were Christians; he remained Jewish and became a very ardent Jew, but maintaining precisely what I just explained to you. A thinking characteristic for an assimilated Jew, a European Jew, although he dropped the habitual manners of an assimilated Jew. He died very young in 1929 within a Jewish ambiance that he had reconstituted fully around himself. He maintained that the Jew is close to the Lord, that the world is not yet close to the Lord, and that Christianity is the manner in which those who are not close to the Lord go across the world toward Him. The figure of Christ turned toward God appeals to all men; in Judaism there is already attainment, but not for everyone. Thus two different but indispensable moments. Whatever be the contestable parts of this argument, the striking event remains: for the first time in religious history, the announcement of a truth in the form of two truths, susceptible of encountering each other without coinciding. There is us, but there are also the others. I am not saying that this duality is easy to live and to think, as a part of daily consciousness. The fact that this could have been thought by a rigorous and total intelligence and by a man who was very pure and of a very integral European culture always impressed me as a precursor of a new peace. That is why events like the text of the "Nostra Aetate" and the visit of the pope to the synagogue in Rome—I regret very much that there is not yet recognition by the Church of the state of Israel[7]—are important and extremely decisive events which attest to new possibilities beyond themselves.

q.: After having spoken of Rosenzweig, let us speak, if you would, of Martin Buber. I believe you know him?

E.L.: Yes, I got to know him personally after the war. My interest in the intersubjective relation, my principle theme, has often been compared to the philosophy of Buber, who distinguished the I-Thou, relation between persons, from the I-It, the relation between man and things. The relation to the other man is irreducible to the knowledge of an object. This is certainly a terrain of reflection where Buber has been before me. When one has worked, even without knowing it, a terrain that has already been worked on by another, one owes allegiance and gratitude to the pioneer. I do not refuse this to Martin Buber, even if, in fact, it is not starting from the Buberian oeuvre that I was led to the reflection on the alterity of the other, to which my modest writings are consecrated. Gabriel Marcel also came independently to this reflection. I do not know if he recognized the paternity of Buber, but he spoke sincerely of a relationship. Thus I am very close to Buberian theses, despite the burst of genius that his books bear and the poetic potential of his very inspired expression. His thinking is universally known and has exercised a great influence across the world. Multifaceted genius, Buber consecrated a considerable work to Hasidism, which is altogether foreign to me, and which he practically introduced into the European sensibility. He wrote stories and novels in which his philosophical thinking was also expressed. I read his *I and Thou*, a fundamental book, where the interpersonal relation is distinguished from the object relation in a very convincing and brilliant way, and with much finesse. The great thing that separates us, or the little thing—when one speaks of someone whom one is said to resemble, one often says, "On little things, there are differences between us"—the principle thing that separates us is what I call the asymmetry of the I-Thou relation. For Buber the relation between the I and the Thou is straightaway experienced as reciprocity. My point of departure is in Dostoevsky and in the phrase I quoted to you earlier: "Each of us is guilty before everyone and for everything, and I more than the others." The feeling that the I owes everything to the Thou, that its responsibility for the other is gratitude, and that the other has always, and rightfully, a right over me: all that I said to you earlier about this "I" submitted to obligation, about this "I" commanded in the face of the other—with this double structure of human misery and word of God—all this perhaps represents a theme basically different from the one that Buber approached. I don't want to develop this further; one of my texts on my relation with Buber will soon be republished.[8] I believe that I have been able to identify many points of difference with him. But what is central is the theme of asymmetry, which determines our different manners of speaking. Consequently, I have read Buber with much respect and attention, but I am not always in agreement with him.

I will recount for you a recent reading where Buber astonished me greatly. It was a text in relation to his biography. There was an encounter with an old pious Jew, who asked him a question relating to 1 Sam. 15:33, a verse where the prophet commands King Saul to erase from the map and from History the kingdom of Amalek, which in the biblical and talmudic tradition incarnates radical evil. Is not Amalek the first to have attacked, cowardly, the Israelites coming out of Egypt, the just-liberated slaves? We are discussing neither history nor historicity. The meaning of biblical hyperbole is to be sought in the context of these hyperboles, whatever be the distance between the verses! There is in Deut. 25:19: "When the Eternal, Your God, will have rid you of all your enemies all over the land that he gives you . . . You will blot out the remembrance of Amalek from under heaven." It belongs to the man who has been freed from evil to strike the ultimate blow against evil. Saul does not accomplish his mission; he does not know how to blot out. He spares Agag of Amalek and he brings back spoils, the best pieces of the Amalekite herds. A scene in which the prophet Samuel asks for an account. Dialogue: "What means this bleating of sheep which strikes my ears and the lowing of cattle?"—"It is to sacrifice to the Eternal, your God."—"The Eternal does not delight in burnt offerings as much as He delights in those who obey his voice."—"Bring to me King Agag" (1 Sam. 15:33). Samuel kills him on the spot. Cruelty of Samuel, who is nonetheless son of the most gentle woman in the world, Hannah. The question asked to Buber: How could he have done this? Buber's response: The prophet did not understand what God commanded him. No doubt Buber thought that his conscience informed him better about the will of God than did books. And why did he not read in 1 Sam. 15:33, "As your sword has made women childless, so shall your mother be childless among women"? I am not always in agreement with Buber, I have told you. I continue to think that without an extreme attention brought to the Book of books, one cannot listen to conscience. There Buber did not think of Auschwitz.

Q.: I would like you to speak now about the man whom you met shortly after the war and who was very important to you, Monsieur Shoshani.

E.L.: After the war I was very attached to a man who was extraordinary, due to the height of his thinking and his moral elevation. He died several years ago in Israel. He lived very close to here; he was a gynecologist; his name was Henri Nerson, Dr. Nerson. My book, *Difficult Freedom*, is dedicated to him. It was he who, directly after the war, introduced me to another exceptional being, exceptional in all senses, and also in the literal sense of the term. He was not like others: in his appearance, in his exterior manner, he did not belong to the order of everyone else. He was not a hobo, but it happened that, according to the common—very common—sense of mortals, he resembled a hobo. His name was Monsieur Shoshani, but I'm not sure if that was his real name. Dr. Nerson had been his student for twenty years before he met me—forty semesters, as my friend used to say, laughing with pleasure. He had got to know him in Strasbourg; Nerson was Alsatian. He warned me too, introducing me to what one could call the atmosphere of M. Shoshani, that the one who vindicates the yoke of the study of the Torah is dispensed from the yoke of civility, and that, in any case, M. Shoshani was the only human individual to whom this ancient and strange apothegm could be rigorously applied. He called himself Monsieur Shoshani. Nerson wasn't sure either if that was the true name of his master, who thought that everything which concerns a man on a personal level was only interesting for himself, and only in very determinate circumstances. The enormity of this man was, first of all, his knowledge of the Jewish texts, the Holy Scriptures, of course, but who would dare to turn that into a merit? Shoshani knew by heart the entire oral tradition to which the Scriptures gave rise. He knew by heart the Talmud and all its commentaries, and the commentaries on the commentaries. I don't know if you have ever seen a page of a treatise of the Talmud. The text of the Mishnah, written down in the second century, debated in the Gemara, written down toward the end of the fifth century, commentaries by Rashi of the tenth and the eleventh centuries, prolonged by the commentaries of those who are called the Tosephites, prolonged further by commentaries from all sides and from all times. Typographically these pages hold something prodigious—a mixture of characters, references, referrals, reminders of all kinds. In Shoshani's course, into which I was admitted, the master never had a book in front of him. He knew everything by heart, and he could interrupt me if, in front of him, I was reading or deciphering with difficulty in the corner of some page the small characters of a Tosephite: "Listen, you back there, you missed a word at the end of the line." His courses were fascinating, despite their length—or because of their length—they ended around two in the morning after five or six hours. But here I'm just telling you about the playful side, the juggling of this considerable genius, which is a bit undignified in its somewhat monstrous format, it is true. One would realize suddenly afterwards that this knowledge of texts was nothing. Alongside this purely exterior knowledge, by memory, M. Shoshani was gifted with an extraordinary dialectical power: the quantity of notions thought together and combined left an impression of savageness, in their unpredictable inventions. The manner in which the texts and Scripture are treated by the Talmudists is already extremely complicated and wise, but Shoshani knew how to prolong it to other textual horizons in order to make an always restless dialectic rebound sovereignly. I knew that outside of this incomparable knowledge of the sources—oceans of knowledge in a way—he had acquired very quickly a vast culture of mathematics and modern physics. I learned that after having disappeared from Paris—he died at Montevideo in South America—I learned that he had given courses there in nuclear physics. A strange man in everyday manners, I have already told you. Sometimes we asked ourselves from what he lived. Certainly from lessons, but sometimes he would find someone passionate about his science who in turn tempted a rich amateur stemming from the destroyed communities of Jewishness of Eastern Europe where the Torah had "a good reputation" and was appreciated for its sublime games. He would thus confiscate Shoshani and provide him with bed, board, and servants in exchange for his discourse. But at a certain moment Shoshani would say "*basta!*" and he would disappear and would find other people of different social groups, paying or nonpaying. M. Shoshani accepted a room at my place; he would come once or twice a week. This lasted several years, two or three, I cannot tell you exactly how long, and then one fine day, without saying goodbye, he left.

Q.: That was when?

E.L.: During the years which immediately followed the war, around 1946–47. He disappeared without saying goodbye. Some time later, one evening, at eleven o'clock, the doorbell rang. I went to open and he said, "It's me." He disappeared again, and we again found his trace in Montevideo, where he died. So that's how he was, this man, someone for whom Scripture and the commentaries were not at all a field of virtuosity. Without always grasping the ultimate sense of his wisdom, one would be impressed by the perfect art of his dialectics. What remained for me of this contact, made out of restlessness, marvels, and insomnia? In short, a new access to rabbinic wisdom and to its signification for the human. Judaism is not the Bible; it is the Bible seen through the Talmud, through the rabbinical wisdom, interrogation, and religious life. This science has two modes. First, there are all the texts which concern duties and the juridical life, those which develop, properly speaking, the Law. This is called *halakhah*, which prescribes, if you wish, everyday conduct: religious, political, social. A lot of casuistics complicate all these problems, but precisely open up the new perspective which transforms all the facts of the fundamental problem. A thinking which proceeds by examples, rather than by the abstraction of the concept, a fundamental part—and certainly the most difficult, the most rude part—of the Talmud. At the same time, it contains a part which one calls *haggadic*. *Haggadah* signifies narrative, legendary narrative. These are variations of the tradition, very ancient variations, very venerable, probably originating or at least taken up again in the first centuries of the Christian era.

Q.: Could you make precise the difference between the juridical texts and the legendary narratives?

E.L.: Next to the juridical parts, there are passages which one calls haggadic, as I told you, which are narratives which appear to be legendary and which expand on many of the stories told in the historical parts of the Old Testament, conversations which are neither given nor mentioned and which have an edifying character, in a certain way of course. But at the same time it is within this haggadic form that the metaphysical or perhaps philosophical prolongations of the law itself are recounted. It is recounted how at the moment when the people left Egypt, Moses looked for the bones of Joseph to bring them back to the Holy Land. Has this narrative no signification beyond the Jews? Does not Joseph represent a certain moment of exile and the wisdom of an ingenious economic administration which nevertheless remains faithful to the Promised Land where one must transport his bones? Are not all these allusions important? How, in the moment of haste when one tried to bring back Joseph, did things happen? This very haste is told in a much fuller manner than in the biblical narrative. I cannot tell you the story itself, but I can give you an example from the *haggadah*. You have in the Talmud a story where the details have a signification which is probably symbolic, but to which one does not always pay attention. The capacity that M. Shoshani had of amplifying or interpreting these passages was very impressive. I don't know if I learned much from him about the manner in which purely juridical texts must be interpreted, but something remained, not the contents but the manner in which these haggadic stories must be approached. I worked on this a lot, first by returning to the talmudic text and trying to understand it. I never expected to write a book about it, but I would know how to teach it. In particular, in this spirit I give a course at the school which I formerly directed every week on Saturday from eleven to noon. I comment in this perspective, searching out the inspiration that he taught me to research in the texts of the weekly sequence.

In Jewish liturgy, you might know this, the Pentateuch is divided into fifty or fifty-two sequences which follow the Sabbaths of the year. In the sequence of each week, I choose some verses which I comment on in front of the students of the school and also in front of a group of all kinds of people who come to listen, to prolong the spirit of Shoshani.

In all modesty really, because in oneself one is not much, but next to this man, one is nothing. I am extremely grateful for what I learned from him. In a haggadic text of the treatise *Pirke Avoth*, there is this phrase: "The words of the sages are like glowing embers." One can ask, why embers, why not flame? Because it only becomes a flame when one knows how to blow on it! I have hardly learned to blow. There are always great minds who contest this manner of blowing. They say, "You see, he draws out of the text what is not in the text. He forces a meaning into it." But if one does it with Goethe, with Valéry, with Corneille, the critics accept it. It appears more scandalous to them when one does it with regard to Scripture. And one has to have met Shoshani in order not to be convinced by these critical minds. Shoshani taught me: what is essential is that the meaning found merits, by its wisdom, the research that reveals it. That the text had suggested it to you.

Q.: What relation did you have with Judaism at the time you met M. Shoshani?

E.L.: I have always been Jewish, you know! I took the religious and the historical adventure of Judaism to heart, taking it as the central adventure of the human. I myself was not at Auschwitz, but finally I lost my entire family there. Even now I ask myself if there is not a strange teaching— may God forgive me for saying this: a teaching of Auschwitz—strange teaching, according to which the beginning of faith is not at all the promise, and faith is not at all something that one can preach, because it is difficult to preach—that is to say, to propose to the other—something without promise. But one can preach it to oneself, one can ask it of oneself: I am not saying that I always manage to consent to it. It is necessary to recall what I was saying to you about symmetry and dissymmetry: to tolerate Auschwitz without denying God, it is perhaps permissible to ask that of oneself. But perhaps also: there would even be an offense in contradicting the despair of those who went to their death. One can ask oneself if even to oneself one is permitted to speak of a religion without promise. Certainly the history of the Holocaust has played a much bigger role in my Judaism than the encounter with this man. But the encounter with this man gave me back a trust in the books. This formula which I use now, "more profound than consciousness, than interiority, are books," came to me during this period with him. I told you this morning the story about Buber, recounting my indignation about the fact that Buber thinks that his conscience knows more about it than books do: this relates directly to the signification of the book which I was just speaking about.

Q.: How did your reflection evolve after this period? What changed, what continued, and what became more profound?

E.L.: These kinds of reckoning are pretentious; they have always to be redone. I remained all the same faithful to what I call the phenomenological manner, but perhaps the importance that I attribute in the analysis to alterity seems to me to stem more from my manner of taking up again the analysis of Scripture. In Scripture one can find other things also! But Scripture speaks to us first of all—Christians say so as well—about the other man and detaches us from this attachment of being to itself. In any case, all the passages in Scripture where one encounters the other seem essential to me. Here I am no longer in the sermon, I am in the confession! It is another genre that one should distrust.

Q.: One does not really know what rapport you have had with the intellectual contemporaneity or with contemporaneity in general. I'm thinking especially, for example, of what one has called structuralism.

E.L.: No, structuralism, I still do not understand today. Of course the most eminent mind of the century is Lévi-Strauss, but I do not at all see where the target of his vision is. It certainly responds, from a moral perspective, to what one calls decolonization and the end of a dominating Europe, but my reaction is primary—it is, I know, worse than primitive: can one compare the scientific intellect of Einstein with the "savage mind," whatever be the complications, the complexities, that the "savage mind" may gather or accomplish?

How can a world of scientific thinking and of communication through scientific thinking be compared to it? No doubt I have not read as I should. It is certainly not structuralism that was able to tempt me. I know that it has had a prodigious influence. There are very distinguished minds, the best of our epoch—such as Ricœur—who take it very seriously.

Q.: But what, between the years of 1945 and today, has tempted you, if I may say so, what intellectual or political event?

E.L.: Outside the masters of phenomenology, I read first of all the texts into which M. Shoshani initiated me, that seemed to me much more important. I have memories of Léon Brunschvicg, but there has also been Blanchot, Jean Wahl, Ricœur, Derrida, and also Vassily Grossman and the Israeli novelist S. Y. Agnon.

Q.: Could you talk to us about your experience as a professor? I know that the theme of teaching is dear to you. How did you arrive at the idea of becoming a professor?

E.L.: I encountered many difficulties in preparing my courses. I always felt better when I was borne by a text and a commentary. The construction of a systematic course, the anticipation of all questions and objections, always seemed to me abstract and artificial. I used to say, jokingly, that the position of a professor of higher education would be entirely beautiful if there were no courses, and this concerned the courses which were an interruption of research. Above all, a teaching that wants to communicate something proper—I am not saying something completely new—but to find something personal, one has to see and revise, to let one's notes mature. This manner of having vanquished all problems which one has to give oneself when one is a professor is a difficult thing and a bit anxiety-producing too. On the other hand, everything that has been thought by someone else, even if it leaves some questions unresolved, is on the contrary welcome; that is more exciting to prepare. The preparation of the lecture course is the difficult task of teaching, and I always admire colleagues who do it with elegance, as if they had resolved everything.

The most exciting part is the explication of a text which poses its questions to you as much as to your auditors, and where the effort consists in reanimating dissimulated questions. One must, in a way, blow on the embers, so that the flame rises. My official career—in 1976 I left the Sorbonne, where Ferdinand Alquié had got me to come from Nanterre—was prolonged, at the request of the university, with seminars until 1984. For these seminars, I almost always taught Husserlian themes; I ensured the continuity of Husserl after the years of my regular teaching.

During one year I also gave seminars on Michel Henry's *L'essence de la manifestation*, an entirely exceptional book. During my years of regular teaching, I approached problems of ontology always with this difficulty, which consists of speaking of things which are born as if they were already born, of leaping over birth. The Husserlian themes allowed the making of a horizon of post-Husserlian actuality also.

Q.: The era between 1946 and 1986 had its ideas, its schools, its doctrines. How did you traverse these movements? Were you interested or indifferent?

E.L.: Reader and spectator rather than *engagé*.

Q.: In relation to the great seriousness of an epoch where everyone was Marxist, everyone was Sartrian, everyone structuralist...

E.L.: I was less astonished, more faithful to my research than seduced by what I just skipped through. I spoke to you of my gratitude with respect to Sartre, the pleasure I took in his intellectual dynamism, in his attention to the real...

Merleau-Ponty and the young phenomenologists—like Ricœur—held my interest more. But is it necessary to name those whom everyone recognizes as essential moments of this period between 1946 and 1986, that is to say, of these forty years?

The great book which impressed me a lot, I have to say, is the book by Vassily Grossman, *Life and Fate*, translated from the Russian, which I read in Russian. Grossman is very important, outside his value as a great writer; he is witness to the end of a certain Europe, the definitive end of the hope of instituting charity in the guise of a regime, the end of the socialist hope. The end of socialism, in the horror of Stalinism, is the greatest spiritual crisis in modern Europe. Marxism represented a generosity, whatever the way in which one understands the materialist doctrine which is its basis. There is in Marxism the recognition of the other; there is certainly the idea that the other must himself struggle for this recognition, that the other must become egoist. But the noble hope consists in healing everything, in installing, beyond the chance of individual charity, a regime without evil. And the regime of charity becomes Stalinism and [complicitous] Hitlerian horror. That's what Grossman shows, who was there, who participated in the enthusiasm of the beginnings. An absolutely overwhelming testimony and a complete despair.

There is something positive in this book also; positive, modestly consoling, or marvelous, there is precisely goodness [*la bonté*]; goodness without regime, the miracle of goodness, the only thing that remains. But goodness appears in certain isolated acts, like, for example, the extraordinary movement with which the book ends, where a woman—the most mean, the most miserable—in a mob unleashed against a conquered German soldier, the most detested in a group of prisoners, gives him her last piece of bread. Horrible scene where the captives are bringing out of a cave the cadavers of those they had captured and tortured. And here is an act of goodness exterior to all system. The scenes of goodness in an inhuman world are disseminated throughout the book, without transforming it into a virtuous book for virtuous readers. The love-plot itself which traverses the novel is dominated by this pure goodness going from human being to human being . . .

There is also in *Life and Fate* a terrible lucidity, there isn't any solution to the human drama by a change of regime, no system of salvation. The only thing that remains is individual goodness, from man to man. You find elsewhere this word *goodness* in my work, in *Totality and Infinity*, which preceded significantly my reading of Grossman. Ethics without ethical system.

Q.: We are nearing the end of this conversation: Israel as a state, is it for you a testimony, a problem, a source of happiness, of hope, of anxiety? What does the existence of the state of Israel represent for you?

E.L.: You are touching there on too many strong feelings! I would only say that now, under the given circumstances, as a State is the only form in which Israel—the people and the culture—can survive.

Q.: Does the way in which Israel exists pose problems for you in relation to the way in which you see the world?

E.L.: I will say to you that there are many things about which I cannot speak because I am not in Israel. I forbid myself to speak about Israel, not being in Israel, not living its noble adventure and not running this great daily risk.

Q.: Today there is renewal of Jewish studies, in Europe and in France in particular, and Emmanuel Levinas has become the obligatory reference.

E.L.: I must tell you that I do not have the impression that my name serves as this kind of reference, and in any case, this role would certainly crush me if I tried to play it. In my opinion, to play this role one would have to have been closer to the halakhic texts of the Talmud.

Q.: But you read it and hear it from the mouth of a dozen people, whom I will not cite: the renewal of Judaism is the work of Emmanuel Levinas, who brought it about. Do you have a sense of this?

E.L.: No, I must tell you that in practice, I don't know anything about it; not at all due to modesty, but truly, I think that much more is required for the renaissance of Judaism.

Q.: Are you trying to say that there is not yet a renaissance of Judaism?

E.L.: No, much more is necessary. There is perhaps an opening in my history, but everything that must be found there has not yet been estimated; one should distrust people who repeat what one opens up to them, and who do not enter into where the opening should happen.

I cannot say it otherwise, not because it would be crazy to say it otherwise, but because I say what I think reality is. I think that certain things which appear in my analyses and which are not citations, which are not references to biblical verses, have perhaps a certain importance, more than the mere repetition of the text I referred to.

Q.: You have disciples?

E.L.: I don't know! I have many friends; I have some friends—let us avoid what is contradictory in these terms—I have some friends. The friend about whom I spoke, Doctor Nerson, who died several years ago in Israel, I miss him every day. From him I took courage. He transmitted to me an absolute trust in the books of our Jewish tradition of which his teacher, M. Shoshani, had shown him—and me a little—the *résistance*.

Q.: Being alone appears to you less enriching?

E.L.: Yes... Listen, I don't want to discourage people who read me. It is not at all that I am content with little, but I know that what they need is much more than I can do for them.

TRANSLATED BY JILL ROBBINS AND MARCUS COELEN
WITH THOMAS LOEBEL

Interview with Myriam Anissimov

Q.: Did the type of education you received predispose you to ask philosophical types of questions?

E.L.: I spent my childhood in the old country of Lithuania where one breathed in Judaism with the air. My parents spoke Yiddish and knew a lot of Hebrew, but they always spoke Russian with the children. Biblical Hebrew was the basis of study. I also had a reader, called a chrestomathy. My first teacher came to the house twice a week to teach me Hebrew. At a time when Judaism was approaching modernity and Zionism was in the air, the fact of being Jewish was as natural as having eyes and ears. Interpretation was bound up with the written word. It wasn't what one today calls hermeneutics, but interpretation was close to the text of the Bible. Much later I studied Talmud; I do not know whether it was a matter of preparation for philosophy, but I have always attributed my philosophical tastes to the precociousness of an interpretation bound up with the text.

Q.: How did you study Hebrew?

E.L.: I learned directly in Hebrew: *Ivrit belvrit* [Hebrew in Hebrew]. But the teacher spoke, interpreted, and translated in Russian.

Q.: Did you go to a yeshiva?

E.L.: Unfortunately not, but—thank God—the town was surrounded by famous *yeshivoth*. I should tell you that Lithuania was not an Hasidic country; it was the preserve of the *mitnagdim*, where intellectual study was essential. At the time I didn't know that these riches were all around me. I appreciated them only when I began to regret not having benefited from them. But after the war, I did make contact with some exceptional teachers who introduced me to the talmudic mind.

Q.: Was the majority of the population of Kovno, where you were born, Jewish?

E.L.: No, but it was the Jewish population that one noticed in the streets. It was a town of seventy thousand to a hundred thousand inhabitants, where 30 percent were Jews. During the First World War, the Jews were expelled from this "border residential zone." There were strongholds near the border and the Jews were not trustworthy in the Russian view. They took precautions: no Jews when the Germans began to approach. We spent most of the war in Kharkov in the Ukraine. I entered a Russian gymnasium with the "five best Jews" who had made it through the *numerus clausus*. In 1916, my father, a bookseller in Kovno, thought that this event merited a celebration. We were very attached to Russian culture, to Pushkin—I knew Pushkin by heart. It is still today the literature that is my life blood.

In 1920, we returned to Lithuania, and I entered a Hebrew *lycée* where in the upper grades the instruction took place in Hebrew. We spoke Hebrew there as one speaks it today in Israel—although not with the same ease nor the same accent. It was in Lithuania that I had my first contact with what I called Europe. The director of the *lycée* was a German Jew. He had discovered Eastern European Judaism during his captivity in Russia. He had a doctorate in literature, and it was he who taught me German. When he used to say, "das ist goethisch" (this is Goethean), everyone shivered. This was a point in my life when I found it truly shameful not to have seen Cologne cathedral! That was my early adolescence.

Q.: When did you come to Strasbourg?

E.L.: At seventeen, for university education. In Germany, this would not have been possible. In 1923, there was already inflation and anti-Semitism over there. They refused to take [foreign] Jews in the universities. France was much more hospitable than Germany.

Q.: Who were your teachers there?

E.L.: Charles Blondel, an anti-Freudian psychologist. It is due to him, no doubt, that I have remained outside of psychoanalysis to this day.

Q.: You didn't know about psychoanalysis?

E.L.: I was won over by more important things. In Strasbourg, there was Henri Carteron, a Catholic professor. Thanks to him I had a revelation of what Christianity was all about. There was also Maurice Pradines, who became a professor of philosophy at the Sorbonne, and Maurice Halbwachs, professor of sociology, who had previously been a student of Durkheim and Lévy-Bruhl. He married the daughter of Victor Basch. Blondel studied with Bergson and Lévy-Bruhl. That was the university of yesterday. Unfortunately, today Bergson is in purgatory, and no one cites him.

Q.: Let's come back to your childhood. Do you remember any distinctive events?

E.L.: The death of Tolstoy was a significant event in my circle. This man, born to a great Russian aristocratic family, had at the end of his life left the comfortable world in which he lived to preach nonviolent resistance to evil. He died in 1910 in the Stapovo train station. Few people know that.

Q.: How did your religious sentiment evolve as a young boy who studied Hebrew?

E.L.: What I can tell you constitutes only an external approach. I was living in a world where the forms of religious Judaism were the norm, and the households were kosher. My grandparents were pious; my parents had what one calls modern views, but it goes without saying that they kept kosher. The attachment to national Jewish traditions was also very clear in other respects. It is certainly much later that I came into direct contact with the texts and with the whole religious perspective of Judaism. Hebrew, for me, is less the Hebrew of the synagogue than that of the Beth Midrash. So in this sense I was completely prepared for my subsequent studies.

Q.: You said earlier that Zionism was in the air.

E.L.: The ideas of Zionism constituted a natural prolongation of sacred history. In Kovno, there was the old city and the modern section of town. In the old city, traditional religion was still quite vibrant. Those who were living in the modern section of town were the children of those who had lived in the old city. They were connected with the Haskalah, with Hebrew language and the new Hebrew literature. Yes, we did speak of Bialik[1] during my childhood, but this wasn't at the expense of midrashic commentary as the background for biblical instruction.

Q.: You evoked earlier the teacher who initiated you into midrash.

E.L.: It was Monsieur Shoshani who taught me this way of blowing on the text to revive its fire. There is a Talmudic passage that says: "The words of the sages are like glowing embers." Why not fire instead of embers? Because one must blow on them to revive them. Shoshani, whom I often quote in my writings, was a Jew in the strong sense of the term on account of the great extent of his knowledge, the subtlety of his analyses, his abilities in modern European science. He was always dishevelled—he looked like a beggar, and he always taught the Talmud without having the text in front of his eyes. He knew it by heart. When I used to read aloud in his presence, he could tell when, in the third line down, I had skipped a word in small letters. He had, moreover, an intellectual penetration, a sense of the question, of the polyvocal character of ideas. Among the important encounters of my life, this man was essential. Shoshani was not a mere teacher; he was a visitation. He spent twenty-four hours a week at my house. We would meet in a group; Elie Wiesel has written some pages about him. Shoshani used to go to his house too, but I didn't know about him at that time. Shoshani recounted nothing. One didn't know what his life had been. It was as if he fell from the sky; I never knew his address. This is not to say that he had anything to reproach himself for; it was simply his manner of being. When he used to come to my house, he would spend the night and I would disregard all other involvements; he was the center. He didn't teach piety; he taught the texts. The texts are more fundamental—and vaster—than piety.

Q.: How did you meet him?

E.L.: I had a good friend, Doctor Nerson, now deceased. He studied with Shoshani for many years, and it was he who brought Shoshani to me. I don't know if Shoshani was particularly pious. He had a prodigious mind. He made a living from the lessons he gave, whenever he found ready students. He knew how to speak all languages, with an accent, mind you, but he had an enormous vocabulary. He was able to express very complex things in French, English, and German. He also spoke Lithuanian Yiddish. Doctor Nerson used to follow him everywhere, and when Monsieur Shoshani died it was Nerson who said kaddish as if he had been his father. I remember when he would telephone he used to say: "Hello, I am here; are you there?" Somehow both he and his interlocutor knew where "here" and "there" were. That was the fantastic side of it all.

Q.: How were the study sessions spent?

E.L.: I was always with Doctor Nerson, and from time to time someone else would also come. We would read the texts and Shoshani would do the talking. We could stay together until two or three in the morning. He had a good knowledge of mathematics and modern physics. There are extraordinary minds who don't need to learn much.

Q.: To return to your comment that Zionist ideas were in the air, what about the Bund?

E.L.: The Bundists would allow nothing, neither Hebrew nor Palestine. At that time, Palestine didn't signify what it signifies today. In the marvelous film, *Les révolutionnaires du Yiddich Land*, one sees all that was authentically Jewish in the Bund. I remember the testimony of a woman who tells how she learned new things when she came into contact with the Bund; for example, that God does not exist. She says this in the same matter-of-fact tone as she says, "Yesterday, there was an attack." Up until that time she had lived in a world in which one could not doubt the existence of God, as one could not doubt the sun that rises every morning. It's a very moving film; it shows the purity of this faith in the October Revolution that was supposed to provide all that humanity could hope for, the fulfillment of humanity's dreams. Marxism was much more than a doctrine, much more than an ideology. It represented a devotion to the other man. It wanted to save all men, not to abandon them. Although Stalinism has compromised all of this, in Marxism there is this movement toward the other man.

Q.: In Lithuania, did you have contacts with the non-Jewish world?

E.L.: There was no contact with non-Jews. They were clients of my father's bookstore, which for the most part sold Russian books. In the old city, there were bookstores that only sold Jewish books. My father, who was called Levine and not Levinas (the *-as* ending is Lithuanian), didn't socialize with Russians; he only sold to them. In Kharkov, Jews were more assimilated than in Lithuania. For my part, I studied Russian culture and I was dazzled. To understand this universe, you should read Vassily Grossman. I admire him a great deal. In *Life and Fate*, he tells how his mother didn't follow the rest of the family, which emigrated to South America, because for her the poetry of Nekrasov and Pushkin was essential. She tells how she cried during a performance of *Uncle Vanya*. Many Jews were like her. Anti-Semitism was a common thing in Russia, but there was a Russian intelligentsia which was very leftist and very welcoming. There were no ghettos in Lithuania, but socially Jews lived in a ghetto.

Q.: You speak of Vassily Grossman; did you read Russian novels?

E.L.: The Russian novel was my preparation for philosophy. Pushkin, Lermontov, Turgenev, Dostoevsky, and Chekhov.

Q.: Do you still read in Russian?

E.L.: I read Grossman in the original text. The essential thing in this book is simply what the character Ikonnikov says—"There is neither God nor the Good, but there is goodness"—which is also my thesis. That is all that is left to mankind. The whole novel is woven like that. Grossman has a view of "humanity" which has rarely, if ever, been attained. Even he never attained it. He also says: "There are acts of goodness which are absolutely gratuitous, unforeseen." For example, the woman who leaves her husband because she loves another, but who comes back when he is persecuted by the Special Section of the Soviet Front Headquarters. Or, toward the book's end, when Stalingrad has already been rescued, the German prisoners, including an officer, are cleaning out a basement and removing the decomposing bodies. The officer suffers particularly from this misery. In the crowd, a woman who hates Germans is delighted to see this man more miserable than the others. Then she gives him the last piece of bread she has. This is extraordinary. Even in hatred there exists a mercy stronger than hatred. I give to this act a religious significance. This is my way of saying that the mercy of God occurs through the particular man—not at all because he is organized in a certain way or because he belongs to a society or an institution. There are acts of stupid, senseless goodness. Grossman shows us this throughout the whole book. *Life and*

Fate does not call for any political action; it does not preach any doctrine. Ikonnikov is feeble-minded. But a feeble-minded person can be inspired. This is a type that exists in Russia. It is *The Idiot* of Dostoevsky... The human pierces the crust of being. Only an idiot can believe in this goodness. I do not have a philosophy of history. I do not want to say that the world is heading toward holiness; men are not saints. However, each man understands holiness. One cannot dispute it. Ikonnikov says that what is important is that evil does not manage to vanquish holiness. I am not at all saying that the good will vanquish evil. Grossman writes that all organization is already ideology. When Christ begins to preach, there is already the Church, and with the Church the whole organization of the good. The opposition of Ikonnikov to Christianity is not directed against this or that part of the teaching of Christ, but against the history of Christianity and of the Church with all the horrors it allows.

I also think of the character in the novel who discovers Judaism when he receives a letter from his mother remarking the presence of a friendly dog when they took her to the ghetto. In the Bible, there is a passage that says: "If you find a dead carcass in the field, you will give it to the dogs" (Exod. 22:31), which isn't simply to say that Jews must not eat it. "You will give it to the dogs" is an order. Why? Because when the Jews left Egypt, "no dog barked" (Exod. 11:7), and still they were given nothing... I can speak to you about my own captivity in this regard, about the dog who accompanied the prisoners. It was a dog who descended from the dogs of Egypt.

When I was in the army I was taken prisoner and put in a Jewish commando unit of about one hundred people. (What would have happened to us if Hitler had won the war?) The French army obtained protection for the Jewish POWs under the Geneva Convention. We received parcels; our commando worked in the German forest, but it wasn't a matter of convicts' work. One day, this dog latched on to us. I don't know where he came from. He liked us. Each time we returned, he jumped for joy; when we returned from the forest, he walked in front of us. He was the only one who recognized us as men.

Q.: Did you know about what was happening to the Jews in the extermination camps?

E.L.: We knew nothing. When rumors reached us, they seemed exaggerated. Toward the end, sometimes one, sometimes another received news that his family had disappeared. But we could not imagine… and yet we were so close to Bergen-Belsen.

Q.: You cited Apollinaire, one of his poems is entitled "Il y a."

E.L.: For Apollinaire, this *il y a* has a sense of abundance. For me, *il y a* has the sense of desolation, of being that is anonymous. *There is [il y a]* being in the same way that it rains [*il pleut*]. In Heidegger *es gibt* signifies a gift. There is a kind of generosity of being. Being is the initial generosity. What I described with respect to my childhood is the "vou… ouh… ouh," the anonymous silence, is it not?

Q.: Can you tell me about your arrival in France, in 1923?

E.L.: The first thing I gain is freedom. For me, freedom of speech is the first freedom. I arrive, and equal in my mind with my arrival, I have the memory of the Dreyfus Affair. My teachers had been young during the time of the Dreyfus Affair. They were all supporters of Dreyfus, of course. When Pradines, in his course on ethics, cited the Dreyfus Affair, he made a strong impression upon the newcomer that I was. There was also the grand slogan of the Revolution: "Liberté, egalité, fraternité." When you come from the East, all this resonates with the fullness of new words, even though on the steps of city hall they are somewhat worn out, don't you think? This feeling can be compared to when I heard the voice of de Gaulle during captivity.

I was impressed by French intelligence, the clarity of ideas, the perfect way of setting things apart, the elegance in the presentation of instruction, the charm of the French language. France is a country where the attachment to cultural conventions seems equivalent to the attachment to the land. I read Descartes, Malebranche, Maine de Biran, and Bergson.

Q.: How did you learn French?

E.L.: Upon arriving in Strasbourg, I knew how to read. With the dictionary, I began to read a text of Corneille and another by Georges Sand; they were those little editions with notes.

Q.: Aside from your professors, did you socialize with other Frenchmen?

E.L.: I met Maurice Blanchot, who was a student there, and we became friends. At that time, Blanchot was not at all on the left. He is a great critic, a novelist. He was part of "cent-vingt-et-un"[2] at the time of the Algerian war. He was very radical. But he left certain movements with which he was associated in 1968, because these had contested Israel. What he did is very great. Blanchot is not an ordinary man, a man whom you can meet in the street. In his eyes, the criterion in politics of what is just and unjust is the unconditional recognition of Israel. That is something quite moving. The injustice committed against Israel during the war, that one calls the *shoah*—the passion of Israel in the sense in which one speaks of the passion of Christ—is the moment when humanity began to bleed through the wounds of Israel. Someone asked me the other day if, as a Jew, I didn't feel like an outsider in France. I replied to him that wherever I am, I feel like I'm in the way, and I quoted a Psalm: "I am a stranger upon the earth" (Ps. 119:19). Strangeness is situated in relation to the earth.

TRANSLATED BY JILL ROBBINS AND THOMAS LOEBEL

Interview with Salomon Malka

Q.: I know you don't like to elaborate upon biographical details; however, a word to say that you were born and grew up in Lithuania. What does that mean for you?

E.L.: First of all, it's a Judaism that wasn't Hasidic. Not that there was any hostility toward Hasidism, mind you. I don't want—God help me—to revive the eighteenth-century quarrel between the *hasidim* and the *mitnagdim*, nor to take up again the battle of the Gaon of Vilna. Besides, I don't have the energy for that. Lithuanian Judaism is this predilection for a certain sobriety—not as opposed to feeling, but as opposed to a certain intoxication of spirit on a popular level. It has a certain intellectualism also. This might surprise you given what I think about reason passing for the essence of spirit. But one of the elements of this Lithuanian Judaism is a certain intellectual discipline which takes precedence over immediacy. Now there is a great tradition of Hasidism which goes all the way back to the Kabbalah. You know that the Gaon was himself a great Kabbalist. But he always thought that the Zohar was in agreement with the Talmud. And as far as I am concerned, the true measure of the Jewish mind and even of the Kabbalah is given by the Talmud.

Q.: Let's talk about the great masters who influenced your work. There is first of all Husserl, whose student you were in Freiburg and whom you were one of the first to introduce to France.

E.L.: I studied Husserl and phenomenology a lot. In phenomenology—I still think so today—there is a method for philosophy. There is a reflection upon oneself which wants to be radical. It does not only take into consideration that which is intended by consciousness, but also searches for that which has been dissimulated in the intending of the object. From this moment on, the object in phenomenology is reconstituted in its world and in all the forgotten intentions of the thinking that absorbed itself into it. It is a manner of thinking concretely. There is in this manner a rigor, but also an appeal to listen acutely for what is implicit. Even when one doesn't apply the phenomenological method according to all the recommendations given by Husserl, one can call oneself a student of this master by special attention to what is allusive in thinking.

Q.: The other great master is Martin Heidegger. What is your debt with respect to Heidegger?

E.L.: What is important for me is the excellence of his phenomenology. I especially admire his early book, *Being and Time*. It is actually a series of marvelous analyses testifying to what phenomenology is capable of. It is always with a feeling of shame that I admit my admiration for the philosopher. We know what Heidegger was in 1933, even if he was so during a brief period, and even if his disciples—many of whom are estimable—forget about it. For me, it is unforgettable. One could have been everything except Hitlerian, even if it was inadvertent.

Q.: This was Heidegger's case?

E.L.: I cannot say whether it was inadvertent. To what extent did he not also belong to that which in a certain Germanic culture and in certain circles is profoundly strange and hostile to us? But there was a genius which I cannot deny. Monsieur Jankélévitch is much more radical and more consequent than I am.[1] I strongly admire his whole character, his firmness in relation to this point. I myself cannot forget what Heidegger was—with *Being and Time* well before 1933—in my education.

Q.: The third name one can cite is Franz Rosenzweig.

E.L.: Rosenzweig, yes. It is the critique of the idea of totality in the *Star of Redemption* that I purely and simply took up again. It is the rupture with Hegel. The rest of his thinking is also very seductive for me, because it is the thinking of a modern Judaism which has gone through assimilation. He is not at all someone who did not enter into it; he's a European Jew who left, without shaking off his European history as one would shake off dust from one's feet. That is very important. Modern, but modern in a certain sense, that is, before puberty. For men of our time, I am calling "puberty" the fact of having known Hitlerism and the Holocaust. Rosenzweig missed the ultimate ordeal. Nor did he get to know the state of Israel, although he admired Zionism, which he opposed, while recognizing the greatness of Herzl's idea. But for me, as I said before, he is modern because he is situated after assimilation.

There is another thing I retain from his thought, and which is essential. That is the idea of a reconciliation with Christianity. Not at all a synthesis but a symbiosis, or if you prefer, a privileged neighborliness, a shared life. He thought that there is a whole part of our life which is enriched by this symbiosis; for example, our access to art, which for him did not belong essentially to the Jewish genius. Great art, that was non-Jewish art, accessible to Jews concretely by means of their coexistence with Christians. This is neither confusion nor syncretism; it is a symbiosis, which for Rosenzweig is profound and linked to the very structure of truth. It is as if there were a supplementary enrichment, an increase. The truth of Judaism would be the one which is given to a people who are always already "near to" the Lord, but who do not see the world. Christianity would be the truth of the one who is on the road to the Eternal, traversing the world. But this experience of the road and the world is also given to Judaism thanks to this neighborliness. A heretical theology? Or rather a possible understanding of destinies which are incontestably and essentially intertwined. At least that is how I conceive it. And these are concrete things, because the state of Israel must cohabit with the Christian world, read Christian authors—Shakespeare and Racine and Victor Hugo—all of Europe, which is irrecusable and which is Christian. That is also what Rosenzweig means for me.

Q.: Husserl, Heidegger, Rosenzweig. This trilogy is missing a name which is less well known: that of Shoshani. Was it he who helped you to discover the Talmud?

E.L.: I don't know if what I know is even a discovery, but it was he who showed me how one must read it. Next to his genius, his knowledge, his dialectical power, everything else pales. I had not learned much of how to read the *halakhah*, which as you know is essential to the Talmud. I had begun to read a bit of the *haggadah*, but Shoshani used to say, "As you read the *haggadah*, you must read the *halakhah*." Which did not mean that one had to take it as a web of symbols or allegories. Moreover, one must read it with imagination. Monsieur Shoshani was very strict in his requirements for me as for everyone else. A master without pity! But when he had a smile of encouragement, that said a lot. And he sometimes had this smile for passages of the midrash I was trying to comment upon. He thought that one should not speculate in the abstract, but in the imagination. One has to think of the worlds which are evoked by each image of the text, and it is in this way that the text begins to speak.

Q.: In listening to a series of interviews with Philippe Nemo on French radio, I was struck by one thing. Presenting your writings, Nemo distinguished between the philosophical works and those he qualified, I think, as "religious." And I myself have the impression that the entire work is of a piece, that it draws from one and the same inspiration.

E.L.: One cannot become the historian of one's own philosophy. That is difficult and pretentious. It is incontestable that in every philosophical reflection, in every philosophical essay, there are memories of a lived experience which is not rigorously intellectual. But starting from this, one must arrive at the language of all philosophers, which I call the Greek language, even if one is not a Hellenist, a language which uses, in sum, terms which are never incomparable, which do not lead back to something confidential. This was discovered by the Greeks, and our European languages adapt to it. Certainly in our European languages there is the folkloric language that we like a lot, but there is this other language through which one explains what has been said in the folkloric language. The great intuitions are often in the commentator's text. But the final signification is an explication in a communicable language and which, once again, says everything that is confidential in another manner. Very often I have asked myself whether semiosis—namely, the attempt to go back to the origin of the meaning of every expression, which logically cannot stop anywhere because everything to which one goes back already uses words—I have asked myself whether a true arresting of this procedure of explication would not be in a philosophical language which is, in this very general sense, a Greek one. Or, if you prefer, whether the work of the great masters of philosophy does not consist precisely in having found—one doesn't know how—the first words. That is how I would draw the difference: There are texts in relation to which I am not bothered by the recourse to verses which rely on the authority and force which comes out from under their confidential form. And there are other texts where it happens that I cite a verse as illustration, but where the analysis itself speaks in an entirely other language. In the same way I would also say—and this will be a bit paradoxical—that philosophy can use religious experiences, but then it is already a Septuagint, which translates them into Greek. And, if you wish, the work of the Septuagint remains unfinished.

Q.: You say that philosophy is "an indiscretion with respect to the unsayable," a quest for the first word...

E.L.: Yes, an open word, a word which is not secret.

Q.: In your most accomplished philosophical book, *Otherwise than Being or Beyond Essence*, the dedication and the last lines of the work give, nevertheless, a Jewish key to your work.

E.L.: But I do not contest that it is a Jewish ordeal which is translated. I prefer the word "ordeal" (*épreuve*) over "experience" (*expérience*), because the word "experience" expresses always a knowledge of which the I is master. In the word "ordeal" there is at the same time the idea of a life and of a critical "testing" which exceeds the I which is its scene. The ordeal of Jewish existence is certainly present in my work, but nowhere in my philosophical essays is there any attempt to prove a dogmatic truth. Only after the fact can one discover a certain spirit there; but Judaism is an essential modality of all that is human. In *Otherwise than Being*, my point of departure is the order of natural existence, the order of beings which hold fast to their being, which persevere in their being. In the right to be which is presupposed in this perseverance—in the good conscience in which a being pursues its thread of being—erupts the question of the justification of being, the question of justice. Not the question of the conformity or nonconformity of the being of beings to a law, but an idea of the priority of the other, the question: In being has one not oppressed someone? As if, at that moment, an identical being reposing in itself (a being that I am), persevering in its identity, asks itself whether it has a reason to be, whether the true vocation of the human, overthrowing its being, does not consist in breaking with this good conscience. That is what I wanted to say a bit everywhere in my books. There are, naturally, numerous complications this account receives.

Is the human I first? Is it not he who, in place of being posed, ought to be de-posed? Does not the true meaning of subjectivity consist in devotion to the other (and in this way, a subjection to the next), rather than being a substance? But—is not this subjection the negation of freedom which seems to be the true definition of the human? It is then necessary to ask if the possibility of nonfreedom suggested in devotion to the other is, if not servitude, precisely obedience to God. If God is not this other—or this excluded middle—who breaks with the alternative between freedom and nonfreedom. Consequently, does not a path begin where the word *God* takes on its meaning, where God "comes to mind," starting from this putting into question by the other, a putting into question which is not lived as oppression? This is the matter of *Otherwise than Being*, which asked of me a more complicated language, a philosophical one, but whose simplicity—evoked just now—became visible only in retrospect.

Q.: One is struck by the very first lines you wrote directly following the war in the preface to *Existence and Existents*: "This study examines a certain number of broader research topics concerning the problem of the Good, time, and the relationship with the other as a movement toward the Good." This is the first book in which is established what will become the kernel of your work to come: the approach of the face of the other as the ethical relation par excellence. How could this morality—optimistic, after all—have been born in the destruction of the war?

E.L.: Why optimistic? I will tell you, optimism and pessimism are not the ultimate categories of evaluation. Is the idea that the human takes on its meaning in the relation of a man to the other man optimistic or pessimistic? It is, perhaps, first of all an ironic proposal immediately after the horrors of 1933–45. Or it is utopian. I'm not afraid of this term. For I really think that the human in its proper sense cannot but awaken in "man as he is." An uncertain awakening, an uneasiness at having taken the place of another. This putting into question of my place—of my site—in being, is it not utopian? Utopia and ethics! A reversal of a being content with its own good conscience of existing, a subversion which I call "otherwise than being." All that a pessimism? Or an optimism, because an awakening to the human? The one who imposes himself as an "accomplished reality," saying "I" without remorse, always certain of himself—this is not very nice! It is in this sense that I always understood "the I is detestable" of Pascal, who also said—and I used it as an epigraph in my book *Otherwise than Being*—"This is my place in the sun—there lies the beginning and the image of the usurpation of the entire earth." And I think also of another philosopher, Simone Weil, who never managed to do justice to her own original Judaism but who, in such an excessive way (and so Jewish too), pushed back in herself the "triumphant I": "Father, tear from me this body and this soul in order to make out of them things that belong to you, to leave me with nothing but this tearing."

Recall, in relation to this quotation of Pascal, the war of 1939, which broke out because Nazi Germany demanded a vital space, its "place in the sun," the order where being strove to persevere in being. But to rediscover the human, not in the real where it sinks and becomes the political history of the world, but in the ruptures of this history, in its crises: this is not to say that the human is nothing. The otherwise than being is attested to by exceptional people, by saints and just ones and by the "thirty-six unknown just ones"[2] to whom the world owes its continued life. This otherwise than being is also attested to by the norms of our language, which even in its hypocrisy and cynicism recognizes the priority of the other man.

In 1968, I had the feeling that all values were being contested as bourgeois—this was quite impressive—all except for one: the other. Nobody ever said that the right of the other man—despite all the liberation of the spontaneous ego, despite all the license of language and contempt for the other as other—remained unpronounceable. Even when a language against the other resounds, language for the other is heard behind it.

Q.: One can be a bit put off, in the later developments of your work, by the notion of "expiation for the other."

E.L.: First of all, one should not understand this expiation in a mystical manner. It is not a manifestation of the sacred. One has to take it as the perspective of holiness, without which the human is inconceivable. This means that man is responsible for the other man and that he is responsible for him even when the other does not concern him, because the other always concerns him. The other's face always regards me. And this is *de jure* limitless. At no moment can you leave the other to his own destiny. I sometimes call this *expiation*, extending all the way to substitution for the other. I am thinking of the talmudic statement, "Do not judge the other without putting yourself in his place." I am not thinking of confusion with him—the relation remains relation to the other, *hesed* or gratuitous charity.

Now, there is the appearance of the third who is a limitation on this measureless *hesed*. Because the other for whom I am responsible can be the executioner of a third who is also my other. Thus the necessity of a justice, of *tzedakah* behind the *hesed*. And this carries with it institutions, and even a State... There is no anarchy in this priority of the other who remains the ethical measure of a necessary politics. Once the State is created, it has its own proper reality. One must then be able to stop it when the anonymousness of the law suppresses "charity."

Q.: But in expiation for the other, there is a notion of suffering.

E.L.: It is always unpleasant to be responsible for the other. There is in the human condition as such an element of the unpleasant. But the good is not simply pleasant. The alternative between optimism and pessimism is not the place of ultimate judgments.

Q.: Responsibility which can extend all the way to persecution?

E.L.: In principle. Against the persecution which targets others and especially those close by, one has to have recourse to justice. Some reproach me with leaving nothing to hope, to the great virtue of expectation. But that is a religious value. Perhaps religion knows more about this than the rigor which tries simply to define the human by its dignity. Isn't God the One for whom I am other? That is possible. But I cannot separate myself from the exceptional situation of the ego. That is to say, of being obligated. I always quote Dostoevsky: "We are all guilty for everything and toward everyone and I more than all the others."

Q.: There is also this refusal of history for which you are so often reproached. And it is true that you refuse in any case a sense [*un sens*] of history, in the double acceptation of this word: direction/signification.

E.L.: It is history which controls me. But I don't think that the judgment of history is the last judgment. I think that man should be able to judge history. If you will, the only history which proves that one must be able to judge history is that which holy history teaches us. Hence the existence of the Jewish people. That is not at all an accident of history. There has been there a humanity which very early awakened itself to the other.

Do you know the little talmudic story? Baba Batra 10a tells that God created ten mighty things: the mountain, but iron hollows out the mountain; iron, but fire melts the iron; fire, but water puts out fire; water, but clouds carry the water; clouds, but wind disperses the clouds; wind, but the human body is the master of the wind; the human body, but fear breaks the body; fear, but wine dispels fear; wine, but sleep drives out the wine; sleep, but sleep is one one-hundredth of death. Therefore, death is the most mighty. But charity saves from death, as it is written in the words of Ps. 10:2: "Charity saves from death." This is all very well, but *where* have you seen charity which saves from death? The Gemara does not answer. But with a little imagination: it is Abraham, to whom death is present, who says, "I am but ashes and dust" (Gen. 18:27), who prays for the safety of Sodom.

This is what I understand by being awakened, early on, to the other. Abraham is only ashes and dust, but this doesn't take from him the courage to pray for others.

Q.: One has the feeling that you are the only one to have attempted to go right to the end of the adventure of a secular Judaism. There is in your work the idea of a God without divinity, of a religion without piety.

E.L.: Religion certainly knows more about this than philosophy does, and one has a different comportment as a religious person. But what I do is the opposite of what would be the quest for a God without divinity. The attempt of my latest essays consists in "describing" the circumstances in which the word *God* comes to mind. Normally, ideas come to us from a knowledge, and knowledge from a certain objectification, where the parts of the real are inscribed. Starting from a thematization. I always thought that the invisible God of monotheism is not only a God who is not visible to the eyes. It is a nonthematizable God. When can a positive sense be given to this negative notion? When I am turned toward the other man and when I am called not to leave him alone. It is a turning contrary to my perseverance in being. This is the circumstance in which God has spoken.

To the extent that I say that the commandment of God starting from the face of the other is something different from and better than thematization, that one can be tempted to say that I have a religion without God. Or the contrary, if you wish. But all of this is too quickly said.

What I seek is the first moment of "epiphany." The God of Nietzsche who is dead is the one who intervenes in the world like all other forces in the world, and which had to be oriented like these forces.

Q.: Someone said of you, "Levinas is a teacher for maturity rather than for youth." What do you think of that?

E.L.: That is very flattering for me. I think that all these things should be said with a great deal of precaution: even the manner in which I look for the circumstances where God "comes to mind" could be taken for an atheism.

More generally: contrary to what my friend Derrida says, philosophy is not a subject matter for children of preschool age or in the first grade.[3] The Gemara says, one should not teach a student who is not *hagoun*, or ready. It is not only a question of morals, but of maturity. And my teacher Shoshani had an expression which he probably borrowed from Maimonides: "One should not give steak to newborns."[4]

TRANSLATED BY JILL ROBBINS AND MARCUS COELEN

PART II

Ethics as First Philosophy

The Vocation of the Other

Q.: You situate the other as the first principle of your philosophical reflection. It constitutes the center, the ultimate preoccupation of man's spiritual adventure, which crosses individual and communal history. For you, the thinker of alterity, the other is an imperative.

E.L.: That is so. It is a matter of a question that one can situate at least on the same level as the famous question of being, around which all of philosophy in the West developed. Rest assured that, by thus changing words, I do not wish to renew philosophy, but I like to insist, nevertheless, on the primordial intellectual role of alterity. In a general manner, the thought of being is the thought of that which is meaningful, affirming itself against impressions: mad, fugitive thoughts which are without unity. The meaningful would be the concordant, the permanent, that which remains—that which is in and for itself, as the philosophers say. One affirms the fact of remaining in oneself, returning to oneself, positing oneself as a oneself, as the sense of the world, as the sense of life, as spirit. As if the meaningful or the reasonable always came back to the event of the perseverance in existence, which finds its full expression in the apparition of an "I" understood at the same time as an "in-itself" and a "for-itself."

But within this priority of being, this insistence on the oneself, isn't there something like a threat against all others, a war inherent in this affirmation of oneself? An atom which is closed unto itself and which, after fission, physicists call "confinement": hardness, cruelty, materiality in the physical sense of the term—shock and pure pressure in the guise of an exteriorization which would be the negation and misrecognition of all alterity?

In contrast, to think the other as other, to think him or her straight-away before affirming oneself, signifies concretely to have goodness. A banal word, which in Vassily Grossman's book *Life and Fate* makes a great impression: in this book the human overwhelms the inhuman in being, always preoccupied with itself. Certainly, the human continues its ap-purtenance in being for a long time. It persists in being: all wars are there. But at the same time, the human—this is extraordinary—cedes its first place. *Après vous, Monsieur!* Ontological courtesy, being-for-the-other.

The other is not other because he would have other attributes, or would have been born elsewhere or at another moment, or because he would be of a different race. The other is other because of me: unique and in some manner different than the individual belonging to a genus. It is not difference which makes alterity: alterity makes difference. The recog-nition of the other happens beyond being, beyond essence, without these formulations taking on a sophistic signification. The possibility of respect and of goodness are extraordinary possibilities with regard to nature, with regard to the perseverance in being: the possibility of holiness which, be-yond the perseverance of a being in its being, would recognize the prior-ity of an irreducible alterity. I think that the true humanity of man begins in this recognition, before any cognition of being, before onto-logy. That is why I said to you that the question of the other seemed to me to be an-terior to the problem of ontology.

Q.: It is thus a matter of conferring on the other his essential and sin-gular place in the very heart of thinking, where his upsurge is imposed by the mediation of language, language which bears the sense and the prin-ciple of relation.

E.L.: In the course of a remarkable article on Heidegger in the period-ical *Le Messager Européen*, Elisabeth de Fontenay, a philosopher whom I admire very much, recently wrote that thought can begin just as well from the starting point of the idea of being as from the idea of the other.[1] She conceded me the right to choose. Elisabeth de Fontenay thinks, how-ever, that contemplation itself implies the idea of being. Given that all thought comprises contemplation, being should thus be situated at the beginning. At the same time, I wonder if contemplation does not already presuppose a dis-interestedness,[2] a relaxation of the allegiance to being, and if this dis-interestedness is not already a relation to the other, already the *for-the-other* of language. I wonder then if language is not the very condition of human thought, if thought is not straightaway on our lips before it goes toward things—if we do indeed go toward things before having *given* them to the other, before having shared them with the other. Being and the other, this does not constitute an alternative: thought would depend on the saying.

Language preceding thought, what a scandal! What good fortune for the garrulous! But certainly, that is not what I mean. Thinking supposes that being, instead of giving itself and instead of being taken, instead of being immediately at my disposal, is that which is thought. That would signify that in my relation to being there is first of all the intention to give. This passage accomplished by matter, which takes off from its fact of being, the fact of being thought, the fact of being contemplated—namely, to appear in a disinterestedness, supposes a dis-inter-estedness which is precisely with respect to the other. Intellectual disinterestedness is possible only because of ethical dis-interestedness, by the dis-interestedness of holiness.

Q.: In the relation of man to man, it may be a matter of announcing *shalom*, peace.

E.L.: One declares peace. Yes, I have said that for me, reason is peace. In my preface to the German translation of *Totality and Infinity*, I define reason by peace.[3] The word *shalom*, in this case, is very important.

Q.: In this surprising upsurge of the question of the other, of which we are witnesses and protagonists, it is justifiable to ask about this attention that pushes us in some fashion toward the other.

E.L.: What would push us? You want humanity to be born from processes that are purely material? Humanity is not some kind of explosion, egoist in the original egoism of being itself. It is the voice of God which reverberates in being. I would maintain the revolutionary character of the apparition of the human. In the discovery of the human, there is awakening of thought and contemplation. But this is the possibility of hearing behind being someone to whom one can give. This is the moment of human awakening in being.

Q.: This human awakening is revealed, thus, in the ethical preoccupation manifested on behalf of the other, in the responsibility which imposes itself as recognition of the other.

E.L.: Someone concerns me; the other concerns me. From the inter-estedness which is the rapport to being, as concern for being, there is passage to the human, the discovery of the death of the other, of his defenselessness and of the nudity of his face, and in turn the response to this discovery: goodness. This discovery of his death, or this hearing of his call, I term the face of the other. Dis-interestedness is taking on oneself the being of the other. I also term this "responsibility." Responsibility is the first language. The "absurd" thesis that I maintain, let me repeat, is that language bears thought.

Q.: What relation would you establish between responsibility and love?

E.L.: I think that responsibility is the love without concupiscence of which Pascal spoke: to respond to the other, to approach the other as unique, isolated from all multiplicity and outside collective necessities. To approach someone as unique to the world is to love him. Affective warmth, feeling, and goodness constitute the proper mode of this approach to the unique, the thinking of the unique. And doubtless, this thought of the unique is only concrete, and hence originary, when it goes *from the one to the other*, in the guise of a society of two, outside the relations that regulate individuals who belong by appurtenance to the same genus. Individuals who constitute the unity of a genus return in love to their unicity, are disengaged from genus. Responsibility is transcendence from the one to the other, the newness of a rapport going from the unique to the unique. Responsibility in effect is inalienable; the responsible self is no longer the self closest to itself, but the first one called. Unique as elected. No one could replace this self nor absolve it from its responsibility. Transcendence from the unique to the unique, before all community: love of the stranger, hence holier, higher than fraternity. This is the originary place of the identical.

Q.: The exigency for justice also intervenes.

E.L.: Justice, which comprises comparison between men and judgment upon men, and consequently the return of the unique to the individual, the return of the unique to the community of genus and therefore the genesis of the political, of the State and its institutions, all of this at the same time presupposes the for-the-other of responsibility which was our starting point. It would take too long to retrace here the articulations of this genesis. But that the first, fundamental, and unforgettable exigency of justice is the love of the other man in his uniqueness, that seems to me decisive.

Q.: This love culminates when the necessity to recognize the other in his strangeness is conceived as evident.

E.L.: Alterity is strangeness, as I said earlier. The other has a tribal link with no one. That is precisely his departure from the community of genus, the total alterity. I spoke of holiness as the ascension to the human in being, higher than all fraternity. The moment in which fraternity attains its full sense is when, in the brother himself, the stranger is recognized: the beyond-the-tribal. It is not that the tribal is proscribed; it comprises many virtues. But in principle, the human is the consciousness that there is still one more step to take: to appease the tribal, scandalous exigency!

Q.: Your thought is founded on the biblical tradition which situates the imperative of alterity, of recognition, and of the love of the other on the level of a filiation and spiritual exigency.

E.L.: In effect, the children of Israel are introduced as the descendants of the patriarchs. Consequently, the virtues of Abraham, Isaac, and Jacob, the glory of their relations to other men, are presented as very elevated. But truly, in the Bible, the essential moment in the development of ethical conscience and of the dignity of man consists in recognizing oneself as a son of God: the filiality of transcendence. This is the superior form of piety, above any tribal link: to address oneself to God as to a Father.

There is a magnificent meditation of Jean Paul II relative to Christianity, teaching us that God would be incarnated not solely in Christ, but through Christ in all men. This divine filiality of humanity is nothing new for Jews: the divine paternity experienced by Jewish piety, as it has been formulated since Isaiah, should be taken literally. In Isaiah, the Israelites are called sons of God, and in the liturgy the words "Our Father" constantly return.

The Bible is also the book of a people, whose unity *as* a people does not suffice. It is necessary that this people receive the Torah. It does not suffice for this people merely to be a descendant of Abraham, Isaac, Jacob: it must be led to Sinai. The departure from Egypt is accomplished at Sinai.

Q.: This divine filiality proceeds in spite of the individuation which is indispensable for man to assume a project in history, at the heart of the human community. This identification of the person participates in his recognition of the other, in his confrontation with him, but equally in the expression of a responsibility manifested on his behalf.

E.L.: The responsibility for the other is the originary place of identification. There are two ways in which one can understand the identity of man. First, as a being who is particular in his genus. By genus, I mean every genus to which the individual human belongs: nation, profession, race, place and date of birth, etc. Consequently, a principle of individuation is necessary to identify a specific—or more exactly, an individual—difference. Humanity comprises exactly a principle of individuation, as do tables, chairs, or stones. These pieces indicate identity for humans. There is individuation of human bodies, but one can also individuate souls, by character, by tastes, by intellectual level, by good qualities or by psychological faults. This is still to individuate or to identify within a genus. However, the other way of being identified is the one that permits one to say "I" or "me" without any consultation with regard to the genus to which one would belong, nor with regard to the differences that one will have constated within oneself in relation to others. One does not confuse oneself so much with others. Everything happens as if one were seized straightaway in one's irreducible uniqueness.

Am I referred to myself as to a substantial identity, invariable under the flow of sensations? Have I experienced this invariable substance, or have I recognized myself in the very spontaneity of my response to the face of the other man, as if he had awakened me and called me? The self is the one who is called as irreplaceable. I am concerned by the face of the other, by the mortality which his nudity exposes and expresses. The other always concerns me; he's my business. Individuation within responsibility, to which I am elected, as it were. Individuation by election! As in the response to the call of God. Consciousness of my election, consciousness of my humanity, consciousness of my noninterchangeability: reponsibility for the other is the original identification.

Q.: Racism could be defined as a refusal or an incapacity to assume the dimension of conscience—thus the love, from which this identification proceeds.

E.L.: In the expression of racism, one experiences human identity uniquely on the basis of its persistence in being, while turning qualitative differences and attributes into a value, as in the appreciation of things that one would possess or reject. But that is not to encounter the face of the other, not to respond to the uniqueness of the other, not to recognize the possibility of sacrifice which in the event of being is the very overwhelming of the human. To experience the death of the other as a more serious matter than my own is humanly possible. The violence of war is the prolongation of the pure persistence in being. It is not that at every moment one dies for the other; even that is quite difficult. I apologize for always speaking of holiness. But it is the ideal of holiness which renders possible the love of the neighbor. The man who is affirmed in his humanity can still be considered a rational animal, but he is not a complete man. The recognition of the unique, the recognition of the other, the priority of the other is, in a certain sense, unreasonable. One may even be astonished that men would manifest goodness, each on the part of the other. There is no grace as astonishing as this peace.

Q.: The holiness in man would be the altogether spiritual faculty of being in peace, in relation, in a permanent and efficient encounter of love; humanity would be established and would find its advent, full of this grace.

E.L.: Humanity precisely as grace, in the passage from the one to the other: transcendence. Passage from the one to the other, without concern for reciprocity, pure gratuity, from the unique to the unique. That is also reason, or peace, or goodness. Reason as generosity above reason as calculation. This human generosity is certainly not a statistical given. All men are not saints, neither are saints always saints. But all men understand the value of holiness. Even when men contest holiness, it is already in the name of another, greater holiness. The fact of admitting that the death of the other is more important than mine, that it takes precedence over mine, is the very miracle of the human in being, the basis of all obligations.

Q.: But in our contemporary reality do you perceive such a preoccupation manifested on behalf of the other, when in fact an individualism most often indifferent to the fact of the life and the death of the other seems to persevere?

E.L.: As I said, this isn't a statistical truth, but the hope of a complete humanity, and the hope of European man. The European spirit—the Bible and the Greek tradition—as realized through the just State, through an extension of the love of the human to the human collectivity. An order which is certainly submitted to the necessities of genus, of space, of the individual, all of which is so admirably thought by the Greek logic, but whose first moment is goodness and comes from altruism, from the gratuitous love going from a uniqueness outside of genus to the absolutely other. Perhaps here I invent new words for old ideas which are a bit flat. But altruism has to be taken seriously. It contains the word *other*, and there is no other more authentically other than the unique.[4] One calls the other position "egoism." But the true ego is the ego which discovers itself precisely in the urgency of responding to a call. Once again: this citation of Dostoevsky: "We are all guilty, the one toward the other, and I more than all the others." It is not in order to recognize itself as more guilty by specific acts committed that the I who speaks here accuses itself. It is as *me*, always the foremost one responsible, experiencing inexhaustible obligations, that the I is in the wrong, and recognizes in this wrong the identity of its "I."

Q.: But to be more precise, racism would be not only the refusal but, moreover, the contestation, the negation of all possible alterity. According to your categories, it could refer to the condemnation and to the murder of the other.

E.L.: One wishes to make him disappear; he is irritating. Among human beings who are disturbed by others, one resents the national order just as one resents the tribal order. The disinterestedness is when in the other to whom I respond I love not the same blood but the human alterity which is beyond all parentage. That should not be taken for a utilitarian or technical thought. When we organize the world, we are obliged for practical reasons to make concessions. But disinterestedness is included in the responsibility in which no one could replace me and in the alterity of the other. That is the first, foremost, truly human link. It is to recognize human dignity, not according to my weight as a being, but according to my presence to the other.

Q.: Across this recognition, does the meaning of life emerge?

E.L.: When I speak of the meaning of life, I mean precisely that by which the human accomplishes its destiny of being human. The human accomplishing its destiny of being human; that is strange enough—by the fact of standing up and no longer being concerned with the self. It is extraordinary and it merits the name *spirit*. It is with the other man that this spirit rises up in being.

The struggle for life, the plants that want to push up everywhere, drying out the other plants, the animals who struggle for life, this is man still immersed in being where the powerful seek to conquer others. And yet the fact—seemingly insignificant—of no longer being concerned with the self constitutes a rupture. Being persisting in its being, the way in which Spinoza characterized the divine: the being which has no other essence than the wish to be, being which is the very effort of being (does not Heidegger also say that being is an issue for *Dasein* in its being?), becomes what I call *spirit*, man devoted to the other man, to the love of the stranger, to someone who belongs as it were to another logical genus.

Q.: The preoccupation with the other is the very force and the fact of the human.

E.L.: I would also say this in another way. Sociality is not a missed union. Often in their treatment of love, writers complain (this idea is very much in fashion today) that love is deceiving because it hopes for coincidence with the other without being able to achieve this coincidence. Deception of love. At the end of a life shared with someone, one constates that one remains separate. I think, however, that human sociality is not at all a missed coincidence, but a superior excellence. Peace is a mode of unity superior to the unity of the One.

Q.: Love should then intend peace?

E.L.: I call love *peace*. It is extraordinarily important, particularly in Judaism. The last word of the Talmud is the word *peace*. The first word of the meeting is also peace, *shalom*. Peace is sociality; it is to attend to the other. It means not to close one's shutters, not to close one's door, but to put a *mezuzah*, a sign of welcome, on the doorpost. In a society placed under the sign of *shalom*, man always cedes his place to the other.

TRANSLATED BY JILL ROBBINS

Being-for-the-Other

Q.: How would you state the point of departure for your ethical philosophy? What distinguishes it from those philosophies which are prevalent in earlier or contemporary meditations on morality?

E.L.: I have not come to renew things. But let us say very schematically that one habitually begins with the universality of the moral law: the great Kantian idea. For Kant, it was a matter of reattaching ethics to a rational principle, the universality of the maxim of action being, for Kant, the criterion of moral value. Or one may depart from the notion of utility, positing that "what is good is that which is useful or advantageous to me." A reflection upon this order of personal utility culminates in the idea that the best thing is to come to an understanding with others and to share what is useful. Founded on this idea, there are ethical doctrines which are altogether sublime: egoism understood properly would lead to altruism. In fact, from this angle one also rejoins the idea of universality: the sharing certainly imposes sacrifices in which the advantage "to myself" decreases, but in which it is no longer contested by the other, who has his share there.

My manner of approaching the question is, in effect, different. It takes off from the idea that ethics arises in the relation to the other and not straightaway by a reference to the universality of a law. The "relation" to the other man as unique—and in this way, precisely, as absolutely other—would be, here, the first significance of the meaningful. Thence the importance of the relation to the other man as the incomparable, as emptied of all "social role," and who thus, in his nudity—his destitution, his mortality—straightaway imposes himself upon my responsibility: goodness, mercy, or charity.

This nudity which is a call to me—an appeal but also an imperative— I name *face*. It is doubtless necessary to insist on the concrete figure in which the notion of alterity acquires its meaning. It should not be confused with that which has only a formal signification. Logically, within all multiplicity, *a* is the other of *b* and *b* is the other of *a*, but each remains what it is in the ensemble formed by the multiplicity of *terms* which are formally united.

Can the alterity of the other take on a sense otherwise, except by a positive modality of the unique and the "incomparable," excluding the other from the synthesis constituting the ensemble? A modality which opposes to the "logos" founding the synthesis of ensembles a refusal even of termino-logy? Is it not the alterity of the other which, in its difference, would forbid *addition* within an ensemble but would maintain the possibility of a non-in-difference with regard to the other, excluded or excluding itself from addition, excluding itself from the extension of genus?

At the time of my little book entitled *Time and the Other*, I thought that femininity was this modality of alterity—this "other genus"—and that sexuality and eroticism were this non-in-difference to the other, irreducible to the formal alterity of terms in an ensemble.[1] Today I think that it is necessary to go back even further and that the exposition, the nudity, and the "imperative demand" of the face of the other constitute this modality that the feminine already presupposes: the proximity of the neighbor is the nonformal alterity. The original meaning of the meaningful would thus reside in an obligation with regard to the neighbor— with regard to the other—who, before all reflection, concerns me or "regards me," is imposed upon my responsibility, in which I am not interchangeable, in which I am irreplaceable and, in a sense, called and "elected." Principle of the proper uniqueness of the I. The I is concrete in the prereflexive "here I am" of its response. The other man in himself is my neighbor, the proximity of the other is my responsibility for him.

But we are never, me and the other, alone in the world. There is always a third; the men who surround me. And this third is also my neighbor. Who is the nearest to me? Inevitable question of justice which arises from the depth of responsibility for the unique, in which ethics begins in the face of that which is incomparable. Here is the necessity of comparing what is incomparable—of knowing men. First violence, violence of judgment, transformation of faces into objective and plastic forms, into figures which are visible but de-faced; the appearing of men: of individuals, who are certainly unique, but restituted to their genera. With intentions to scrutinize and acts to remember. And perhaps, at the basis of a necessary justice, the very ascending of knowledge, of objectifying and objective rationality, of the very idea of universality. The other is no longer the unique person offering himself to the compassion of my responsibility, but an individual within a logical order or a citizen of a state in which institutions, general laws, and judges are both possible and necessary.

But would ethics disappear in the justice that it requires and in the politics that justice requires? A permanent danger which threatens goodness and the originary compassion of responsibility for the other man. A danger of being extinguished in the system of universal laws which these laws require and support. But also the eventual possibility for "goodness" to be understood in the guise of prophetic voices reverberating imperiously beneath the profundity of established laws. Voices that do not come, like a legislation beneath a legislation, to be formulated once again in the guise of logical rules, whatever be their invitations to generosity and mercy—to *hesed* and to *rahamin*, according to the biblical expressions, which are understood within the rigorous meditation of the just law. But mercy-for-the-other-man, going beyond the rigorous limit which designates justice, responds to these invitations, whether by the resources—or by the poverty—of my uniqueness as an I, in which God can come to mind. Creative, it pierces the hard crust of "the being persevering in its being" which risks burying everything forever.

Q.: Your work mixes in a concerted manner philosophy—Greek and Western (as its name implies) philosophy—and the Jewish tradition. How do you see this "marriage," this demand or this interpellation of one tradition by the other?

E.L.: Greek thought, of Greek origin, is not simply Greek folklore, that is to say, it does not belong simply to an ethnic particularism. In exactly the same manner, I think that the Bible is not Jewish folklore, proper to Jewish particularism. But there is a difference between the two civilizations. I think that Greek spirituality is first of all in knowledge. It is a matter of grasping—in both senses of the term—a being: to comprehend and to apprehend him, to unveil and to dominate him. The Bible "breathes" differently, bringing the idea of social proximity as an original mode of spirituality, meaning, and intelligibility. Certainly the Greeks knew about proximity, but for them the truth of being is in contemplation, knowledge, and theory. To this I oppose the dialogical proximity, fraternal or social, of the Bible, different from the adequation between knowledge and the thing known, different from coincidence within the truth of representation. Proximity without coincidence, which, for all that, is not experienced as a truth that has been missed.

Certainly, in thus presenting "dialogical" proximity in my discourse I let the discourse embrace or collect in an "ensemble" the very proximity that I am claiming, at the same time, is irreducible to syntheses. But is this not the philosophical marvel of Greece, its grace and lucidity? Its discourse lets distances or proximities appear without altering them by the synthetic forms of the logos. Its saying does not submit what is said to its formal constraints; it lucidly leaves the said the freedom of un-saying and resaying. In suggesting earlier that in the love of the other is the foundation of justice and that in justice there is a recourse to objectivity—and perhaps its dialectical birth—we have sketched the passage from proximity to knowledge without compromising proximity, and hence also the manner for spirituality and the Bible to be reconciled with Greece or to claim to be European.

Q.: You have reflected a lot on the alterity of the other in the ethical relation. What about the other pole of the relation, that is, the subject?

E.L.: The ethical attitude takes on a meaning that I call the face of the other man: nudity, exposition unto death, and in the being of the I, infinite obligation and obedience to the imperative. You may object, saying: to be able to assume this absolute responsibility vis-à-vis the other in his destitution and in his mortality, it would still be necessary already to be affirmed "on one's own account" as an I. To be posited.

Certainly. But one must make precise just *how* the I is posited or affirms itself. Is this "I" affirmed just as one who is posited as standing with full rights to be where he is; who, in the world in which he is found, is "doing well" [*qui, dans le monde òu il se trouve, se trouve bien*]; who "perseveres in being" and who has no scruples about persevering? Or is the I posited straightaway for-the-other, straightaway in obligation and straightaway as the only one who is ready to respond and to bear this responsibility, like one who is the first to have hearkened to the call and the last, perhaps, to have listened to it? For the I this amounts to its very identification in its uniqueness as an I: its uniqueness, its exteriority from the extension of any genus, and in this sense, its freedom. It will hold to this primordial election before being affirmed for-itself. It is this moment of election, this "non-interchangeability," which is the originary subjectivation.

Q.: In your work, in contrast to the majority of contemporary philosophers, one finds neither reference nor allusion to psychoanalysis. What is your relation to this knowledge and to this practice?

E.L.: I have a very great suspicion with regard to the practice of psychoanalysis and to its abuses. The non-knowledge that characterizes the ethical relation of which I was speaking has a proper, positive meaning of humility and abnegation. It is respect, not repression; nor is it simple ignorance. But if the concept of the unconscious were to signify a lived mental experience which is not reducible to re-presentation and to the present, thus giving it all the significations of temporality, then it suits me fine.

I have always admired Heidegger's analysis of "The Word of Anaximander."[2] The present—the presence of the present—appears there as violence in its very persistence, repelling past and future, without the suggestion of any "remorse" about this exclusive *Dasein*. To let time signify according to its diachrony, disengaged from the simultaneity through which knowledge would grasp it, is to think time under the figure of the ethical, under the figure of the responsibility for the other in the gratuitous generosity of love renouncing reciprocity. This responsibility is established neither beneath the simultaneity of the givens of knowledge, contemporary for the gaze which apprehends everything, nor in the reciprocity of exchanges within economic society.

The relationship between me and the other is asymmetrical, like the irreversibility of time, the non-in-difference to the other going beyond contemporaneity, and proximity not being a matter of having missed out on coincidence. All this may have been glimpsed in the discovery of the unconscious. But I am disgusted by the arbitrariness to which the patient is submitted in psychoanalytic practice and by the crudeness of a psychology that explains each intuition as eventually suggestive. One speaks of a man who has "worked through his Oedipus complex"—who would have symbolically killed his father and married his mother—as of one who has just made his first communion.

Q.: How do you envisage the relationship between philosophy on the one hand and on the other art and literature, which pass for being a "contestation" of the preeminence of reasoning reason?

E.L.: In a certain sense one returns to the logos of reasoning reason once the very negation of its reign is thematized or enunciated or renounced by gratuitous generosity. The logos has the ultimate power of the last word within the reflection on the very signification that escapes it, that is to say, within philosophy. But as we have said, the logical narrative of reflection does not leave ineffaceable traces in the structure of signification which is narrated or deformed in reflection. The possible unsayings and resayings limit the definitive saying of reflection. Moreover, there are doubtless situations in which the signification which acquires meaning absorbs the understanding and adjourns reflective thought. This would already be the definition of music, of literature, of the art of poetry, of that which sings. Except that in poetry and in music too, but after the fact, hermeneutics explicates the song of works that sing and discovers in them a message and folds the poem into the logos while depriving it of poetry. But there can be poetry in the hermeneutic logos itself before logic can render an account of this hermeneutic song. And there can be urgency in the ethical vocation of the face, which adjourns reflection on this urgency. An urgency which does not necessarily belong to the contingencies of the beautiful and the good.

Q.: How would you qualify the relations between ethics and aesthetics? Do they exclude one another?

E.L.: The beautiful is not the ultimate. One can speak of the beautiful as a face. But in so doing, there is also the possibility of fascination and henceforth of an indifference or an ethical cruelty.

Q.: The question of history. Is there for you a meaning of history?

E.L.: For me the great event of history—but this is already or still an event of sacred history—would be the apparition of the human which would signify the interruption of the pure perseverance of a being in its being. It is this that we have been speaking about since the beginning of our interview. Interruption of the *conatus essendi* and of the struggle for existence which draws man into evil and into war. But by understanding the vocation of being-for-the other, which must be thought in all its acuity, that which is human in man has also put into question the *conatus es-*

sendi. In this possibility of disinterestedness, in this goodness, the awakening to biblical humanity is produced: to respond to the other, to the priority of the other, the asymmetry between me and the other, him always *before* me, man as an irrational animal, or rational according to a new reason.

But I don't have any philosophy of history. Would this breaking through of nature by the human assure the triumph of the human? Does the vocation offer a guarantee? Generosity is always menaced by the inhuman necessities of being in man and in economy, even and up through the ideologies that issue from generosity. Let us think of the experience of the twentieth century, is it destined for success? I don't know. Certainly I sometimes think that the disinterestedness of love unwittingly allows one to think so. But can one circulate such thoughts without adding to them any consolation?

I have been very struck by Vassily Grossman's book *Life and Fate*, which describes all the horrors of the inhuman, of Stalinism and Hitlerism. In this extraordinary book the essential teaching is articulated by a strange, socially marginal person who has lived through it all. Halfway between simplemindedness and holiness, between madness and wisdom, he doesn't believe in God anymore, nor in the Good which would organize an ideology. And if he does not see any system capable of vanquishing evil, he does claim that evil cannot vanquish the senseless, incidental goodness in the human, the compassion proceeding from one private man to another, but outside all redemptive institutions, political or religious. And in the highest and purest manifestation of this goodness, stronger than the Good, he still distrusts the moment it becomes preaching and when, in this ideological beginning, already it ceaselessly risks betraying itself.

TRANSLATED BY JILL ROBBINS

The Philosopher and Death

Q.: It is always the living, is it not, who speak of the dead and of death? Philosophers who question themselves about death do so necessarily about the death of the other, since, like each of us, they have no experience of their own. Even Socrates had not yet lived through death when he carried out his last conversation with his disciples, though hemlock was flowing in his veins, and he was dying as he spoke of death. It is Plato who spoke of the dead Socrates.

E.L.: I believe you are touching there on an essential point. Death is utterly unknown. It is, moreover, unknown otherwise than any [other] unknown. It seems to me, whatever the subsequent reactions within philosophy, and even within opinion, death is firstly the nothingness of knowledge. I do not say that it *is* nothingness. It is also the "plenitude" of the question, but first one says, "I do not know." These are the first words that come, and which are fitting.

Q.: For us in our world, death is a definitive disappearance. And with it, notably, the word of him who disappears is finished. One cites someone's "last words," but it is still a matter of the words of a living person. Posthumous memoirs are redacted prior to death: the dead are silent.

E.L.: Death is a disappearance for the others. But in itself, it is a dilemma: to be or "not to be." The description of the phenomenon of death is made while one is alive. And if something comes to pass afterwards, we must agree that it is not of the order of the experience of the living. The possibility that there be something that comes to pass afterward is situated beyond our reach. The idea that it is a matter of an excluded third term, or something other than being and nothingness, itself provokes fright. We speak of death without ever being sure that death is what we are speaking of. It is, no doubt, something that does not enter into human thought.

Q.: And yet, death is the sole point of certainty upon which thought could anchor itself, the sole indubitable event of our destiny?

E.L.: That it happens: yes. Death is the inexorable.

Q.: The sole certainty, but inexorable?

E.L.: Everything else is inexorable as a function of death. Of itself, it is inexorable and in this sense, again, frightening. It is that which comes and that which one cannot assume. For a thought moving continuously in the midst of interdependent notions, death is the hole which undoes the system, the disturbance of every order, the dismantling of every totality. You go toward death, you "learn to die," you "prepare" yourself for the final event; but in the last quarter of an hour—or the last second—death is there, travelling its part of the route alone and ready to surprise. In that sense death is not a possibility like all other possibilities, where there is always something preliminary, always a project. To be unassumable belongs to death's very quality. It is an event without a project insofar as the "project" that one might have of death is undone in the last moment. It is death alone which travels the last part of the route. Not us. One does not, properly speaking, encounter it.

Spinoza will say, as you know, that philosophers ought to think of death least of all things. By contrast, Heidegger referred philosophical thought to death most extensively. The philosopher's mortality marks his thought as it marks his existence. A finite existence. A finite human thought, though it be philosophical. A philosophical thought because of this finitude. Heidegger calls the extreme possibility of death the possibility of impossibility. Without wishing to play on words, I have always thought that possibility implies a human power, whereas dying is unassumable: it is rather "an impossibility of possibility."

Q.: One which is inevitable and which nevertheless is impossible for us in the strict sense of the term?

E.L.: The inexorable, in the sense in which I was using the word earlier. The unassumable. Under this aspect, death is refractory to knowledge, in an exceptional manner. It is unknown but not because knowledge is limited, since knowledge could one day be enlarged miraculously. Death shall never be able to be known. It was in that sense that I stated earlier that the unassumable belongs to its quality. Those who come back from the last extremity and recount it have not really been there. That is not serious.

Q.: The world of the cave remains closed upon itself and on its shadows. We know no more today, according to you, than did the tenth book of Plato's *Republic*, no more than our grandsons will know about this essential point of human destiny. Death is the sphinx whom one questions but who does not respond.

E.L.: Yes. And the word *mystery* is fitting here. Death is the site of this category: mystery. An unknown that poses a question. A question without givens. It is not a matter of emphasizing indefatigably the banal evidence of the fact that we are unaware of the beyond of death. We are even unaware of the meaning that the word "beyond" could have here. Even the famous nothingness on which one agrees so easily poses a problem. Can one break with being? Can one exit being? Does not negation, and even annihilation, leave in subsistence the very scene in which negations and annihilations are played out? Is not the outside in some sense inside? Isn't one always closed in existence? Absolutely no evasion.

In his magnificent and strange work, Maurice Blanchot thinks death starting from this impossibility of breaking off. And there lies—upon the mystery of death—a profound and obsessional view. Ontology as obsession. In the anguish of death, the impossibility of nothingness. An impossibility of "stopping the music" or interrupting the "hustle-bustle" of existence! And yet an impossibility of continuing.

Q.: But within this perspective precisely, could one not also say in a positive manner that nothing entirely new occurs in our existence other than death? Death is precisely the intrusion of the unknown, of what has never happened, in a world where, sooner or later, everything happens. The mystery of death is also the possibility of something else.

E.L.: We will speak of this other aspect of death. Something new is in effect produced, but only for us who attend to the death of the other. We shall never know what death signifies for the deceased himself. We do not even know what legitimacy there might be in saying "for the deceased himself." But for the survivor, there is in the other's death both the disappearance of the deceased and the extreme solitude that results. I think that the human consists precisely in opening itself to the death of the other, in being preoccupied with his death. What I am here saying might appear to be a pious thought, but I am persuaded that around the death of my neighbor is manifested what I called the humanity of man.

Q.: To receive in thought and heart the perspective of the other is certainly an act of piety, but is it also one of thinking?

E.L.: Yes.

Q.: Gabriel Marcel said that to love is to say to the other: "You shall not die." It is to recognize, thanks to the gaze of love, that the death of the other is impossible and, at the same time, to recognize that which is impossible in death. In this sense, can we say that death arrests the project of being? It is otherwise prolonged, yet it is nevertheless prolonged, and not only in our memory and our thought. Can we not reintegrate into a new project even the death of the other?

E.L.: Gabriel Marcel believes in the metaphysical efficacy of love and does not think that the excluded third term might be thinkable.

Q.: Plato also has Socrates say that he accepts running "the fine risk of immortality." Isn't this a form of the project's continuity across the rupture? One changes level, and even life, but he who is merely mortal glimpses the opening of the possibility, the eventuality of becoming immortal through the passage of death: to run this risk, but also to take on this hope, is that not precisely what is human, terribly human?

E.L.: Alexander Kojève was fond of recalling that moment where Socrates is on the point of convincing his interlocutors of the immortality of the soul. They were divided, consequently, between the hope of seeing Socrates again after his death and the despair over the separation about to take place. But Plato, not present at the conversation, did not share the emotion of these interlocutors. Did he not indicate from the beginning of his dialogue that he had been absent due to illness? We shall never know, then, whether he was convinced about immortality by the proofs of the *Phaedo* or whether he had run the risk of believing them.

That is, if we believe Kojève, who was not lacking in ingenious and penetrating ideas.

Q.: Yet is it not the case that a philosopher's reflection can and must "risk" itself in the unknown, envisioning this "fine risk of immortality" which death makes us run? Isn't this to take account of that which is most human in thought?

E.L.: I consider that this alternative between being and nothingness on which the proof of immortality is based does not pose the first question. "To be or not to be" is not the ultimate alternative and, in any case, not the ultimate nor the most urgent question. We will come back to that. To be sure, to speak of questions of life and death is to speak of urgent questions. But is life and death as a pair reducible to being and not being? Is it not a metaphor? We must come back to the concrete consideration of death.

Q.: Concretely, life and death are inseparable. One cannot think of life as if death did not exist. But human life, insofar as it is human, poses questions to human death, which is not a death of just anything. What is this the death of? Love which is more than being? To love or not to love is certainly the most profound form of the question "to be or not to be." We know that death is an end, but we do not know of what, and we also do not know whether it is also a beginning.

E.L.: When death is there, we are no longer there. Is this an end point or a beginning? Let us say in effect that we know nothing about it. One has perhaps never yet measured to what degree all that is unknown. The idea of the excluded third term of which I spoke earlier is entirely gratuitous, yet it is a measure of the unknown and the mystery of the question of death. I mentioned the metaphor life-death. In our everyday life, we use these two words constantly, driven by our perseverance in being, forgetting the properly human vocation of disinterestedness, disengagement from being, and our concern for the being of the other. I always try to introduce, moreover, the idea that mystery is ineluctable in the description and terminology of death. In effect, we must consider mysterious the other side of this violence which is perpetrated in death; this is precisely because it is not assumable by anyone. But before the death of the other who is my neighbor, mysterious death appears to me, in any case, as an isolation in regard to which I could in no way remain indifferent. It awakens me to the other.

Heidegger deduces all thinkable signification from the attitude of man in regard to his own death. He thinks to the end, in both senses of the term. He takes his thought to its final consequences, and he thinks that my death can only be, for me, the ultimate "of-itself." I ask myself whether that is truly the limit of thinking. Is there no thinking that goes beyond my own death, toward the death of the other man, and does the human not consist precisely in thinking beyond its own death? In affirming this, I am not trying to adopt the stance of some sort of beautiful soul. What I mean is that the death of the other can constitute a central experience for me, whatever be the resources of our perseverance in our own being. For me, for example—and this will not astonish you—the Holocaust is an event whose meaning remains inexhaustible. But in every death to which one attends, and in each approach of someone who is mortal, the resonances of this extraordinary unknown are heard. We apprehend this unknown irresistibly in the other man's encounter with death. An event the significance of which is infinite, and the emotion of which is thoroughly ethical.

Q.: The death of the other whom we love confers upon death all its dramatic intensity because the life of the other has shone with all its intensity. It is not only the death of the other, it is apparently the death of love, in which the other had taken on for us the plenitude of his being and his life, as well as an identity irreducible to any other one. It is impossible that this pass unnoticed, that it be hidden from view, and when the other we love is touched by death, it is our common love which is touched, it is our own death which is announced to us. When one has lost someone close, one enters in some sense into intimacy with death, and we discover more intensely to what degree it is a part of the fabric of our lives.

E.L.: I am not thinking of intensity and my analysis does not begin in a relation to the death of those who "are dear to us," still less in the return to "oneself," which would bring us back to the priority of my own death. In starting from the Holocaust, I think about the death of the other man; I think of the other man for whom one may already feel—I don't know why—like a guilty survivor. I have asked myself, as perhaps you know, what the face of the other man means. I have taken the liberty of saying that there is in the face above all an uprightness and a rectitude, a being face forward precisely as if it were exposed to some threat at point-blank range, as if it presented itself wholly delivered up to death. I sometimes ask myself whether the idea of the straight line—the shortest distance between two points—is not originally the line according to which the face that I encounter is exposed to death. It is probably the manner in which my death regards and intends me, but I do not see my own face. The first thing which is evident in the face of the other is this rectitude of exposure and defenselessness. In his face, the human being is most naked, destitution itself. And at the same time, he faces. It is in the manner in which he is completely alone in his facing us that we measure the violence perpetrated in death.

Third moment of the epiphany of the face: it makes a demand on me. The face looks at me and calls to me. It lays claim to me. What does it ask? Not to leave it alone. An answer: here I am. My presence vain, perhaps, a gratuitous movement of presence and responsibility for another person. To respond "here I am" is already the encounter with the face.

Q.: Its very singularity only appears in extreme and ultimate moments. One often says, "He resembles so and so." At the same time, one sees clearly that he resembles no one but himself, and no other can take his place for us, whether we love him or not.

E.L.: When one wants to define this famous love of the neighbor—an often used term—I think one must return to the relation with the face as the mortality of the neighbor and the impossibility of leaving him to his solitude. The positive definition of the love of the neighbor is distinguished from everything that is erotic and concupiscent. A love without concupiscence—that is sociality itself. In this relation with the face, in this direct relation with the death of the other, you discover that the death of the other has priority over your own and over your life. It is not merely the banal fact that one can die for someone: this banal fact—which is no mere banality—is the breakthrough of the human putting into question the ontological necessities and the persistence of a being that perseveres in its being. To throw oneself into the water to save someone, without knowing how to swim, is to go toward the other totally; without holding anything back of oneself; to give oneself to the other totally; to respond to his unformulated demand, to the expression of the face, to his mortality and to his "thou shalt not kill." But above all, it is no longer simply a matter of going toward the other while he dies, but of responding through one's presence to the mortality of the living. All this is ethical conduct. At the limit, ethics is the supreme scruple not to drive the other into some third—or fourth—world by occupying a place in the sun. Pascal said that my place in the sun is the image and the beginning of the usurpation of the whole earth. It is as if, by the fact of being there, I deprived someone of his vital space, as if I expelled or assassinated someone. It was also Pascal who said, "The I is detestable."[1] He was not simply giving a lesson in courtesy or style, but in ontology. As if the principle of identity positing itself triumphantly as I contained an indecency and a violence; as if the I impeded, by its very position, the full existence of another; as if in appropriating something, the I risked taking it away from someone else.

Q.: Simone Weil said, "I regard the world as if I were not there." This form of supreme detachment and of contemplation, which lies at the point opposite from indifference, perhaps seeks in the world and in man an original and infinite purity. It is an effort to deliver the world from what is opaque in our presence, from the obstacle that our presence creates between a pure gaze and its veritable object. Is it not in the same sense that Racine's unhappy Phaedra concludes, at once guilty and ashamed of being so, "And death, to my eyes fleeing the light, renders to the day which it had sullied all its purity" (act V, scene vii, ll. 50–51)?

E.L.: I think that these quotations accord on many points with what I would like to suggest. Behind the relationship with the death of the other a very strange problem emerges: among us humans does our very being already legitimate our wish to be? It is not a matter of asking ourselves in the name of some abstract law whether or not we ought to give up our lives, but finding reasons for being, for meriting being. Bad conscience of being coming to light before the death of the other! Is this not a listening to the commandment to love which the faces of mortals transmit to us? There can be no doubt of their right to be, but the I is the singular site at which this problem awakens. The effort to exist, the aspiration to persevere in being, the *conatus essendi* according to philosophers like Spinoza, is the beginning of every right. This precisely is what I attempt to put into question—starting from the encounter with the mortality, or the face, of the other—when I insist upon the radical difference between the others and me. The anguish for my own death reveals my finitude and the scandal of an existence that always dies too early. Within this finitude, the good conscience of being remains intact. It is the death of the other man which challenges this good conscience.

Q.: Nevertheless, all the others do not exist equally for us. They exist more or less, and their deaths affect us more or less, depending on how far away or close they are to our lives. And for all sorts of reasons. But when one has seen death touch the face of a beloved being, death becomes at once more horrible and more easy, almost desirable: life itself becomes foreign; and we pass from the horror of dying to the horror of living or surviving. Death takes on, in a certain sense, the traits of this loved face and thereby becomes attractive instead of fearsome. To share such a destiny becomes enviable, all in all, in the name of love. All the great lovers throughout history want to follow the other into the grave. In a death that truly touches us, are we not stripped of the I?

E.L.: Death, in this case, has lost its threat.

Q.: Death engenders something like an appeal from the other, something like an appeal of love. In any case, it appears as a deliverance; it saves us from living halfway.

E.L.: But that is not an ethical attitude. I was speaking on the contrary of the ethical attitude which is the ground of sociality. Not an attitude which regards the death of a being already chosen and dear, but instead the death of the first one to come along. To recognize that I let the other—whoever he might be—pass before I do, that is the ethical.

Q.: It is to break with an ontology in which our own being conditions the access to being and beings. Ultimately, the existence of the other, and therefore the death of the other, alone counts?

E.L.: It is starting from the existence of the other that my existence can be posed as human. By starting with the relation to the death of the other, I am trying to imagine an anthropology different from that which starts from the *conatus essendi*. But I believe that it is not only to the death of the other we respond but also to his life. And it is in responding to his life that we are already with him in his death. I have sometimes wondered if in order to reveal the human which strives to break with ontology, that ontology must either be founded or undermined.

TRANSLATED BY BETTINA BERGO

Being-Toward-Death and "Thou Shalt Not Kill"

Q.: You have been able to track contemporary French philosophy over the last decade. Phenomenology and existentialism dominated the postwar years, structuralism followed. Can you still imagine today a definite trend of French philosophizing? Or do there exist wholly heterogenous approaches, which cannot be brought under one umbrella anymore?

E.L.: Everything was animated during the postwar years. Traditional philosophizing meant German idealism; there were Hegel students; phenomenology was new. Phenomenology had a distinct evolution in France. Not that there were movements which were obligatory for all philosophers. There certainly were distinguished thinkers like Claude Lévi-Strauss, whom one read with much interest, but no norms for thinking followed from them. It seems completely mistaken to phrase the question as if there had been some sort of dominant movement. Naturally, the arrival of phenomenology was something utterly new and, as method, something very necessary and illuminating. The personality of Heidegger carried a great deal of weight in France at the time, and still now many read and interpret Heidegger. Heideggerian language has become universal—just as it has become in Germany. The people I meet from Germany always, even when they attack Heidegger, speak a Heideggerian language.

Q.: What was for you Heidegger's central thought—the thought you have developed further?

E.L.: I have admired in particular the way in which Husserlian method was employed in *Being and Time*. For instance, the demonstration of states-of-mind [*die Befindlichkeit*], in their theoretical sense, was something quite extraordinary, a flowering of the Husserlian method. Also very important, of course, was a truth, an eternal truth, of the difference between Being and beings, and therefore, to have a feel for the ontico-ontological difference: the return to Being as verb. There was a frequent mix-up because the French *être* means "being" as well as "Being." Again, this moment is taken up even by those who neither believe in the event [*das Ereignis*], nor accept the fourfold [*das Geviert*] as the focus for all thinking.

Q.: In extending Heidegger's thought, you have attempted to thematize a region presupposed by every experience, and which constitutes knowledge. You have formulated it as the experience of the other.

E.L.: I cannot say that this is as important a discovery as that of the ontico-ontological difference, but the relation to the other for Heidegger is present only as a moment of being-in-the-world. This strange relation to another person as the beginning of new concepts, and a new comportment, and a new finality of thinking is absent in Heidegger. The purely ethical has had, perpetually, a bad reputation. It was always resisted, either by ontology or by religion. For religion, and primarily for Christianity, the ethical appears to be only an approach, a beginning: the religious stands over the ethical. For thinking, the sacred appears as something which stands in essence higher and belongs to the metaphysical. I believe, on the other hand, that the ethical is the spiritual itself and that there is nothing that surpasses the ethical. The surpassing of the ethical is precisely the beginning of all violence. It is especially important to recognize this after the events that occurred between 1933 and 1945, which is not to justify philosophically or to take some new position on the evil done then. To recognize the unsurpassable quality of the ethical is, rather, the fundamental lesson and the first truth.

It seems to me extremely important in this connection that the relation of myself to the other not involve a collapsing together of the two, but that the two-ness, the non-unity, is actual in the ethical. Proximity is a value in and for itself. Literature accustoms us to believe that the lovers are *unfortunately* still separated, that love would hence be only truly fulfilled if the duality were overcome. There would be a certain tragedy of solitude. On the other hand, I think that not collapsing the lovers together is an excellence in itself; it is the good in-itself, the very place of goodness. In deprecatory terms, ethics is always taken as a moral for children: to be good. One speaks of it with a smile. In *Life and Fate*, Vassily Grossman believes that the *eschaton* is approaching because everything European appears to be moving into a final crisis with Hitler and Stalin. The only thing which still remains is the goodness of one human being toward another. His book recounts the de-Europeanization of Europe, this de-humanization of the human in all its forms. The sole thing which remains is goodness. From 1933 to 1945, it was crucial to render help. Please excuse me if it seems as though I am preaching.

Q.: You have said that the ethical unfolds itself in the relation to another person. If I recall correctly, you wrote that ethics cannot posit out of itself any norms. Hegel developed the ethical dimension out of the relationship of recognition: they recognize themselves as mutually recognizing each other:[1] Would you be able to agree to such a structural formulation of the ethical relation?

E.L.: For me, certainly, that is already the Bible. The Old Testament already said this perfectly. What does the Bible in fact say? The text says: "Thou shalt not kill." It also says that there are a variety of ways to kill. It isn't always just a matter of killing, say, with a knife. The everyday killing with a good conscience, the killing in all innocence—there is such a thing as well! "Love thy neighbor" and "thou shalt not kill" mean the same thing.

It is completely extraordinary that being as such is always a *conatus essendi*, the tendency to self-perservere in being. The Bible comes right along and adds—for it has to be read this way—to be human means to have a responsibility for the other. The other is properly nothing to me. In French, this is expressed well: *il n'est rien pour moi, il ne me regarde pas* (he is nothing to me, he does not concern me). This "not-concerning-me" is the non-human. The human enters into being in order to say the ontological absurdity: the other *does* concern me, the death of the other *does* concern me. Ethics in the West always assumes the other is a limit for me. Hobbes says that it is precisely *from* this reciprocal hatred that one can come to philosophy. That is to say, without love for the other, we can therefore reach a better society in which allowance is made for the other. This would be a politics capable of leading to an ethics. I believe, conversely, that politics must be held in check by ethics: the other does concern me. I have a modern expression for this, namely: I am the hostage of the other. I am the hostage of my other. One recognizes the other insofar as one is oneself a hostage. The important thing here is that *I* am the hostage. In this connection, it is important—and this was not seen by German idealism—that the I is without reciprocity. It cannot be said that we are "I"s in the world. The way in which my "I" is an I is something utterly singular in the world. And therefore, *I* am responsible, and may not be concerned about whether the other is responsible for me. The human, in the highest, strictest sense of the word, is without reciprocity. I didn't discover that, Dostoevsky did. It is his great truth: "We are all guilty in everything in respect to all others, and I more than all the others." This last "I more than all the others" is the important thing here, even if that means in a certain sense to be an idiot. Well, I see my preaching continues.

Q.: You are tying ethics to the relation to the other human being. Do not ecological problems, such as the destructive consequences of the techno-sciences, also present the task of producing a relation to nature as the other of the human? Would your approach encompass that?

E.L.: I have thought about that as well. If there were only the two of us in the world, you and I, then there would be no question, then my system would work perfectly. I am responsible to the other in everything. In this anthropology, the other's death, his being-toward-death, is more important to me than my being-toward-death. For a man—certainly not for an animal—but for a man who has heard the word of God, this is so. But we are not only two, we are at least three. Now we are a threesome; we are a humanity. The question then arises—the political question: *who* is the neighbor? Then it is necessary to reflect about such things; *il faut délibérer*. And now, everything is new and different. The other was precisely what I call the "face." For me, he is singular. When the third appears, the other's singularity is placed in question. I must look him in the face as well. One must, then, compare the incomparable. For me, this is the Greek moment in our civilization. We could not get by with the Bible alone; we must turn to the Greeks. The importance of knowing, the importance of comparing, stems from them; everything economic is posed by them, and we then come to something other than love. For until now, I have been speaking of love. This responsibility for the other is the grounding moment of love. It is not really a state of mind; it is not a sentiment, but rather an obligation. The human is first of all obligation. Every feeling, every state of mind, presupposes a being-hostage! It is a mistake to think that this responsibility would be no burden, but it is not only a burden. It is frequently asked: how could Kant consider love an obligation? In the presence of the face of the other, love is obligation. Only afterwards do I come to meditate and to compare. Then violence enters the scene because justice's judgment is violence.

Europe is the Bible and the Greeks. When we come to the Greeks, and that means to our world, in which there has to be a state, a court, and an economic law, the relation of goodness to the other does not, of course, vanish. In the very consciousness of justice in Europe this is disclosed: justice is not yet completely just. And this justice, which is better than justice, is our European consciousness. It has to be made better! I mean that the feeling that there is still violence evokes a search for a better justice. A progressivism of justice belongs to this, as does the possibility of creating out of my singularity something for the other. The relation of the one to the other does not vanish in justice, but rather the I always hears the call to create something. However, this cannot become a universal principle, because, were it a universal principle, it would be a *moment* of justice, a law. In this sense, *caritas* is near to law. But after Auschwitz, one can no longer preach in this way, because the traditional European, and also Christian, sermon expects a *happy end*. When this is accomplished, we are redeemed. And being-redeemed always means that one has come into a world of equality; there is satisfaction in practically the material sense. But after Auschwitz, even though it doesn't "pay" to be good, one cannot deduce from that that one should not be good. Hence, to stop preaching for the good would not suffice. Stop preaching, but accept the obligation to say the good, to want the good, to do the good. This is to call on what is human, the human as precisely the place where humanity has become a difficult matter. Such calling on the human is no longer a sermon, because the sermon always has a *happy end*. Even if the priest does not always say this, it is invariably understood.

Q.: Where does the obligation to the good stem from? Where does it issue from?

E.L.: Where does it stem from? A principle. The face of the other *is* pure alterity, pure strangeness, the other freed from every particular difference and so for the I straightaway obligation. In Deuteronomy 10:19 we read: "Love therefore the stranger." In the otherness of the other lies the beginning of all love. It is always believed that the source of an obligation in the world has to include the *happy end*. If I propose the difficult burden of responsibility for the other, I naturally cannot deduce its source out of some kind of promise of the *happy end*. It's not pleasant, it's not enjoyable, but it is "good." Responsibility for the other is the experience of the good, the very meaning of the good, goodness. Only goodness is good. If I cannot automatically deduce this from happiness, it still does not yet signify violence. It is God's command.

Q.: The experience of the face of the other stands for you in connection with the experience of God and also with the infinite. Why?

E.L.: I wrote a little book entitled *Of God Who Comes to Mind*. I attempted to speak of this God of whom we speak—who is the true God, even though I cannot prove his existence—and to say where his concept originates. How does he come to me? I do not deduce him from causality, nor from the ground or origin of being, but rather from the face of the other. He comes to me, when I encounter the face.

Q.: Can you be more specific?

E.L.: The relation to the face of the other, or seeing the face of the other (I don't know that the word "seeing" fits here exactly, one always "sees" an object), means that I approach the other so that his face acquires meaning for me. The meaningfulness of the face is the command to responsibility. To say this in a Heideggerian way: when Heidegger taught us that tools, like the knife, the fork, and also, for example, the street, "fall into my hands," and are ready-to-hand for me before I objectify them, it is not because this possibility is based on knowledge.[2] This possibility is not to be grounded in a meaning either, because here meaning itself is grounded "in the hands." I think the face in exactly this manner. The face is face not because I see it, nor because I recognize the color of your eyes, or the form of your lips. That wouldn't be seeing the face or approaching the face. When I see the face approaching, I am already completely contemporaneous, exuberant. The nose, I recognize this nose. In the West, this is certainly the way we *regard* a person. But I think that to approach the face of the other is to worry directly about his death, and this means to regard him straightaway as mortal, finite. The directness of death *is* the face of the other because the face is being looked on by death. It is like the origin of the straight line. One can neither prove the origin, nor define it. It is directness in itself, the directness of death. And his death, your death, is immediately present to me, even though I do everything possible in order to forget it. What nonetheless remains behind the scenes is the ethical, an original being delivered over to the other—love. Only justice can modify that, in that justice brings this being delivered over unto the neighbor under a measure, or tempers it by thinking it in relation to the third or fourth, who are my "others" as well. Justice is already the first violence.

Q.: Is there then a kind of knowing or a thinking which is in itself peaceful, and which does not conceal in itself the seed of acts of violence?

E.L.: Certainly. I have already told you. We are always searching for a justice which is more just than justice. And the great pitfall is there as well for Europeans, when they would rebuild all society on an ideological basis. It is terrible because then everything reverts to deduction, to administration and to violence. I am very cautious about ideological socialism. I am preaching, though, as I say all this.

Q.: You spoke of the other as an original experience which presents itself in death.

E.L.: I am very cautious with this word. Experience is knowledge. The presence of the other touches me ("touches," as in *je suis touché*, is better because then I am actually passive). I am concerned. You say beautifully in German: *Der Andere geht mich an* ("The other concerns [lit., goes to] me"). This concerning-me-of-your-death is the *éclatement*, the shattering of being. Spinoza believed it to be the first truth that being is concerned in its being with this being. That is also the first word of Heidegger; I have not forgotten it. *Dasein* is a being for whom, in its very being, being is an issue. Later, in the encounter with Beaufret, in the *Letter on Humanism*, he says that *Dasein* is a being for whom the meaning of this being is an issue. I was reading Heidegger before you were born. The entire book, *Being and Time*, was so extraordinary, because this being abandoned to Being, this care for being, leads indeed to the way in which everything possesses meaning. In 1927 it appeared to us as if he were beginning with a kind of Darwinian struggle for existence. *Dasein* is a being for whom this, his being, is an issue. Later he changed this a little: *Dasein* is a being for whom the meaning of being is a concern.

Q.: Heideggerian being is, however, anonymous, not personal like the original experience of the face of the other?

E.L.: True, he discovered that; but I would not condemn him for it. The Heideggerian being-with-one-another [*das Miteinandersein*] appears to me always like marching-together. That is not for me; there is no face there. However, being-toward-the-other is not an anonymous relation.

Q.: How does a philosophical concept of God relate to a religious conception, such as to the Christian or Judaic God?

E.L.: I recognize what is Christian as what is biblical. As a Jew, what I have to say to Christianity is a bit complicated. Within Christianity the barbarity of history has never disappeared; it is even because of Christianity that there has never ceased to be endless enmity toward Jews and ceaseless wars. Then something new came along, and one called it the Holocaust. The great "experience" of Judaism. I call it *passion* in the same sense as one speaks of the suffering [*Leiden*] of Christ under the Romans. So *la passion des juifs sous Adolf Hitler* still belongs for me to the Passion of Christ and to holy history, although in it something new comes to pass. Of course the torture and murder in Auschwitz was carried out by men who all knew the catechism, a fact that one cannot forget. But at the same time, a moment of what one calls Christian *charité*, or the love of the neighbor, also appeared to Jews. Wherever one saw a black cassock, one knew that one could find protection. My wife and daughter were saved in a cloister. All this produced a new relationship to Christianity. What came to pass in history as Auschwitz interminably sickens Christians themselves; I am convinced of this. This is a new suffering and, for the Church, a new way.

Europe, then, is the Bible and the Greeks. It has come closer to the Bible and has come into its own destiny. It takes in everything else in the world. I have no nostalgia for the exotic. For me, Europe is central.

Q.: Do you mean that those of us in this tradition should remain in this tradition of thought?

E.L.: Yes. I mean this. One can express everything in Greek. One can, for example, say Buddhism in Greek. Speaking Greek will always remain European; Greek is the language of the university. With this I am thinking neither about the Greek roots of words nor a Greek grammar. The way of speaking in the university is Greek and cosmopolitan [*allweltlich*]. Certainly, in this sense, Greek is spoken at the University of Tokyo. It is central, because Greek is not one language among others.

Q.: Your ethical thinking sets itself off from a philosophy of reconciliation, of unity, and perhaps also from fusion. You plead for multiplicity and, in this sense, want to break with the Parmenidean element in the European philosophical tradition. Isn't the invention of the thought of unity decisive for the European tradition?

E.L.: No. When I speak about Europe, I think about the gathering of humanity. Only in the European sense can the world be gathered together! At least, that is my belief. In this sense, Buddhism can be said just as well in Greek. There are just so many more confluences in the European tradition than in the particularities—in the *génie national*—of a people. To speak in a Greek way means, as in Plato, that there is a reply to every objection, and that what is said should not be forgotten. What one said yesterday must be true and important today as well. One must use words whose deeper sense is not simply presupposed: one can preserve them and one can always come back to them. The Greek words are spoken without prejudice; they are not burdened with pre-judgment. One begins in the clarity of an unequivocal sign and only then can the way to what is secret appear. That is the eternal youth and the great maturity of the Greek language. In it Heidegger discovered everything other, but he proceeds from this unequivocal sign.

Q.: Heidegger has criticized thinking since Plato as forgetful of being. Are there not moments that you criticize in European thinking?

E.L.: For me, what is Greek is not pre-Socratic. The pre-Socratic is first made intelligible through the Socratic.

Q.: Whereas you say that for the most part some of your thought was provoked by historical events, on the whole your philosophy appears as a mode of originary philosophy, which—aiming at eternal truths—finds itself in the ethical situation.

E.L.: The ethical situation I consider with gravity. Here lies the beginning of gravity. To me, the original recognition of the other and the beginning of meaning resounds in the "thou shalt not kill." This saying is extremely important: *Vor-Sicht* ("fore-sight") toward the death of the other is the beginning of the recognition of the other. He is certainly mortal; in his presence, the "I"-ness of my "I" is free of being-toward-death! If you read the Judaic commentary on the Bible in conjunction with the biblical text, then you find the following question: How were the Ten

Commandments written on the two tablets? This is, to say it in German, a *meschuggene*—that is, a crazy—question. Concerning this question and its answer, two interpretations are to be found in a commentary from the first century of the Christian era. On the two tablets, the Ten Commandments were written twice. One time on one side and one time on the other. That is one possible opinion. It makes good sense: one is naturally not allowed to interpret the world of the Ten Commandments always in one and the same way. The Ten Commandments can shape diverse worlds, which are not mutually exclusive but do vary from each other. The other opinion is that five commandments stood on one tablet and five commandments stood on the other tablet. Why? Because one could then not only read them from the top to the bottom, but also horizontally. And then you get, "I am the eternal one!" with "Thou shalt not kill!" We were in Holland, in a cloister, and there I saw two tablets. On the one tablet stood three commandments, on the other stood seven. The commandments concerning God were separated from the commandments concerning men—separated from each other! I said to my dear neighbor that I had seen the tablets written otherwise. When he asked why I criticize the three and the seven, I told him my story about the two tablets: the "ten and ten" and the "five and five." It went over pretty well.

TRANSLATED BY ANDREW SCHMITZ

Intention, Event, and the Other

Q.: In his introduction to your philosophy, Stephen Strasser has said that you revealed a deep dimension of phenomenology. I would think that this—I mean, *only* a deep dimension—is indeed too little, if one sees the way you bear a relation to Heidegger.

E.L.: For me, Heidegger is first and foremost the author of *Being and Time*. I mean, the miracle of phenomenology is *Being and Time*. Everything said there is a completely exacting application of the phenomenological method without needing to regress to a constituting consciousness. The pages on state-of-mind, being-toward-death, all this is a wonder. And my appeal to Husserl, to the rules of reduction—in essence, one can remain within the spirit of the problem without imitation.

Q.: I was recently at a conference in Bochum. The early (Freiburg) works of Heidegger were discussed in the presence of Hans-Georg Gadamer and Walter Bröcker. The point seemed to be that *Being and Time* was basically a *stage* for Heidegger.

E.L.: Sure. It appears as a moment in the collected works.

Q.: Nonetheless, as I am sure you know, there are still some things missing from Heidegger which are needed in order to be able to reconstruct his development correctly. But you said something to Bernhard Casper concerning the political Martin Heidegger that surprised me very much—namely, you placed *Being and Time* next to Plato's *Phaedrus*, Kant's *Critique of Pure Reason*, and Hegel's *Phenomenology of Spirit*, but could not and would not forgive the Heidegger of 1933–34.

E.L.: Yes.

Q.: But there are still arguments, and not just a few, claiming that Heidegger's commitment to the Nazis...

E.L.: To Hitler.

Q.: ... to Hitler—you're right—to Hitler could be directly derived from his thinking.

E.L.: I heard Hitler on the radio, and Hitler did always sound a bit like Heidegger to me. I mean in the way in which someone approves of something and proceeds to holler about it. I ascribed that naturally to the Alemannic atmosphere in Baden. I was with Heidegger during one semester in Freiburg as well. I must tell you something here. In 1928–29, as I read him for the first time, it sounded, resounded, *theological* as well. You know, "guilt." It looked as if it were a secularization of theology. Do you know the saying from Max Scheler, "It is a mixture of genius and Sunday school preaching"? That was the echo.

Q.: Yes.

E.L.: Christian.

Q.: That could be behind it.

E.L.: But what for? In which moment was *Being and Time* a feeling of this pre-Hitlerian atmosphere? "Destruktion"![1]

Q.: You have characterized your philosophy by the distinction between Odysseus returning home again, safe and sound, after his wanderings, and Abraham, who sets out without returning home.

E.L.: Odysseus returning—it's a catch phrase.

Q.: I found this image quite illuminating. When one reads Kafka, this idea of homecoming is quite clearly detectable: wanting to integrate oneself and not being able to integrate.

E.L.: I think in Kafka there is no returning; there is a search for a place, *un lieu* somewhere. It is a movement to the past. With Kafka, there is, in general, no place. Do you know how Psalm 119:19 goes? "I am..."

Q.: A stranger.

E.L.: "... a stranger on the earth: hide not thy commandments from me." A stranger on the earth... and then the second half of the verse:

"Give me your law." "I am a stranger on the earth." There it is, exactly, the same word that always appears in the Bible: one must attend to the cares of the "stranger."

Q.: Then both ways—Abraham and Odysseus—do not mutually exclude each other? Naturally, Ernst Bloch says *Heimat* ("home"), in a certain sense a very German word; in French there is no equivalent.

E.L.: On the contrary, *patrie, chez soi, Bei-sich-sein,* "to be with oneself."

Q.: Now, the concept of totality, or the totality of being, in which all transcendence so to speak disappears, plays a central role in your writings. Could one always link "totality" with the concept of the "same"?

E.L.: Totality also has for me a concrete, that is, a phenomenological meaning. What does self-totalizing mean? Totality is not only a philosophical intuition, an observation of things taken as a whole, as an ensemble. The word *ensemble* itself is a mathematical expression. The word *totality* has a ground, a concrete meaning, and I link it strongly to the economic relationship of reciprocal change.

Q.: Exchange?

E.L.: Right, exchange. This adding up of the sum total is the economic life, absolutely: precisely there, the face plays no role, human beings are terms, they come into an ensemble, adding themselves up. The adding up of totality is, concretely, economic life and the State; economic life is concrete in the State, of course. Then there is the search for justice, as the knowledge of terms which stand in this ensemble. I mean, one cannot only criticize this adding up, but must observe the moment it has, perhaps, originally a meaning.

Therefore, totality is constituted in this relationship. And all I have done is to find a relation that is not an adding up. We are so bound to the concept of an adding up that it often appears to us as if dualism were a fall, a decline. Isn't this true? Everything must be one, must become one.

Q.: Therefore, multiplicity.

E.L.: One multiplicity.

Q.: Dualism is actually already multiplicity.

E.L.: Sure. Dualism is a particular multiplicity. If we pair off...

Q.: But a dualism assumes as well a multiplicity.

E.L.: Dualism is always disturbed by multiplicity. If we pair off, then everything becomes the same. Well, that's not good, but at least I am bound to the other. Unfortunately we are three—at least—the third always appears.

Q.: In the novella by Gottfried Keller, *A Village Romeo and Juliet,* there is an absolute connection between two people which excludes all others. And it ends tragically.

E.L.: The exclusion is already the disturbance.

Q.: What function does philosophy have today, do you think?

E.L.: Not what it is in Husserl. In Husserl, philosophy is what is truly human, the function of what is human as such. The philosopher is the functionary of humanity.[2] Certainly today it is not that. I would say this quite plainly: what is truly human is—and don't be afraid of this word— love. And I mean it even with everything that burdens love or, I could say it better, responsibility. And responsibility is actually love, as Pascal said: "without concupiscence." It is preeminently the access to the singular. I always say: with knowledge, in a logical operation, from genus to species to individual, one cannot get to singularity! Love, or responsibility, is instead that which gives meaning to singularity. The relation is always nonreciprocal; love exists without worrying about being loved. That is my concept of dissymmetry. The other is, in this moment, the beloved, singular. And I am singular in another sense, as chosen, as being chosen for responsibility. If I ascribe or delegate this responsibility to someone else, I am no longer in ethics. And philosophy is then consciousness, a speaking *about* it, in order to arrive exactly at this delegation.

Q.: Now, it is also the case that philosophy today has become more and more the history of philosophy. Philosophy has become the contemplation of its historical development.

E.L.: Such contemplation belongs to it, undeniably. One must also know this history.

Q.: Yes, of course, as an element, but not as the main activity of philosophy.

E.L.: Certainly. This contemplation stands apart from what one sees in the West as philosophy, as philosophical knowing. In any event, the moment of knowing as well as the act of narrating cannot be ignored. One has to speak about it, and in so doing, it may appear as though all this had been integrated into speaking. But the conversation as such is addressed *to* someone. It is happening right now. Everything that I am now summarizing and pulling together is addressed to someone; and this always shatters the whole, the totality.

Q.: Löwith, in his postdoctoral thesis with Heidegger, *Das Individuum in der Rolle des Mitmenschen*, had already criticized solitary thinking, like Hegel's, which basically speaks to no one.

E.L.: In Heidegger, man is a "fellow man," he who stands alongside me.

Q.: You've criticized this already.

E.L.: He "marches alongside." And in addition to this the fellow man belongs in Heidegger to being-in-the-world, to worldly understanding. The other: there *is* such a thing as an other who is a logical concept in an ensemble. In an ensemble, every *a* is different in relation to every *b*, and every *b* is different in relation to every *a*, and so on. In my work, there is an attempt to think alterity not only logically, so to speak, but qualitatively, as though it were possible to defend oneself against being a term, to refuse to be a term. Twenty years ago, I thought that the feminine was another genus, in the full sense of this word. The feminine does not belong to the same genus as the "I." Something like this was already in my short text, *Time and the Other*. Yet what until now remains to be thought is being-other not only formally, but with definite content.

Q.: How does this now relate to what you have named the "face"? "Face" is certainly—I don't know if this is correct to say—a metaphor.

E.L.: The face is not at all what has been seen.

Q.: Right. But there is a difficulty in spite of this: we are always seeing a determinate face, a countenance.

E.L.: No. This is not the way I think about the face. One can first of all consider the face, *le visage*, as if it were something seen, although I would then say in French, it is defaced, *dévisagé*. Defacement occurs also as a way of looking, a way of knowing, for example, what color your eyes are. No, the face is not this. "Face," as I have always described it, is nakedness, helplessness, perhaps an exposure to death.

q.: Basically the attempt is to name what cannot be named.

e.l.: Yes. The meaning of poverty, of helplessness, of being exposed to the point of death is a completely simple system, and at the same time— I have written again and again—an imperative: "thou shalt not kill me" and "thou shalt not leave me alone in my dying."

q.: Now, how should I express this? Into this "vacuum," into the un-nameable, something always already enters, since we always want to name, to identify, something. And we cannot do otherwise than to think. That is the crux.

e.l.: It must be seen how thinking is constituted, what comes into it. It must be named with other words. For example, *responsibility* or *obedience*. Obedience? This is theology, you might say. And probably it stems from theology; it has a meaning there. Obedience is an imperative in the presence of the face of the other. That is—how should I put this?—the paradox: the co-existence and co-significance of the poverty and arrogance of the other. That is the word of God and I think it is not so easy to say this. But what comes to pass is something extraordinary.

I would refer this to being. Being always has to be, being is *conatus essendi*. In life being is immediately war. What did Heidegger say at the beginning of *Being and Time*? *Dasein* is distinguished by the fact that, in its very being, that being is an issue for it. He meant then, "being is an issue" which is "an issue of the understanding of being." But in *Being and Time*, it is almost formulated in a Darwinian manner: "Being is an issue for *itself*." Now let us approach something truly mad: I must care for *your* being. I cannot allow myself to abandon you to your death. This madness is what is human.

I was very pleased to find quoted in your letter to me the phrase (from "The Trace of the Other") "an eschatology without hope for oneself." That is perhaps a translation of our experience of the twentieth century in general. And in this relationship to the face of the other there are precisely no assurances. With Buber, reciprocity comes immediately. Buber found in the I-Thou relationship that the I stands in relation to the Thou exactly as the Thou stands in relation to the I. I have, you know, often spoken of this. For the encounter with the face I still reserve another word: *miséricorde*, mercy, when one assumes responsibility for the suffering of the other. This appears, naturally, as the phenomenon of love. When the other suffers, I have sympathy [*sympathie*], the origin of love.

Q.: Do you mean this in the sense of suffering-with [*Mitleid*]?

E.L.: No. Suffering-with as a phenomenon supposes a self. In a sense I would say that *mercy* is a word of God, something which signifies a radical interruption in the undisturbed being of a being. And if I talk then of "eschatology without hope for oneself," I am completely uncertain whether this responsibility is a guarantee, a guarantee that a history will continue flowing, passing on.

Q.: Taken fundamentally, then, you are destroying the alternatives of pessimism and optimism. Theodicy for instance is actually an optimistic conception.

E.L.: Yes. I am providing a theology without a theodicy. Kant had also thought along these lines. It's not to be preached: a religion without preaching. One can ask oneself to assume responsibility for oneself—this is very hard—but this request cannot be made of the other. To preach to the other is not allowed.

Q.: You said once that philosophy is not able to console.

E.L.: No consolation, that is right. Nietzsche said Christianity is consolation. It has a negative significance in his work.

Q.: Hegel is stuck as well in this theodicy, that is, in the problem of theodicy.

E.L.: Yes, certainly, a huge theodicy: everything wicked forms a part of meaning.

Q.: There is, of course, a place in the *Aesthetics* where Hegel speaks of a worthless and unproductive negativity, of a "merely negative." Auschwitz would be for us today an example. Auschwitz is badly suited for the "motor" of history. Hegel indeed speaks in the *Philosophy of History* of the "disgusting and revolting" spectacle of the medieval period, that only philosophy could "conceive and justify."

E.L.: Yes, I saw in the *Aesthetics* that things occur which stand outside of history and therefore have no meaning.

Q.: You say: *no* meaning. Could not one also say: *free* from meaning?

E.L.: That would be "suprahuman." What is suprahuman would then appear. In your letter, you said that if one spoke of all human beings, totality would again receive meaning. Based on what I said about "adding-up," I think this cannot really be allowed. We cannot speak of every human being, especially not of all human beings as every human being. "Every human being" is not "all human beings." I mean, the "all-inclusive" is not at the beginning. Perhaps the all-inclusive is at the end, as an open unity or totality. But, have you read Rosenzweig?

Q.: Do you mean *The Star of Redemption*?

E.L.: It is not my Bible, but I took over the critique of totality, precisely Hegel's totality. And Paul Natorp had spoken of the impersonal pronoun *it*?

Q.: Yes, of the *es gibt*.

E.L.: In Buber's sense?

Q.: There is another interesting context: In Heidegger, the *es gibt* surfaces in connection to the *Kehre*. There, being is a giving [*ein gebendes*], a sending.

E.L.: An *Ereignis* ["event"].

Q.: He expresses it paradoxically: it is a sending and a taking away. But this is very difficult, because being is not a subject; therefore a being which sends to and gives *itself*.

E.L.: That is similar to the Heideggerian *Ereignis*. It is basically the beginning of the *es gibt*.

Q.: The *es gibt* contains in German "to give," but the French *il y a*...

E.L.: ... is a horrible, much more impersonal expression. I always say: "*Il* y a comme *il* pleut." Heidegger says "it worlds [*es weltet*]."

Q.: Now, you speak of the same, *le même*, and of the other, *l'autre*.

E.L.: *Le même*: "I" in its limited sense, "I" as completely other than the other. Not because I feel certain inexpressible things, not because I have, as one says in English, a *secret*, a *mysterium*, an immanence which is my world. Certainly not in this sense. Rather, "I" in the sense that "I" am straightaway delivered over and obligated to the other. Only when I speak of justice, an ethics of multiplicity, do I come to terminology, to the logos of the term.

Q.: But what is so remarkable is that in my connection to the other, I always already have a relation to him. I even understand him. But also, exactly as you say, I am absolutely separated from him through that which you name his "secret."

E.L.: *Le même et l'autre* in this sense is, for example, difference. Yes. But I just barely allow myself to designate this as a "relation." I always put the word—when I remember to—in quotation marks, because "relation" rests on the ground of the ensemble. In the totality, there are "relations." I have an expression: non-indifference. In French one can say, I am non-indifferent to someone. The double negation in "non-indifference" signifies difference; this expression is extremely important to me. This is something completely other than a "relation," which always presupposes a together, a universal genus.

Q.: But isn't relation both unity and difference?

E.L.: "Relation" is always so. And then there is something utterly other that is non-indifferent to me. I thought about this when I spoke of the feminine in *Time and the Other*, where the erotic is the relation to the completely other. The German translation of this text contains an excellent afterword by Ludwig Wenzler, who wrote with such a spiritual sympathy that he speaks about this better than I myself do. If the translation is reissued, I would like to have the afterword changed to a foreword.

Q.: There is a new interest in metaphysics. But perhaps it is only a fashion, like structuralism has been?

E.L.: I think that the truly new moment in the whole of modern philosophy is the recognition that the human is not the knowledge of God, but rather the place where God *works*, where "God lives." Hence, an immanent transcendence. In Heidegger as well: ontology, not God, is at the core of human being. The human being *is* the being of beings, or belongs, in any event, to the being of beings—not as a place of viewing, but as a place of action. In the sense that creation cannot come all at once into the head of God, there is the "life of God" [*Leben Gottes*]. This is in Meister Eckhart as well. It really isn't all that new.

Q.: With your formula "ethics as first philosophy," do you want to articulate a higher value of ethics, perhaps something of an ontology? Isn't there an "ordering" going on in here?

E.L.: I don't see an ordering, but that does not mean that one can get rid of the Greeks. How is that for a confession? I always say—but under my breath—that the Bible and the Greeks present the only serious issues in human life; everything else is dancing. I think these texts are open to the whole world. There is no racism intended.

Q.: "Everything else is dancing"—one could naturally think of Nietzsche.

E.L.: Yes, but you know, television shows the horrible things occurring in South Africa. And there, when they bury people, they dance. Have you seen this? That is really some way to express mourning.

Q.: It, too, is an expression.

E.L.: Yes, of course, so far I am still a philosopher. But it supplies us the expression of a dancing civilization; they weep differently.

Q.: And now to come finally to Nietzsche: you have just received the Nietzsche prize?

E.L.: Yes. A Nietzsche prize—not a Nobel prize. I just came from Sicily. The prize was shared between me, Severino, and another Italian philosopher. I gratefully received it. I have written nothing on Nietzsche, and in my response—I wanted to express appreciation for the prize—I stressed that the ethics of Nietzsche is not my ethics. But then I went on to say that, at the end of the nineteenth century, when all values were classified and put in their place, it was he who foresaw what the twentieth century would make of those values. And then I cited the passages where he recognizes Judaism. He speaks of love in its "humility and wretchedness," which comes "from the small Jewish community."[3] I remarked that just because he speaks of the poor does not mean that we are only concerned with pre-Christian Judaism. Rather, we are concerned with Judaism as I experienced it in Lithuania.

Q.: It is quite remarkable that, as a Jew, you are pointing this out, because Nietzsche is—unbelievably—for many still counted among the anti-Semites.

E.L.: He had Hitler as a reader.

Q.: Yes, from the Förster-Nietzsche version, this terrible edition. But there are places—you know this already—where he characterizes the anti-Semites precisely as "revolting," as "barefaced and stupid bands."

E.L.: There is also a place where he says that one is relieved that when one sees a Jew, one is among other Germans. Remarks like these exist as well. But I must say to you: I take strength from an impression by Rosenzweig. For Rosenzweig at the end of the First World War, Nietzsche is an entirely wonderful example, in his own way, of how to speak to madness as a way to transcendence.

Q.: In this way we could come back again to the theme of "totality." When you earlier characterized thinking as an adding-up... that's how Jews were handled during the Third Reich, as numbers.

E.L.: The final expression of an "adding-up." Adding up is a concrete figure in pure economic life, in purely economic conditions.

Q.: Exchange of wares.

E.L.: To me, all of phenomenology, the final meaning of phenomenology, appears as the search for the concrete figure of a concept, of a determination, of a thought. "Figure" in the scholastic sense—one must repeatedly specify the figure of one's thinking. Figure is the concrete, something concrete in which one can think a thing. So, as I say: *disinterestedness*. It is a good word because it contains the root *esse*, meaning "being." *Interestedness* means to be bound to being, and *disinterestedness* the self's withdrawal from being. I always say: *dis-inter-estedness*.

Q.: A question for clarification: *inter-esse* means as well "between being," that is, "relation."

E.L.: Yes.

Q.: Is not the *dis-inter-estedness* "relationlessness" as well?

E.L. Yet *inter-esse* also means to be inside being [*drinnen im Sein sein*]. "To be inside being": as *being* to be in being. But that's not what I wish to say. The word *désintéressement* is very common in French. Yet what does it mean to think disinterestedness? It means to find the figure, where something like this is a moment, where, for example, the figure of disinterestedness means "to be responsible for the other." We are dealing with abstract things and concepts, and phenomenology—"to the things themselves"—therefore requires some kind of staging, a mise-en-scène. As I like to say, phenomenology is the search for a mise-en-scène. In this sense, *Being and Time* is a "Himalaya," a truly lofty landscape of the concrete.

Q.: Then you would have opened phenomenology, if one wants to put it this way, to a concrete dimension, and not so much a "deep dimension."

E.L.: Yes. But do you believe that height and depth completely diverge? The Third Investigation of the *Logical Investigations*, on the concept of founding, is where the concept of the concrete is worked through. Indeed the entire defined area, for instance, color without extension, is abstract. A piece is concrete, but a color is abstract, etc. This is very important. And what is sought in consciousness is precisely this staging. It is discovered in intention. One must not, therefore, take the word "intention" only abstractly as an act of consciousness. "Intention" must be pursued. Intention means, in French, "disposition"; it reveals what one really wants. Phenomenology is the return to intentions in order to arrive at what one in fact understands. I am always quoting: to arrive at "what one really wants to get at [*worauf es eigentlich hinauswill*]."[4]

Q.: Heidegger, by the way, seems to have preferred Husserl's *Logical Investigations* to the *Ideas*.

E.L.: Yes. Especially—I don't know why—the Sixth Investigation. Because of the way the syntheses, the syntaxes, the forms of the sentences all build together toward a disclosure. The First Investigation is exceptional. In this sense, then, to come back to the beginning of our discussion, I feel very close to Husserl. Insofar as one remarks the ulterior motives of the noeses and doesn't see intention always as the noetic-noematic structure.

Q.: If I might return to another theme: *Totality and Infinity* formulates the thought of a plurality which will not be vaulted over by any Totality. But could it actually not be that the thought of totality is required precisely for the safeguarding of plurality? Something like in Kant. With him, the whole is something double: in the first place as "Compositum"

(Understanding, Categories), which is a reconstruction out of the parts, and in the second place as "Totum" (sensibility, space, time), which is the presupposition of the parts. The many and the one; the one and the many.

E.L.: The chapter on the schematism is exceedingly important with Kant. And do you know why? Because the schematism chapter is the one in which synthesis can receive its mise-en-scène, in what is sensible, in *time*. The concept of "staging" fits this chapter. You may recall why Kant, after the deduction of the categories, must all at once return to the sensible. Only in the schema of time does such a thing become concrete.

Q.: And your thinking would now lie in the future, if I am allowed to name it here, in something to come?

E.L.: Well, if one can think "what is to come," it is already the past.

Q.: Sure, but your term regarding this is "fecundity."

E.L.: That is for me what remains authentically of *alterité* as woman, the *alteritas*: the son. In this sense, something remains of the alterity of the feminine genus. For Hegel, I believe, there is something like this...

Q.: ... in the *Jena Realphilosophie*: "the relationship of love, which has become itself the object."

E.L.: No. That is a completely particular relationship to offspring. What I have in mind is a possibility beyond all possibilities, and straightaway still *my* possibility, a limit-concept, the beyond of "mine-ness." This is what I call a relationship "to the son." I am often asked: why not the daughter? Now... I *have* an adult daughter. But I know I have seen this in Hegel: identity which is non-identity, where the Same and the Other are *together*.

Q.: Nevertheless, is it not true that Hegel is simply the thinker of identity?

E.L.: Yet, thinking together identity and non-identity: that together is identity, right?

Q.: That's right.

E.L.: What I want to say is that identity is in all thinking—I do not say in *my* thinking, because using a possessive here for thinking would be a dangerous vulgarity. I feel that the neighbor is not a fall from coincidence, not a *modus deficiens* of coincidence, regardless of what Plotinus thought. Throughout all of our literature, there has been the theme of two beings who may well coincide, yet do not get there—as if coincidence were the highest, the greatest value. Very important. Can one say, "sociablity"? Can one say, "toward society"? I would like to find a more rigorous concept than "society." In French, there is the word *socialité*.

Q.: And how does it pertain to the difference—much discussed around the turn of the century—between "society" and "community?"

E.L.: "Community" is just as well the search for unity, for the coincidence of what is common among us. Seeking the place and position where one founds society on knowledge is Greek. Knowledge, common knowledge, is "community."

Q.: Since you are speaking about the Greeks: you said that I must fear the death of the other more than my own—doesn't this stand in relation to Socrates, when he says that "doing what is unjust is more to be guarded against than suffering it"?

E.L.: But "guarding against" in this way recalls the terror of the tyrant in revenge. Doesn't this indicate the great value of the *ideas*? The most important thing here is the truth of the matter.

Q.: More often you quote Dostoevsky.

E.L.: Oh yes.

Q.: Is it from there, perhaps, that the saying "weight of the world" stems? In Dostoevsky, it means this: "Every one of us is guilty in relation to all . . ."

E.L.: "for all and for everything, and I more so than all the others." Yes.

Q.: And you speak of bearing the weight of the world as being responsible to everyone. By the way, I have found the formulation "the weight of the world" word for word in *Being and Nothingness*, even though Sartre understands this to mean something certainly different than you.

E.L.: I am chosen. To me this means, "I am the chosen one": as "myself" and not as a Jew. As a "self"! The contrary of this is probably the meaning of chosenness in the theological sense.

Q.: My responsibility to the other is a choice—could I say: an honor?

E.L.: An honor, yes.

Q.: Yet I am not above the other because of this?

E.L.: Naturally not. But in any case, with the sense that I would not be completely superfluous, would not be completely wiped out . . .

Q.: A few additional questions: you studied with Husserl for two semesters?

E.L.: Yes, I lived in Freiburg for two semesters. Husserl had already been made an emeritus professor. Heidegger came for the second semester.

Q.: Yes, from Marburg.

E.L.: With an entire suite of pupils. I heard someone say, "I've studied with Heidegger for twenty semesters"—probably someone accompanying him from Marburg.

Q.: According to a passage from Stephen Strasser, you went through Heidegger, beyond Heidegger, by means of Heidegger; that is, you are in relation to him, however. . .

E.L.: . . . always with pain and suffering. But I cannot deny it. Mont Blanc is Mont Blanc. I often amuse myself by saying which five philosophers are indispensible or constitute all of philosophy. Well, first comes Plato, and then Kant.

Q.: You leave Aristotle out?!

E.L.: Now, I believe it's all Plato: Being, the given, ideas—this goes for Descartes as well. So, then comes Kant, where everything is turned upside down. Next. . . Hegel, where history—of the categories—becomes content. Then come two personal favorites: first Bergson. In the years between 1920 and 1930, it was a fantastic experience.

Q.: He was much more of an event here in France than in Germany.

E.L.: Bergson anticipated at any moment his "comeback" here in Paris. He was neither damned, nor saved. *Purgatoire*, one says in French. If one has a lot of sins, but not enough to be damned, then one must wait it out in *purgatoire*. The Heideggerian concept of temporality, that is, a temporality which is free of those concepts of the exact sciences, would be impossible without Bergson.

And lastly—Heidegger. I must confess, I haven't said Husserl—Heidegger.

Q.: If I may join in with a question here: you say that philosophy as ontology—an ontology from which you do not exclude Heidegger—is a philosophy of power.

E.L.: Yes, insofar as knowing is always mastery. It isn't contemplative. In any event, Heidegger said: technology, the power of technology (is) taking-in-hand.

Q.: Horkheimer had named this "instrumental reason."

E.L.: Not in the sense of technology, though. I don't think the concept is all that original. Bergson had already glimpsed it.

Q.: But—perhaps to ask heretically—when did philosophy ever have power?

E.L.: Plato encountered that himself, didn't he?

Q.: ... as philosophy?

E.L.: Philosophy? No. But from philosophy emerged all of modern science. What is practical was always very important to every philosophy. And philosophy stood by and condoned it.

Q.: Not to act can still be an action.

E.L.: It is extremely important to me that in knowing not only the eyes are there but the hands are always already there as well, in the utility of a being and in readiness-to-hand in its mode of being. The brilliant thing in Heidegger is naturally that he immediately saw in this a *modus essendi*. During the years we were reading Heidegger for the first time, we were impressed not by being in general, but by the possibility of differentiating between the *ways of being*—not the essences. We were impressed in that it could give us presence-at-hand and readiness-to-hand, life and *Dasein*. It is always a matter of the naming of a verb and not the naming of a thing.

Q.: Yes, of a verb: "to be."

E.L.: The 1929 encounter between Heidegger and Cassirer in Davos is often retold. I was invited by Heidegger. And I met up with the "Normaliens" at Davos—the students of the Ecole Normale Supérieure—who had come with Léon Brunschvicg. In France to be a "Normalien" is more important than being a baron. Cavaillès—mathematician, philosopher, and later a martyr of the Resistance—was there, and Maurice de Gandillac. And we read *Being and Time* for the first time in a field which lay under snow. What impressed us at that time were the ways-of-being, the ways not of essences but of being. In his memoirs de Gandillac spoke of this field. A few years ago, he flew there and visited it.

Anyway you see how Heidegger played a role in my life; that cannot be forgotten. I have an expression for this—and I say this under my breath as well: I came for Husserl and found Heidegger.

Q.: Really, *that* you could say outright!

E.L.: No, no. It was Husserl who founded the entire procedure—the high art—of phenomenology. Heidegger just took it up and made it sparkle.

Q.: Heidegger made off with quite a few things.

E.L.: They were so close at the time, and Husserl had no doubts that Heidegger was really his pupil, as I'm sure you know, at least during the first months. It was a huge surprise to him—I read a letter, which Husserl wrote to another pupil. He told of how he discovered that Heidegger was going his own way.

Q.: Also related to this—to my knowledge—was his book on Aristotle. Heidegger wanted to write a book on Aristotle and publish it in Husserl's *Jahrbuch*. But nothing came of it.[5]

E.L.: Husserl wasn't really all that conversant with the history of philosophy. He had read the Überweg...[6]

Q.: It was wholly different with Heidegger.

E.L.: Yes . . .

Q.: The disputation at Davos has become quite famous from the protocol by Ritter and Bollnow.

E.L.: Right. Heidegger spoke on Kant and Cassirer on "being-in-the-world": Cassirer consistently made note of the difference between a "point of departure" and a "hereafter." The Heideggerian position is that the thing is in the point of departure. In this moment, though, the world is another matter. *Terminus a quo, terminus ad quem*—those were the expressions . . .

Q.: If you are saying that Heideigger played a decisive role in your life, then do you mean that in the end the German language did as well?

E.L.: So much philosophy has been placed in this language, from Kant to Husserl, Heidegger and Jaspers, that the language is full of a kind of scent. And all that is expressed as honest thinking carries a wonderful overtone and echo.

TRANSLATED BY ANDREW SCHMITZ

Reality Has Weight

Q.: You have lived in three cultural landscapes—the Russian, the Jewish, and the German.

E.L.: In my childhood, I was immersed in Russian culture, but also in the proximity of biblical texts. I read the Bible in Hebrew very early, I learned to read in this language. I also kept company with Dostoevsky. For a long time I lived in Kharkov, in the Ukraine. I was a child of twelve at the time of the Russian Revolution, and I saw this enormous, dramatic event through quite everyday appearances.

Q.: At seventeen you came to Strasbourg to study philosophy. . . . In 1928, in order to study with Husserl, you left for Germany. There you also met Heidegger, long before he took his unfortunate political positions in favor of the Nazi regime. This event was, no doubt, one of the defining moments of your life.

E.L.: Heidegger literally fascinated me. One had to reserve a place in the morning in order to get a chance to listen to him in the afternoon. This was in the period of *Being and Time*. At that point, one could in no way imagine that Heidegger would take such tragic political positions. Thanks to him, I attended his encounter with Cassirer, author of *The Philosophy of the Enlightenment*. This 1929 encounter was a summit of thinking. I remember that Heidegger was dressed in mountain clothing; Cassirer was more classical, but he made an extraordinary impression; I remember the nobility of his gray hair. In their dialogue, Cassirer often alluded to the Heideggerian conception of being-in-the-world, and

Heidegger spoke a lot of Kant. I was struck by Cassirer's boldness, but just as much by Heidegger's tranquil assurance.

Q.: Could you describe the role played by these encounters in your philosophical training?

E.L.: My philosophy rests upon a pre-philosophical experience, upon a ground that does not pertain solely to philosophy. I believe that what we call the "horizon of meaning" does not depend simply upon our experience of the world.

Q.: Nevertheless you line up with the phenomenological movement in France, a school of thought which returns to the things themselves.

E.L.: To be sure, but to approach the things themselves does not consist in approaching the world such as it is at the moment that I construct, say, a ship or a house. Every experience opens up contexts which are not given by the experience of perception. Every experience opens the world of meaningful things, of other men, to one's relation with the other. The other is always there, no matter what one's perception of him might be. What is meaningful depends upon the lights of the experience of the other, and thinking always contains more than it can effectively obtain. It is here that I part company with a conception of experience that would reduce thinking to a thinking of measurements, to a thinking of equivalences. Idealism has always wanted to interpret experience. In a sense it wanted to think that the real was absolutely equal to consciousness, that there was no overflowing, no deficit, no surplus. However, Descartes shows clearly that the form of God is greater than its psychological meaning. From the outset, we think more than we can think. For me this is exemplary. The things that we have within our horizon always overflow their content.

Q.: Husserl's work is, in some respects, the odyssey of a philosopher who attempts to reconstruct, through reduction, the pure "I." Then, in his later texts, he puts objectivity in question, referring to the "life world."

E.L.: The life world is not a world of measurements. It is a concrete world at the heart of which significations take root. For me, the most important thing is that there is less in the objective idea than in the idea when it is relativized with respect to man. Idealism always imagined that reality was only representation; phenomenology teaches us that reality constitutes more than what captures our gaze. Reality has weight.

Q.: Merleau-Ponty spoke of the flesh of the world.

E.L.: That is an excellent formula. Reality has weight when one discovers its contexts. This is the phenomenological message. The deduction pertains not only to the analysis of concepts; things are not content to appear; they *are*, rather, within the circumstances that give them the weight of their horizons. And this weight is their richness. . . .

Q.: Let us turn now to the Book, to what is for you much more than a book; I am thinking of the Bible.

E.L.: I see a religious element in it, a Passion with a capital *P*. Upon my return from captivity in a camp for French prisoners in Germany, I met a giant of traditional Jewish culture, Monsieur Shoshani. He did not experience the relation to the text as a simple relation of piety or edification, but rather as a horizon of intellectual rigor. I owe him everything I publish on the Talmud today. I place this man, who had the appearance of a beggar, next to Husserl and Heidegger. He was—together with Jean Wahl and my much missed friend, Doctor Nerson—one of my privileged interlocutors.

Q.: You, a phenomenologist, also live in the Judaic world.

E.L.: There I rediscover the fact that every philosophical experience rests upon a pre-philosophical one. In Jewish thought, I encountered the fact that ethics is not a simple region of being. The encounter with the other offers us the first meaning, and in the extension of this encounter, we discover all the others. Ethics is a decisive experience.

Q.: Does it prescribe what ought to be?

E.L.: The law results from the fact that I encounter the other. This fact implies, from the outset, a responsibility toward him. This difference is a nonindifference.

Q.: In the West, philosophy is Greek and Jewish. You live in the midst of these two blocs.

E.L.: The Jewish religious texts speak of the proximity of the neighbor. The encounter with the other engages me and that is something from which I cannot flee. As for the Greeks, they taught me the language of philosophy.

Q.: And how would I know that I must not flee?

E.L.: As for the concrete morals that I ought to derive from an ethics, I believe that if one looks closely at the prophetic texts, one sees that they always describe the other as weaker than you are. I am always obligated to him. In *The Brothers Karamazov*, Dostoevsky says that we are all responsible for everything, before everyone, and I more than all the others. I am always responsible, each I is noninterchangeable. Nobody else can do what I do in my place. The knot of singularity is responsibility.

Q.: What then does it mean to translate the text of the Talmud into Greek?

E.L.: The art of communicating, what in philosophy is called theorizing, is Greek. These philosophers teach us how to speak. But communication is not only a form, and when we think, we speak Greek even if we do not know this language. There is Greek in French. Therefore, in order to speak, we communicate in Greek.

Q.: How about the Talmud?

E.L.: This text appears in an exceptionally tangled form. It is constituted by oral traditions that were subsequently transcribed for reasons of convenience. This text requires us to search perpetually for the signification of what was said. However, you know, I am not a specialist. I restrict myself to commenting on the least arduous, the most narrative parts, the legendary segments. This text is very vast insofar as it is never separated from its examples. It is continually enriched with new aspects.

Q.: For you, the Talmud is also a spiritual exercise, and you have a relation with this text that differs from that which you have with Plato.

E.L.: The Talmud is horribly difficult, as much so as is Plato. You know, there is no punctuation in the Talmud, and one goes unceasingly from one subject to another without transitions. But what interests me is to place the problems of the Talmud within the perspective of philosophy! And yet I have no rule for interpretation.

Q.: Let us take an example borrowed from your *Nine Talmudic Readings*, the one concerning Adam's rib in the Bible, found in your chapter entitled "And God Created Woman." Starting from this text, you attempt to describe the relation of man to woman as one of non-subordination.

E.L.: In Hebrew, "rib" and "side" are one and the same word: *côté*. Against the tradition that reads this story from a surgical perspective, I propose a different version. I propose to read "rib" as "side." If one sees that, one sees that there is no longer a relation of part to whole, but a bifurcation, a division into two. One immediately sees new perspectives appear, of equality, of a same origin. I am not at all saying that the tradition of masculine domination does not exist, but that it is not the only one. Philosophically, the subject is not only a unity. Human subjectivity is dual.

Q.: Could one think of the bisexuality Freud described?

E.L.: It is nonetheless strange that we multiply ourselves this way. Duality is essential and there is perhaps multiplicity in quite a few things.

Q.: In the *Symposium*, Plato recounts the myth of the androgyne, of this double being, alternately man-man, woman-woman, man-woman, this being cut into two by the Titans.

E.L.: One can also wonder whether they were joined nose to nose... There are fascinating points of convergence where many interrogations from the greatest civilizations meet.

Q.: In "Judaism and Revolution," a text from after 1968, you assert that revolution is liberation, a pulling free from economic determinations. The personal would not be negotiable; it would not give rise to bartering.

E.L.: Modernity defines itself through the abundant use of the word *revolution*. There was even a National Socialist revolution! However, the revolution is first of all a necessity, an urgency, something that cannot wait. This idea is born with the appearance of human beings outside their condition, of men who require immediate solutions. To talk about a revolution that institutes a regime of oppression is a contradiction in terms.

Q.: You propose that Jewish texts call for justice.

E.L.: To belong to Judaism is to belong to a tradition, a very ancient one. But, you know, the prophets were not, in the first place, promising eternal life. They were not doing eschatology; they were not analyzing only the final ends, they were stating the social and the moral.

Q.: I, who am not Jewish, admit that I have difficulty understanding the notion of a chosen people.

E.L.: Chosenness does not privilege; it has only a moral meaning. The moral man is the one in a group who does the thing that is to be done. In so doing, he is chosen. The prophet who demands justice is chosen not by others; he is chosen because he was the first to hear the call.

It was a mistake to have experienced chosenness as a privilege. To be sure, during persecution, it could often be an element of consolation, and this awareness of being chosen could become egotistical. Yet I insist that one should not see this notion as a prerogative. The prophet Amos says, "It is you alone that I have chosen of all the families of the earth, that is why I will call you to account for all your sins" (Amos 3:2).

Q.: What do you think of Kant's moral subject who constitutes himself in his autonomy?

E.L.: I like the second formulation of the categorical imperative, the one that tells [me] to respect man in myself when I respect the other. In this expression, we are not in pure universality, but already in the presence of the other. You know, the rights of man are nothing new; we already find their traces in Cicero. Much more important to me is that the rights of the other come before my own. That is much more important. We must understand that the rights of the other do not only begin with the defense of my own rights.

Q.: The Talmud, that art of commentary, raises, in a certain sense, the question of the status of commentary in general.

E.L.: Commentary is the life of the text. If a text is alive today, it is because we comment on it. The meanings are not exhausted in interpretation. This is true of the Talmud, but also for Plato or Goethe. When we read Goethe, we also read the commentaries on *Faust*, wherein the innumerable lives of the text are found. Proust realizes this in regard to his past, and we ourselves realize this in regard to Proust. Further, think of Kafka. He describes a culpability without crime, a world in which man never gets to to know the accusations charged against him. We see there the genesis of the problem of meaning. It is not only the question "Is my life righteous?" but rather, "Is it righteous to be?" This is very important, for we always measure out the good on the basis of the being that is.

Q.: Your commentaries are original insofar as they do not claim to gain access to a final, true, or terroristic interpretation.

E.L.: It is because there are a multiplicity of human beings that the text can have all these meanings. If one of them were missing, a meaning would be lost.

Q.: There is also a multiplicity of cultures, Jews, Greeks, but also the Bororo of the Mongols, the Indians...

E.L.: To be sure, but it is Europe which, alongside its numerous atrocities, invented the idea of "de-Europeanization." This represents a victory of European generosity. For me, of course, the Bible is the model of excellence; but I say this knowing nothing of Buddhism.

Q.: A last question that I hardly dare to ask after Auschwitz. What does it mean to be Jewish? You say that, during the War, certain members of the Resistance were more Jewish than the Jews. How could one explain to a contemporary Chinese person what it means to be Jewish?

E.L.: I understand your apprehension and your prudence. After the persecution, this question is difficult, virtually unposable. But you ask it nonetheless, and I shall only say that to be Jewish is not a particularity; it is a modality. Everyone is a little bit Jewish, and if there are men on Mars, one will find Jews among them. Moreover, Jews are people who doubt themselves, who in a certain sense, belong to a religion of unbelievers. God says to Joshua, "I will not abandon you" [and, in the subsequent phrase]: "nor will I let you escape" (Josh. 1:9).

TRANSLATED BY ALIN CRISTIAN AND BETTINA BERGO

Philosophy, Justice, and Love

Q.: "The face of the other is perhaps the very beginning of philosophy." Do you mean to say that philosophy does not begin with and in the experience of finitude, but rather in that of the infinite as the call of justice? Does philosophy begin before itself, in an experience prior to philosophical discourse?

E.L.: My main point in saying that was that the order of meaning, which seems to me primary, is precisely what comes to us from the inter-human relation, so that the face, with all its meaningfulness, as brought out by analysis, is the beginning of intelligibility. Of course, the whole perspective of ethics immediately emerges here; but we cannot say that it is already philosophy. Philosophy is a theoretical discourse; I have thought that the theoretical presupposes more. It is inasmuch as I have not only to respond to the face of the other but, alongside him, to approach the third party, that the necessity for the theoretical attitude arises. The encounter with the other is straightaway my responsibility for him. That is the responsibility for my neighbor, which is no doubt the severe name for what we call love of one's neighbor: love without eros, charity, love in which the ethical aspect dominates the passionate aspect, love without concupiscence. I don't very much like the word *love*, which is worn out and debased. Let us speak instead of the taking upon oneself of the fate of the other. That is the "vision" of the face, and it applies to the first one to come along. If he were my only interlocutor, I would have nothing but obligations! But I don't live in a world in which there is but one single "first comer"; there is always a third party in the world: he or she is also my other, my neighbor. Hence, it is important to me to know which of the two takes precedence. Is the one not the persecutor of the other? Must not human beings, who are incomparable, be compared? Thus justice, here, takes precedence over the taking upon oneself of the fate of the other. I must judge, where before I was to assume responsibilities. Here is the birth of the theoretical; here is the birth of the concern for justice, which is the basis of the theoretical. But it is always starting from the face, from the responsibility for the other, that justice appears, calling in turn for judgment and comparison, a comparison of what is in principle incomparable, for every being is unique. Every other is unique. In the necessity of being concerned with justice the idea of equity appears, the basis of objectivity. At a certain moment, there is a necessity for a "weighing," a comparison, a thinking, and in this sense philosophy would be the appearance of wisdom from the depths of that initial charity; it would be—and I am not playing word games—the wisdom of that charity, the wisdom of love.

Q.: Would the experience of the death of the other and, in a sense, the experience of death itself be alien to the ethical welcome of one's neighbor?

E.L.: Now you are posing the problem, "What is there in the face?" In my analysis, the face is definitely not a plastic form like a portrait. The relation to the face is a relation to the absolutely weak, to what is absolutely exposed, naked, and destitute. It is a relation with destitution and consequently with what is alone and can undergo the supreme isolation we call death. There is, consequently, in the face of the other always the death of the other and thus, in some way, an incitement to murder, the temptation to go to the extreme, to completely neglect the other. At the same time (and this is the paradoxical thing) the face is also the "thou shalt not kill." This explanation can be taken much further. "Thou shalt not kill" is also the fact that I cannot let the other die alone. There is, as it were, an appeal to me. You see—and this seems important to me—the relation with the other is not symmetrical; it is not at all as in Martin Buber. When I say "thou" to an I, to a me, according to Buber I would always have that me before me as the one who says "thou" to me. Consequently, there would be a reciprocal relationship. According to my analysis, on the other hand, in the relation to the face, it is asymmetry that is affirmed: at the outset I hardly care what the other is with respect to me, that is his own business; for me, he is above all the one for whom I am responsible.

Q.: Does the executioner have a face?

E.L.: You are posing the whole problem of evil. When I speak of justice, I introduce the idea of the struggle with evil; I separate myself from the idea of non-resistance to evil. If self-defense is problematic, the executioner is the one who threatens the belligerent neighbor and calls down violence: in this sense, he no longer has a face. But my central idea is what I called an "asymmetry of intersubjectivity": the exceptional situation of the I. I always recall Dostoevsky on this subject; one of his characters says: we are all guilty for everything and everyone, and I more than all the others. But to this idea—without contradicting it—I immediately add the concern for the third and, hence, justice. The whole problematic of the executioner opens here, starting from justice and defense of the other man, my neighbor, and not at all starting from a threat against me. If there were no order of justice, there would be no limit to my responsibility. There is a certain measure of violence necessary starting from justice, but if one speaks of justice, it is necessary to admit judges: it is necessary to admit institutions and the State, to live in a world of citizens and not only in the order of the face-to-face. But on the other hand, it is starting from the relation to the face, from me before the face of the other, that we can speak of the legitimacy or illegitimacy of the State. A State in which the interpersonal relation is impossible, in which it is directed in advance by the determinism proper to the State, is a totalitarian State. So there is a limit to the State. Whereas, in Hobbes's vision—in which the State emerges not from the limitation of charity but from the limitation of violence—one cannot set a limit on the State.

Q.: So is the State always the acceptance of some level of violence?

E.L.: There is an element of violence in the State, but the violence can involve justice. That does not mean violence must not be avoided as much as possible; everything that replaces violence in the friction between states, everything that can be left to negotiation, to speech, is absolutely essential; but one cannot say that there is no legitimate violence.

Q.: Would a form of speech such as prophetic speech be contrary to the State?

E.L.: It is an extremely bold, audacious speech, since the prophet always speaks before the king; the prophet is not in hiding, he is not preparing a revelation from underground. In the Bible—it's astonishing—the king accepts this direct opposition. Not your ordinary king! Isaiah and Jeremiah submit to violence. Let us not forget the perennial false prophets who flatter kings. Only the true prophet addresses the king and the people without compromise and recalls them to the ethical. In the Old Testament, there is certainly no denunciation of the State as such. There is a protest against the pure and simple assimilation of the State into the politics of the world. What shocks Samuel when the people come to demand that he give them a king for Israel is their wanting to have a king like *all the nations!* In Deuteronomy, there is a doctrine of royal power; the State is supposed to be in conformity with the law. The idea of an ethical State is biblical.

Q.: Is it seen as the lesser of two evils?

E.L.: No, it is the wisdom of the nations. The other concerns you even when a third does him harm, and consequently you are there before the necessity of justice and of a certain violence. The third party isn't there by accident. In a certain sense, all the others are present in the face of the other. If there were two of us in the world, there wouldn't be any problem: the other passes before I do. And to a certain extent—God keep me from being reduced to this as a daily rule—I am responsible for the other even when he bothers me, even when he persecutes me. Since we're talking a lot about prophets today, there is in the Lamentations of Jeremiah a text, not very long, which says: "Let him turn his cheek to the smiter" (Lam. 3:30). But I am responsible for the persecution of my neighbors. If I belong to a people, that people and my kin are all my neighbors. They have a right to defense, just as do those who are not my kin.[1]

Q.: You spoke of the asymmetry that differs from Buber's relationship of reciprocity.

E.L.: As citizens we are reciprocal, but it is a more complex structure than the face-to-face.

Q.: Yes, but in the initial, interhuman domain, wouldn't there be the risk that the dimension of gentleness might be absent in a relation in which there would not be reciprocity? Are justice and gentleness alien to one another?

E.L.: They are very close. I have tried to make this deduction: justice itself is born of charity. They can seem alien when they are presented as successive stages; in reality, they are inseparable and simultaneous, unless one is on a desert island, without humanity, without a third.

Q.: Might one not think that the experience of justice assumes the experience of love which has compassion for the suffering of the other? Schopenhauer identified love with compassion and made justice an aspect of love. Would you agree?

E.L.: Certainly. Except that for me the suffering proper to compassion, suffering because the other suffers, is only one aspect of a relation that is much more complex and much more complete at the same time: the responsibility for the other. I am in reality responsible for the other even when he or she commits crimes. This is, for me, what is essential in the Jewish conscience. But I also think that this is what is essential in the human conscience: all men are responsible for one another, and "I more than anyone else." One of the most important things for me is this asymmetry: all men are responsible for one another and I more than everybody. It is Dostoevsky's formula which, as you see, I quote again.

Q.: And the relation between justice and love?

E.L.: Justice comes from love. That definitely doesn't mean to say that the rigor of justice can't be turned against love understood from the starting point of responsibility. Politics, left to itself, has its own determinism. Love must always watch over justice. In Jewish theology—I am not guided by that theology explicitly—God is the God of justice, but his principal attribute is mercy. In talmudic language, God is always called *Rachmanah*, the Merciful: this whole topic is studied in rabbinic exegesis. Why are there *two* accounts of creation? Because the Eternal—called *Elohim* in the first account—wanted initially (this is only a fable, of course) to create a world sustained solely by justice. It didn't hold up. The second account, in which the Tetragrammaton appears, attests to the intervention of mercy.

Q.: So love is originary?

E.L.: Love is originary. I'm not speaking theologically at all; I myself don't use the word *love* much; it is worn out and ambiguous. Then, too, there is something severe in this originary love; this love is commanded. In my last book, which is called *Of God Who Comes to Mind*, there is an attempt, outside all theology, to ask at what moment the word of God is heard. It is inscribed in the face of the other, in the encounter with the other: a double expression of weakness and demand. Is that the word of God? A word that obligates me as the one responsible for the other; there is an election there, because that responsibility is inalienable. A responsibility that you yield to someone is no longer a responsibility. I substitute myself for every man and no one can substitute for me, and in that sense I am chosen. Let us think again of my quotation from Dostoevsky. I have always thought that election is definitely not a privilege; it is the fundamental characteristic of the human person as morally responsible. Responsibility is an individuation, a principle of individuation. Concerning the famous problem, "Is man individuated by matter, or individuated by form?" I maintain individuation by responsibility for the other. It, too, is severe; I leave the whole consoling side of this ethics to religion.

Q.: Does gentleness belong to religion?

E.L.: What responsibility as a principle of human individuation lacks is that God perhaps helps you to be responsible; that is gentleness. But to deserve the help of God, it is necessary to want to do what must be done without his help. I am not getting into that question theologically. I am describing the ethical: it is the human qua human. The ethical is not an invention of the white race, of a humanity which has read the Greek authors in school and gone through a specific evolution. The only absolute value is the human possibility of giving the other priority over oneself. I don't think that there is a humanity that can take exception to that ideal, even if it is declared an ideal of holiness. I am not saying that the human being is a saint; I'm saying that he or she is the one who has understood that holiness is incontestable. This is the beginning of philosophy; this is the rational, the intelligible. Here it sounds as if we were getting away from reality. One is easily led to suspect pure bookishness and the hypocrisy of bookishness in all this, but we tend to forget the depth of our relation to *books*—that is, to inspired language—which speak of nothing else. The Book of books, and all literature, which is perhaps only a premonition or recollection of the Bible. All humanity has books, be they but books before books: the inspired language of proverbs, fables, and even folklore. The human being is not only in the world, not only an *in-der-Welt-Sein* (being-in-the-world) but also *zum-Buch-Sein* (being-toward-the-book), namely, in relationship to the inspired word, an ambiance as important for our existence as streets, houses, and clothing. The book is wrongly interpreted as pure *Zuhandenes*, as what is ready-to-hand, a manual. My relation to the book is definitely not pure use; it doesn't have the same meaning as the relation I have with the hammer or the telephone.

Q.: On this relation between philosophy and religion, don't you think that, at the origin of philosophizing, there is an intuition of being which would be close to religion?

E.L.: I would say yes, in fact, insofar as the relation to the other is the beginning of the intelligible. I cannot describe the relation to God without speaking of my concern for the other. When I speak to a Christian, I always quote Matthew 25: the relation to God is presented there as a relation to another person. It is not a metaphor; in the other, there is a real presence of God. In my relation to the other, I hear the word of God. It is not a metaphor. It is not only extremely important; it is literally true. I'm not saying that the other is God, but that in his or her face I hear the word of God.

Q.: Is the face a mediator between God and us?

E.L.: Oh, no, no, not at all, it is not mediation. It is the way in which the word of God reverberates.

Q.: Is there a difference?

E.L.: Hold on a minute. Now we're getting into theology... To me, the other is the other human being. *Would* you like to do a bit of theology? In the Old Testament, you know, God also comes down toward man. God the Father "descends," for example, in Genesis 11:7, Numbers 11:17, Exodus 19:18. There is no separation between the Father and the Word; it is in the form of speech, in the form of an ethical order or an order to love that the descent of God happens. It is in the face of the other that the commandment comes which interrupts the progress of the world. Why would I feel responsible in the presence of the face? That is Cain's answer when he is asked: "Where is your brother?" He answers: "Am I my brother's keeper?" That is the face of the other taken as an image among images, when the word of God it bears is not recognized. We must not take Cain's answer as if he were mocking God or as if he were answering like a child: "It isn't me, somebody else did it." Cain's answer is sincere.

Ethics is the only thing lacking in his answer; it consists solely of ontology: I am I, and he is he. We are separate ontological beings.

Q.: In this relation to the other, as you wrote in "The Trace of the Other," "consciousness loses its first place."

E.L.: Yes, responsible subjectivity is a subjectivity which is straightaway commanded; heteronomy is somehow stronger than autonomy here, except that this heteronomy is not servitude or bondage. As if certain purely formal relations, when they are filled with content, could have a content stronger than the formal necessity they signify. *A* commanding *b* is a formula of *b*'s non-freedom; but if *b* is man and *a* is God, the subordination is not servitude; on the contrary, it is a call to man. We must not always formalize: Nietzsche thought that if God exists, the I is impossible. That can be very convincing. If *a* commands *b*, *b* is no longer autonomous, no longer has subjectivity; but when, in thinking, you do not remain in the formal, when you think starting from a content, the situation one calls heteronomy has a completely different signification. The consciousness of responsibility straightaway imposed is certainly not in the nominative; it is rather in the accusative. It is "ordered," and the French word *ordonner* (to order) is very good: when you become a priest, you are ordained, you take orders; but in reality, you receive powers. In French the word *ordonné* means both having received orders and having been consecrated. It is in that sense that I can say that consciousness, subjectivity, no longer has first place in its relation to the other. My view is opposed to the tendency of a whole portion of contemporary philosophy that prefers to see in the human being a simple articulation or a simple aspect of a rational, ontological system that has nothing human about it; even in Heidegger, *Dasein* is ultimately a structure of being in general bound to its vocation, to its gesture of being, to its event of being. The human is not the ultimate meaning of being; man is a being who comprehends being and, in that sense, is the manifestation of it, and only thus is he of interest to philosophy. Similarly, in certain trends in structuralist research, rules, pure forms, universal structures, ensembles which have a legality as cold as mathematical laws are isolated. And then that dictates the human. In Merleau-Ponty, there is a very beautiful passage in which he analyzes the way one hand touches the other.[2] One hand touches the other, the other hand touches the first; the hand, consequently, is touched and touches the touching—one hand touches the touching. A reflexive structure: it is as if space were touching itself through man. What is pleasing here is, perhaps, this non-human—or non-humanist, isn't it?—structure in which man is only a moment. Within the same distrust with regard to humanism, there is in contemporary philosophy a struggle against the notion of the subject. One wishes for a principle of intelligibility which no longer envelops the human; one wants the subject to evoke a principle that would not be enveloped by the concern for human fate. On the other hand, when I say that consciousness in the relation with the other loses its first place, it is not in that sense; I mean to say on the contrary that, in consciousness thus conceived, there is the awakening to humanity. The humanity of consciousness is not in its powers, but in its responsibility: in passivity, in welcome, in obligation with regard to the other. It is the other who is first, and there the question of my sovereign consciousness is no longer the first question. I advocate, as in the title of one of my books, "the humanism of the other man."

One last thing that is very close to my heart. In this whole priority of the relation to the other, there is a break with a great traditional idea of the excellence of unity. Relation would already be a deprivation of this unity. That is the tradition beginning with Plotinus. My idea would consist in thinking sociality independent of the "lost" unity.

Q.: Is that the origin of your criticism of Western philosophy as egology?

E.L.: As egology, yes. If you read the *Enneads*, the One doesn't even have consciousness of self; if it did have consciousness of self, it would already be multiple, losing perfection. In knowledge, one is two, even when one is alone. Even when one assumes consciousness of self, there is already a split. The various relations that can exist in man and in being are always judged according to their proximity to or distance from unity. What is relation? What is time? A fall from unity, a fall from eternity. There are many theologians from various religions who say that the good life is coincidence with God; coincidence, that is, the return to unity. Whereas in the insistence on the relation to the other in responsibility, the excellence of sociality itself is affirmed: in theological terms, proximity to God, society with God.

Q.: Is this the excellence of multiplicity?

E.L.: It is the excellence of the multiple, which evidently can be thought as a degradation of the one. To cite a biblical verse, once created, man is blessed with a command "to multiply." In ethical and religious terms: it is to have someone to love, to have someone for whom to exist, not to be just for oneself. He created them as man and woman straightaway, "male and female He created them." While at every moment, for us Europeans, to approach unity is essential. Fusion is essential. We say that love is fusion, that it triumphs in fusion. In Plato's *Symposium*, Socrates reports that Diotima says that love as such is a daimon, precisely because he is nothing but separation and desire for the other.

Q.: In this perspective, what, according to you, would be the difference between Eros and Agape?

E.L.: I am definitely not a Freudian; consequently I don't think that Agape comes from Eros. But I don't deny that sexuality is also an important philosophical problem; the meaning of the division of the human into man and woman is not reducible to a biological problem. I used to think that alterity begins in the feminine. That is, in fact, a very strange alterity: woman is neither the contradiction nor the opposite of man. The difference between man and woman is not like other differences. Not like the opposition between light and darkness. It is a distinction that is not contingent, and whose place must be sought in relation to love. I can say no more about it now; I think in any case that Eros is definitely not Agape, that Agape is neither a derivative nor the extinction of Eros. Before Eros there was the face; Eros itself is possible only between faces. The problem of Eros is philosophical and concerns alterity. Thirty years ago I wrote a book called *Time and the Other* in which I thought that the feminine was alterity itself; I do not retract that, but I have never been a Freudian. In *Totality and Infinity*, there is a chapter on Eros, which is described as love that becomes enjoyment, whereas my view of Agape, which starts from responsibility for the other, is grave.

Q.: You say that "the responsibility for the other comes from the hither side of my freedom." It is the problematic of the awakening-reawakening. To reawaken is to discover oneself responsible for the other; it is to discover oneself always in debt on the hither side of freedom. To wake up and to respond: are they the same thing? To discover oneself in debt: is that already to respond? Or, between "discovering oneself" and "responding," is there not freedom, a possibility of bad faith, of non-response?

E.L.: What is important is that the relation to the other is awakening and sobering up, that awakening is obligation. You say to me: isn't that obligation preceded by a free decision? What matters to me in responsibility for the other is, as it were, an engagement which is older than any deliberation we can remember and which is constitutive of the human. It is evident that there is in man the possibility of not awakening to the other; there is the possibility of evil. Evil is the order of being pure and simple, and on the contrary, to go toward the other is the breaking through of the human in being, an "otherwise than being." I am not at all certain that the triumph of the "otherwise than being" is assured. There can be periods during which the human is completely extinguished, but the ideal of holiness is what humanity has introduced into being. An ideal of holiness contrary to the laws of being. Reciprocal actions and reactions, compensation for forces expended, the regaining of an equilibrium, whatever the wars, whatever the "cruelties" that take cover in that indifferent language that passes for justice: such is the law of being. No illness, no exception, no disorder, that is the order of being. I have no illusions; most of the time, things happen according to that law, and probably will again. Humanity achieves friendship, even when it seems to be broken off, but also constructs a political order in which the determinism of being can reappear. I have no illusions about it and I have no optimistic philosophy for the end of history. Perhaps religions have a deeper insight into such things. But the human consists in acting without letting yourself be guided by these menacing possibilities. That is what the awakening to the human is. And there have been in history just men and saints.

Q.: Is being also inertia, the fact of not responding, of not awakening to another?

E.L.: Inertia is certainly the great law of being; but the human looms up in it and can disturb it. For a long time? For a moment? The human is a scandal in being, a "sickness" of being for the realists, but not evil.

Q.: The madness of the cross?

E.L.: Yes, certainly, if you like, that suits the idea I just expressed, and there are equivalent ideas in Jewish thought. There is the history of the Jewish people itself. This idea of the crisis of being describes for me something which is specifically human and certainly corresponds to the prophetic instant. In the very structure of prophecy, a temporality is opened up, breaking with the "rigor" of being, with eternity understood as presence which does not pass away.

Q.: Is it the opening up of time?

E.L.: Yes, there is the time that one can understand in terms of presence and the present, and in which the past is only a retained present and the future a present to come. Re-presentation would be the fundamental modality of mental life. But starting from the ethical relation with the other, I glimpse a temporality in which the dimensions of the past and the future have their own signification. In my responsibility for the other, the past of the other, which has never been my present, "concerns me": it is not a re-presentation for me. The past of the other and, somehow, the history of humanity in which I have never participated, in which I have never been present, are my past. As for the future—it is not my anticipation of a present which is already waiting for me, all ready and like the imperturbable order of being, "as if it had already arrived," as if temporality were a synchrony. The future is the time of pro-phecy, which is also an imperative, a moral order, herald of an inspiration. I have tried to present the essence of these ideas in a study that will soon appear: a future that is not simply what is yet-to-come [*un futur qui n'est pas un simple à-venir*]. The infinity of time doesn't frighten me; I think that it is the very movement of the *à-Dieu*, and that time is better than eternity which is an exasperation of the "present," an idealization of the present.

Q.: You see Heidegger as continuing Western philosophy, which maintains the primacy of the same over the other.

E.L.: For me, Heidegger is the greatest philosopher of the century, perhaps one of the very great philosophers of the millennium; but I am very pained by that because I can never forget what he was in 1933, even if only for a short period. What I admire in his work is *Being and Time*. It is a summit of phenomenology. The analyses are brilliant. As for the later Heidegger, I am much less familiar with him. What frightens me a little is also the development of a discourse in which the human becomes an articulation of an anonymous or neutral intelligibility, to which the revelation of God is subordinated. In the *Geviert*, there are gods, in the plural.

Q.: Given the ontological difference that Heidegger establishes between beings and being, would not Heideggerian being correspond to a certain extent to the "otherwise than being"?

E.L.: No, I don't think so. Besides, otherwise than being isn't a "something." It is the relation to the other, the ethical relation. In Heidegger, the ethical relation, *Miteinandersein*, being-with-another, is only one moment of our presence in the world. It does not have the central place. *Mit* is always being next to... It is not in the first instance the face, it is *zusammensein* (being-together), perhaps *zusammenmarschieren* (marching-together).

Q.: True, it is a moment; but at the same time, is it not an essential structure of *Dasein*?

E.L.: Yes, certainly, but we have always known that man is a social animal. That is definitely not the meaning I'm looking for. They say that in my philosophy—I am often criticized for this—there is an underestimation of the world. In Heidegger, the world is very important. In *Holzwege* there is a tree; you don't find men there.

Q.: And a structure or a moment such as *Fürsorge* ("solicitude"), the assistance to the other?

E.L.: Yes, but I don't believe he thinks that feeding the hungry and clothing the naked, that is, giving, is the meaning of being or that it might be above the task of being.

Q.: It is an open question.

E.L.: Yes, it is open. Don't worry; I'm not a fool. I could not fail to recognize Heidegger's speculative greatness. But the emphases in his analyses are elsewhere. I repeat, his analyses are brilliant. But what does fearing for the other mean in his theory of *Befindlichkeit*? To me, it is an essential moment; I even think that fearing God primarily means fearing for the other. Fearing for the other doesn't enter into the Heideggerian analysis of *Befindlichkeit* because in that theory—a very admirable theory of double intentionality—all emotion, all fear, is finally emotion for oneself, fear for oneself, fear of the dog but anguish *for* oneself.

But then what of fearing for the other? Obviously that fear could be interpreted as fear for oneself, on the pretext that in fearing for the other I may be afraid of being in the same situation as the other. But that is not what fearing for the other really is. The mother who fears for the child, or even each of us who fears for a friend, fears for the other. (But every other is a friend. Do you see what I mean?) As if by chance, in Leviticus 19:13, certain verses that end with "and thou shalt fear God" proscribe bad acts concerning the other man. Doesn't the theory of *Befindlichkeit* come up short here?

Q.: Do you think that Heidegger would propose a kind of sacralization of the world, and that his thought represents a culmination of paganism?

E.L.: Whatever the case may be, he has a very great sense for everything that is part of the landscape—not the artistic landscape, but the place in which man is enrooted. It is absolutely not a philosophy of the émigré! I would even say that it is not a philosophy of the emigrant. To me, being a migrant is not being a nomad. Nothing is more enrooted than the nomad. But he or she who emigrates is fully human: the migration of man does not destroy, does not demolish the meaning of being.

Q.: Do you think that, in Heidegger, it is a question of geographical enrootedness? For example, reading your text in *Difficult Freedom*, "Heidegger and Gagarin," one has the impression that enrootedness in Heidegger, as you interpret it, is a local enrootedness, in a geographical space. Is that what Heidegger has in mind, or is it not rather an enrootedness in the world?

E.L.: But the human is lived, is described, always in the same landscape. When you have been on the moon a bit, you certainly return to the world as to your village. But Heidegger has said that one cannot live in geometrical space. Gagarin didn't settle in geometrical space after he returned to earth, but he was able to make geometrical space his place and the place of his professional activity.

Q.: Is it that the world in Heidegger is in fact something other than the terrestrial world, than identification with a landscape?

E.L.: It has been said that my article on Gagarin and Heidegger was "violent."[3] There are texts in Heidegger on the place of man in Central Europe. Europe and the German West are central to him. There is a whole geopolitics in Heidegger.

Q.: What is the influence of Rosenzweig on your thought?

E.L.: It is his critique of totality, his critique of Hegel, that has given me the most, and I have been very appreciative of the idea that initial intelligibility—Rosenzweig's great idea—is the conjuncture of creation, revelation, and redemption. These are not late and derived notions (it hardly matters at what moment they appear in history) but the source of all meaning. I reiterated this in the preface I wrote for Stéphane Mosès's book on Rosenzweig.[4] In Rosenzweig's work, the abstract aspects of time—past, present, future—are deformalized; it is no longer a question of time, an empty form in which there are three formal dimensions. The past is creation. It is as if Rosenzweig were saying: to think the past concretely, you have to think creation. Or, the future is redemption; the present is revelation. What I retain is definitely not that second or third identification, but instead the very precocious idea that certain formal notions are not fully intelligible except in a concrete event, which seems even more irrational than the notions, but through which they are truly thought. This is also certainly one of the ideas presented by Husserlian phenomenology, which Rosenzweig didn't know.

Q.: And the influence of Buber and Marcel?

E.L.: I read Buber very late, and Marcel too; but I said in a little article soon to be published[5] that whoever has walked on Buber's ground owes allegiance to Buber, even if he didn't know where he was. It is as if you were about to cross the border without knowing it; you owe obedience to the country where you are. It is Buber who identified that ground, saw the theme of the other, the *Du*, the Thou. Marcel is also very close to me, but I find that in Marcel dialogue is finally overwhelmed by ontology. There is in Marcel the concern to prolong traditional ontology: God is Being. The idea that God is otherwise than being, beyond being, or without being, as Marion says (have you seen the title of his book, *God Without Being*?),[6] would have frightened him.

Q.: Various attempts have been made, notably in Latin America, to establish a synthesis of your philosophy and Marxism. What do you think of that?

E.L.: I knew Enrique Dussel, who used to quote me a lot, and who is now much closer to political, even geopolitical thought. Moreover, I have gotten to know a very sympathetic group of South Americans working out a "liberation philosophy"—Scannone in particular. We had a meeting here, with Bernhard Casper, a friend of mine who is a professor of theology at Freiburg, and some Catholic philosophers from South America.

There is a very interesting attempt in South America to return to the spirit of the people. Moreover, there is a great influence of Heidegger in the manner—the rhythm—of developing topics, and in the radicalism of the questioning. I am very happy, very proud even, when I hear echoes of my work in this group. It is a fundamental approval. It means that other people have also seen "the same thing."

Q.: Can your thought, which is a thought of love, be reconciled with a philosophy of conquest, like Marxism?

E.L.: No, in Marxism, there is not just conquest; there is recognition of the other. True enough, it consists in saying: we can save the other if he himself demands his due. Marxism invites humanity to demand what it is my duty to give it. That is a bit different from my radical distinction between me and others, but Marxism cannot be condemned for that. Not because it succeeded so well, but because it took the other seriously.

Q.: As a political philosophy, Marxism is nevertheless a philosophy of power, which preaches the conquest of power by violence.

E.L.: That is true of all political ideologies. But in principle those who preach Marxism hoped to make political power useless. That is the idea of some of the most sublime phrases, when Lenin said for example that the day would come when even a scullery maid would be able to lead a State. That really doesn't mean that she will lead the State, but that the political problem will no longer be posed in today's terms. There is a messianism here. As for what it has become in practice... For me, one of the great disappointments of twentieth-century history has been that a movement like that produced Stalinism. That is finitude!

Q.: In the nineteenth century, there was already that schism between anarchist socialism and Marxist socialism.

E.L.: Of course. But the degeneration of generosity into Stalinism is infinitely more serious.

Q.: In modern Marxism, the idea of a withering away, which was dear to initial Marxism, has disappeared.

E.L.: Perhaps, but there is room for a just State in what I say of the relationship to the other. Our conversation began with that subject.

Q.: Do you think that such a State could exist?

E.L.: Yes, there is a possible harmony between ethics and the State. The just State will come from just persons and saints rather than from propaganda and preaching.

Q.: This love might make the very existence of the State unnecessary, as Aristotle says in the treatise *On Friendship*.

E.L.: I think rather, as I said at the beginning, that charity is impossible without justice, and that justice is warped without charity.

TRANSLATED BY MICHAEL B. SMITH

The Awakening of the I

Q.: You have had occasion to say, "Europe is the Bible and the Greeks." In a sense, this formula could apply to the totality of your intellectual approach, in which the philosophy coming from the Greek heritage confronts the Judeo-Christian tradition. Could you indicate first what "the Bible" represents in this phrase?

E.L.: It is, evidently, only a matter of indicating the great directions, and not a precise designation of historical wholes. The Bible, or, if you prefer, the Judeo-Christian source of our culture, consists in affirming a primordial responsibility "for the other," such that, in an apparent paradox, concern for another may precede concern for oneself. Holiness thus shows itself as an irreducible possibility of the human and God: being called by man. An original ethical event which would also be first theology. Thus ethics is no longer a simple moralism of rules which decree what is virtuous. It is the original awakening of an I responsible for the other; the accession of my person to the uniqueness of the I called and elected to responsibility for the other. The human I is not a unity closed upon itself, like the uniqueness of the atom, but rather an opening, that of responsibility, which is the true beginning of the human and of spirituality. In the call which the face of the other man addresses to me, I grasp in an immediate fashion the graces of love: spirituality, the lived experience of authentic humanity.

Q.: The attitude that you describe evokes holiness. The least one might say is that nearly all human beings are quite distanced from this attitude.

E.L.: Holiness is nevertheless the supreme perfection, and I am not saying that all humans are saints! But it is enough that, at times, there have been saints, and especially that holiness always be admired, even by those who seem the most distant from it. This holiness which cedes one's place to the other becomes possible in humanity. And there is something divine in this appearance of the human capable of thinking of another before thinking of himself. With humanity, holiness thus comes to transform the being of nature by constituting this opening of which I was speaking earlier. Very briefly stated, this is what, in the formula from which we started, "the Bible" designates.

Q.: And the Greeks? For Socrates himself asserts that it is better to be the victim than the executioner, or again, that no one volunteers to be bad. In what sense are the Greeks different from the Bible, then?

E.L.: It is true that by certain traits the Greeks were capable of being "biblical," if I dare say so. To the examples you mention, we must also add the idea of Plato, who places the Good above being, which is altogether extraordinary. In the European heritage that is ours, we must therefore not radically oppose the Judeo-Christian and the Greek sources.

There is, nonetheless, one specific dimension in which the Greeks have excelled, in centering their reflection upon the question of harmony and the order of being. This is the dimension of the State, justice, and the political. Justice is distinct from charity, since with it there intervenes a form of equality and measure, a set of social rules to be established according to the judgment of the State, and therefore according to politics. This time, the relation between me and another must leave place for a third party, a sovereign judge who decides between equals.

Q.: Could you illustrate that with an example?

E.L.: Let us imagine that it is a matter of judging a man and rendering sentence. In order to determine this sentence, one finds oneself again face to face with the other, and one must look only at the face. But once the sentence is pronounced, once it is made public, one must be able to discuss, contest, approve, or combat it. Public opinion—other citizens and the press—can intervene and state, for example, that this sentence ought to be reviewed.

Therein lies the very foundation of democracy. One can debate decisions; there is no human decree that cannot be revised. Charity is thus put to the test of public verification. Even if there exist examples of such an attitude in the texts of the Bible, it is above all on this point that the Greek contribution to European culture is situated.

Q.: What would you respond to someone who said that he did not admire holiness, did not feel this call of the other, or more simply that the other left him indifferent?

E.L.: I do not believe that is truly possible. It is a matter here of our first experience, the very one that constitutes us, and which is as if the ground of our existence. However indifferent one might claim to be, it is not possible to pass a face by without greeting it, or without saying to oneself, "What will he ask of me?" Not only our personal life, but also all of civilization is founded upon this.

Q.: Nevertheless, do not the rule of money and the extension of business values tend to modify, even to cause us to forget, this relation to the other which you judge fundamental?

E.L.: I don't think so. There are, of course, the frightening aspects of capitalism and of excessive attachment to money. But one must not fall into the error that consists in believing that money is accursed and that one must declare it systematically malignant.

I am convinced that there is an ethical significance to money and that it can contribute to a humanization of the world. We must not forget that it is never only things that we sell and purchase, but also products created by human relations and labor. The exchange, the allocation, and the forms of equality and circulation among humans which money makes possible create, in my view, a factor for peace and healthy relations. Barter and trade are, on the contrary, a source of confrontations and war. And money is the end of barter and trade.

Q.: Should we conclude that the disappearance of the socialist states and the return of the Eastern European countries to market economies might constitute, in your eyes, factors for humanization and peace?

E.L.: It is not in these terms that the question should be posed in my opinion. On account of Stalinism, the bureaucratic terror, and all the crimes tied to communism's existence, no one deplores the fall of communist power. It is impossible to mourn Stalin, who commanded atrocities in the name of Marx's humanitarian promise and committed injustices in the name of a justice to come.

Yet despite the horror of this regime, there subsisted a hope. One could always tell oneself that all these crimes were perhaps not committed in vain. One could still imagine that, after a period both obscure and difficult to cross, better times would come. For, even if the Soviet state had become the most terrible of all, it remained the carrier of a promise of deliverance, of a hope for liberation.

The disappearance of this horizon appears to me as a profoundly troubling event, for it overturns our vision of time. Since the Bible, we are accustomed to think that time is going somewhere, that the history of humanity is directed toward a horizon, even across wrong turns and vicissitudes. Europe built its vision of time and history upon this conviction and this expectation: time promised something. The Soviet regime, despite its refusal of transcendence and of religion, was the inheritor of this conception. After the 1917 revolution, one had the feeling that something was still augured, was still afoot despite the obstacles and the errors. With the foundering of the Soviet system, even if this event presents a number of positive aspects, categories profoundly embedded in the European consciousness are troubled. Our relation to time finds itself in crisis. It seems indispensable that we Westerners situate ourselves in the perspective of a time bearing a promise. I do not know to what degree we can manage without this. This appears to me to be the most troubling aspect in our present situation.

Q.: Do you not believe that this experience might carry over to another horizon?

E.L.: For the moment I do not see how. Unless we conceive of our liberal society as a form of fulfillment of all promises. One could say in effect to oneself that, in Western democracies, all tomorrows are guaranteed, peace reigns, and true misery hardly exists anymore. We see developing, moreover, a life of comforts, security, vacations, and also of culture, music, and art. There is here an ideal for humanity which one would be wrong to consider contemptible. When one has known other regimes and other modes of life, one can even consider this ideal a form of human perfection. One could thus imagine that the continuation and development of this liberal society might become the principle of historic action. It is a possibility. But this is no longer the same sort of hope as existed before…

Q.: Do you not fear that liberal democracies would be undermined by the resurgence of murderous "hopes," tied to the return of nationalism, xenophobia, anti-Semitism?

E.L.: I believe in the force of liberalism in Europe. But I also have too many memories to be certain in my answer.

Q.: Among your memories, your teacher, Heidegger, occupies a prominent place. It is in a critical relation to his thought, moreover, that you have constructed your own work. How do you view him today?

E.L.: I always recall with the greatest emotion my studies with Heidegger. Whatever the reservations one might formulate about the man and his political engagement at the side of the Nazis, he was incontestably a genius, the author of an extremely profound philosophical work which one cannot dismiss with a few sentences.

Q.: May I ask you, for all that, to indicate what is the connection—if one exists—between his thought and his political engagement?

E.L.: For Heidegger, being is animated by the effort of being. For being, in its effort of being, it is simply a matter of being, above all and at all costs. This resolution leads to an entry into struggles between individuals, nations, or classes—while remaining firm and unshakable like steel. There is in Heidegger the dream of a nobility of the blood and the sword. Now, humanism is altogether different. It is a response to the other that cedes him first place, that gives way before him rather than combating him. The absence of concern for the other in Heidegger and his personal political adventure are bound up together. And despite all my admiration for the grandeur of his thought, I could never share this double aspect of his positions.

Q.: Did you tell him this?

E.L.: I will answer you simply with a brief personal recollection which happens, likewise, to be a historic scene. In the summer of 1929, I attended the celebrated encounter at Davos that was marked by the philosophical confrontation between Ernst Cassirer and Martin Heidegger. As you know, it was following this historic confrontation that there disap-

peared from Germany the thinking inspired by Kant and the Enlightenment heritage which Cassirer principally represented. Now, one evening,
during this meeting, we put on a revue, a little play which Cassirer and
Heidegger attended, and in which we enacted their controversy. For my
part, I incarnated Cassirer, whose positions Heidegger constantly attacked. To translate this noncombative and slightly desolate attitude of
Cassirer, I repeated continuously, "I'm a pacifist..."

TRANSLATED BY BETTINA BERGO

In the Name of the Other

Q.: You are often called a moralist. How do you respond to that?

E.L.: A moralist is a preacher: he gives sermons, attempts to elevate the level of morality, supports the arguments put forth in favor of a desired moral effect. This role assuredly requires a subtle mind, but also ruse. And this most certainly is not a philosophical virtue! The moralizer can only succeed by having recourse to models—as exemplified by the moralizer himself who, repeatedly quoting himself, ends up refuting himself.

Q.: Today, when you see Lithuania engaged in a battle for its independence, what old memories come back to you?

E.L.: Mostly memories of Jewish life. You cannot imagine the extent to which the two societies were separate. The Jews lived in the old town of Kovno, but without feeling entrapped in a ghetto for all that. If the Lithuanians themselves kept their distance, it's also true they never carried out a pogrom, unlike certain regions of Holy Russia. My parents had settled in the Ukraine during World War I. Following the revolution, they decided to return to Lithuania. This was in 1920; I was fourteen and a half at the time, and with sadness said to myself, "I am leaving a messianic country."

Q.: How so?

E.L.: I saw myself drifting back toward a bourgeois existence. Do not think for a minute that I had transformed myself into a militant Marxist revolutionary. But I was under the impression that in Russia history was reaching its ultimate goal, a bit like the ultimate flowering of justice. This, of course, was before Stalin.

Q.: Seven years later, in Germany, you discovered Heidegger. In a recently discovered letter of his, dating back from 1929, the language used is already openly anti-Semitic and foretells his support of Hitler.[1]

E.L.: At the time, I would have been stupefied. In 1928, when I arrived at Freiburg-in-Brisgau to join Husserl's seminars, I discovered that everybody was reading *Being and Time*, which had just been published. Heidegger was all one talked about. I will not deny my first impression. It was, most certainly, as I think back to it now, that of standing before a Plato or a Kant. He seemed to have the same sovereignty. It was he who informed me, in 1929, of the debate that was to take place in Davos between Ernst Cassirer and himself.

Q.: For Heidegger, was this not, above all, a matter of confronting his great rival—this humanist heir apparent to Kant—who, at that stage, dominated the philosophical scene?

E.L.: At that time, I was far from being up to comprehending the stakes. My political education, in the technical sense of the word, was nonexistent. I found myself in this Germany without so much as knowing the color of the stones of the Church of Freiburg. The truest reality to me was what Heidegger said, his disagreements with Husserl, and the latter's responses to him. What's more, in those days, the threats were far less clearly felt than they are today. In Davos, Heidegger reigned. I still see him walking in his ski outfit, and Cassirer, so courteous, yet reduced to the defensive.

Q.: Could you sense that he was heading towards defeat, taking with him all the values for which he stood?

E.L.: I must admit that I did not even pity Cassirer. For years afterward, the scene haunted me. Naive as I was then, I imagined that only vulgarity and hatred could lead to Nazism. And thus for it to be linked to a man like Heidegger, of such standing, was inconceivable to me!

Q.: What is your understanding of his behavior? There must be a number of explanations, including the most ordinary vanities.

E.L.: Listen, that is too easy an answer. It was evident that his background was modest, and he was very flattered by his personal triumphs, the high esteem in which society's leaders held him. On another level, in his writings, and in particular his etymologies, I now forever hear the common theme of the German soil. I also became aware of a surprising lacuna in his work: the only thing which he did not examine phenomenologically was money. In *Being and Time*, you will find the hand, the worker, the craftsman, but there is no mention of money.

Q.: How do you interpret this?

E.L.: I think that the notion of exchange as such reflected too explicitly on the Jews.

Q.: Do you agree with Heidegger's understanding of modernity as a form of decadence?

E.L.: I do not. For him, it is tied to a denunciation of technology. I claim that without technology, we would be in no position to feed the Third World. I know of no more frightening images than some of the scenes of African life shown on television; and those children! Nothing is nobler than exposing man's misery.

Q.: Therefore, you do not lend your voice to the popular lament on the stupidity and inanity of the media.

E.L.: It all depends on talent, and talent exists in this domain as well. Neither do I share with Heidegger his abhorrence of the big city, of the bourgeoisie.

Q.: What do you conceive to be the role of philosophy in our society?

E.L.: Once again, it is not one of moralism. Charity arises in a consciousness awakened by the encounter with the other. Charity—goodness effected without expectation of recompense. Already the paradoxes in the Bible! This is wisdom, which interrupts the good sense of the interested animal. It is the inception of man in man. Philosophy—love of wisdom—prevents one from going back to sleep. But it took Plato, Descartes, Kant, Hegel, and Bergson for charity to become one of the universal laws of justice, and to give these laws legitimacy. The meeting with the other man would thus find itself not merely as a little province of the psychic landscape, but rather as the very source of spirituality—if we can still bear that overused term. Here indubitably lies my primary theme, where I express my reservations about a tradition that claims knowledge to be the supreme fulfillment of the human. I do not underestimate the importance of knowledge, but I do not consider it to be the ultimate axiological judgment.

Q.: Take man's scientific knowledge, for example, does it not show enough respect for its object?

E.L.: The achievement of knowledge consists of grasping the object. Its strangeness is then conquered. Its newness, the opening up of its otherness, is reduced to the "same," to what has already been seen, already known. In the ethical relation, the other man remains other to me. Despite our exchanges, he remains that which I—closed up in myself—am not.

Q.: Meaning?

E.L.: We are all enchained to ourselves, in the grips of our concern to be, which Heidegger summarized by saying, at issue for a being—*Dasein*—is this being itself. I do not call this constant tension of a being over itself egoism, but within this tension lies the source of egoism. The being of the living, the life of the living being, is a struggle for life. And matter is hard, enclosed upon itself, confined within its atoms. Ultimately, with man comes a history—forgive me this platitude—of tears and blood. And yet, it does happen that a man dies for another, that the being of the other is dearer to him than his own. This is only possible within the order of the human, and is found nowhere else. "Après vous, Monsieur," as it is said in French manners.

Q.: Except that we are well beyond courtesy.

E.L.: The priority of the other person begins in this self-effacing gesture, in our ceding our place. This is the road that can lead to holiness. To meet another, one must first welcome a face. This means more than looking at the features in the other face, or the color that characterizes the surface of his skin, or the iris of his eyes—as if in doing so one could perceive, grasp, know. Is not the face first of all expression and appeal, preceding the datum of knowledge? Is it not the nakedness of the other—destitution and misery beneath the adopted countenance? One scene from Vassily Grossman's book *Life and Fate* has always impressed me. It takes place in Moscow, in the middle of Stalin's era, in the Lubianka, in front of the only window that officially still allows access to the friends and family who are either incarcerated or facing deportation. People are standing in line, and Grossman talks about these human beings who glue their eyes to the nape of the neck of the person in front of them and read on that nape all the anxiety in the world.

Q.: As one says, barefacedly [*à visage ouvert*]?

E.L.: Exactly. In the innocence of our daily lives, the face of the other signifies above all a demand. The face requires you, calls you outside. And already there resounds the word from Sinai, "thou shalt not kill," which signifies "you shall defend the life of the other." An order of God, or an echo, or the mystery of that order, "you will answer for the other!" It is the very articulation of the love of the other. You are indebted to someone from whom you have not borrowed a thing: a debt that precedes all borrowing. And *you* are responsible, the only one who could answer, the non-interchangeable, and the unique one. Within responsibility there is election, the original constitution of the I, and the revelation of its ethical meaning. I am chosen. But the other, the loved one, the loved one as loved, is unique to the world. This is beyond the individual, beyond the shared belonging to the genus. In this relation of the unique to the unique there appears, before the purely formal community of the genus, the original sociality.

Q.: Is one to understand that there is no morality without religion?

E.L.: God speaks to the I starting from the face of the other. It is from there that the meaning itself of the word *God* comes to mind. Before the concept of creation, starting from the commandment, starting from pure ethics.

Q.: Such as you present it, there is a great violence in this order. What happens, then, to your autonomy as an individual?

E.L.: I recall that Ricœur would say to me, "Your 'I' has no esteem for itself." One thus reproaches one's freedom for losing itself in the burden of responsibility for oneself and others; and concern for others can, of course, appear as a form of subjection, as an infinite subjection. But is freedom—which asserts itself against natural finalities, against what is natural in nature—measured against its leisure? Is freedom not that which is most remarkable in the mortal, finite, and interchangeable being who then raises himself to his unique identity as a unique being? This is the meaning of the notion of election. To be aware of it, to be able to say "I," is to be born to a new autonomy.

Q.: For you, what behaviors are implied by this responsibility for the other person? Compassion, solidarity, attentiveness toward human rights?

E.L.: I gladly use here a Hebrew term, *hesed*. This is an ancient word, since it appears in a particularly suggestive fashion in the Hebrew Bible, in what is termed (by Christians) the "Old Testament." It means charity in its absolute gratuity. The responsibility for the other, of which I am speaking, does not expect reciprocity.

Q.: Neither dialogue nor exchange?

E.L.: On this point, I might add, I am very wary of the philosophy of dialogue—such as Martin Buber conceived it—which starts from the reciprocity between the interlocutors: that which I am for you, you are for me. But let us return to the Hebrew, to this complex expression from Micah 6:8, *ahavath hesed*. How does one translate it when both words have a very close literal meaning? *Ahavath* means "love," or "love of," and *hesed*, likewise, means "love." Does this result in "love of love"? It would, unless one remembers that the latter term can also be used as an adverb. This would give us "love lovingly."

Q.: Love of charity?

E.L.: That is close to the version of André Chouraqui, although he chose to refine it. He proposes, "love of cherishing." I prefer "love without concupiscence," to quote Pascal, which, I grant you, can create a strange effect in a Hebrew Bible translation. But we would thus be closer to the gratuity of love which this formula underscores.

Q.: How can you defend this level of demand? The others, unfortunately, are innumerable.

E.L.: There lies a new difficulty, which invites us to a new development. We are not a pair, alone in the world, but at least three. Two plus a third. If I heed the second person to the end, if I accede absolutely to his request, I risk, by this very fact, doing a disservice to the third one, who is also my other. But if I listen to the third, I run the risk of wronging the second one. This is where the State steps in. The State begins as soon as three are present. It is inevitable. Because no one should be neglected, yet it is impossible to establish with the multiplicity of humanity a relation of unique to unique, of face to face. One steps out of the register of charity between individuals to enter the political. Charity pursues its fulfillment in a demand for justice. It takes a referee, laws, institutions, an authority; hence the State, with its tyrannical element. Without justice or the State, charity runs the risk of being wrong. However, it is clear that from the point of view of justice, preference for the other is no longer possible.

At this point, I would like to share with you a very beautiful portion of a talmudic text. The rabbis focused on what seemed to them to be contradictions in the Scripture. One verse, Deuteronomy 1:17, says, "Do not, in justice, show partiality to someone"—which literally reads in Hebrew: "Do not look at his face when judging." Another verse, Numbers 6:26, adds, "May the Eternal One turn His face toward you." A contradiction, or close to it! The rabbis resolve it this way: "Do not look at the face before the verdict. Once the verdict has been given, look at the face." Charity can accomplish a lot, even after a rigorous justice has been passed. Since justice constantly has a bad conscience, the demand of charity which precedes it remains and beckons it. And justice, the justice that deserves its name, does not forget that the law is perfectible. It leaves open the possibility of a revision of a judgment once pronounced. And this is very important. Because justice—summoned by charity—nevertheless founds the State and its tyrannical component. By admitting its imperfection, by arranging for a recourse for the judged, justice is already questioning the State. This is why democracy is the necessary prolongation of the State. It is not one regime possible among others, but the only suitable one. This is because it safeguards the capacity to improve or to change the law by changing—unfortunate logic!—tyrants, these personalities necessary to the State despite everything. Once we choose another tyrant, we imagine, of course, that he will be better than his predecessor. We say this with each election!

Q.: What do you think of the individualism which reigns in our democratic societies?

E.L.: That is not as deep a concern. Each concrete situation brings modifications to what we have said. Without going into too much detail, in today's comments I imagined myself reflecting on the very apparition of the human in man.

Q.: To Miguel Abensour you are a misunderstood political philosopher. How do you tie your moral philosophy to the consideration of political questions?

E.L.: Listen, I am a democrat. What more would you like me to say?

Q.: Nevertheless, when you posit democracy as the necessary prolongation of the State, this warrants further examination.

E.L.: Necessary but not natural. It is its ethical prolongation. I know that one can consider it rather scandalous to support this logic, in the face of a reality where one finds false bills and suspicious amnesties. But how do you expect me to move from the absolute splendors of *hesed*, of charity, to an analysis of the state procedures at work in our democracies?

Q.: Which nation most closely correlates with your concept of a State and democracy?

E.L.: That's easy: France. But you can see from here the commentaries to which we are exposing ourselves with such a response: "You are happy, thus all is well!" Never mind. When I arrived here, in 1923, and I started my philosophical studies at Strasbourg, the big event for me was to meet shortly thereafter, aside from my professors, my colleague Maurice Blanchot. It is with him that I discovered, echoing or at times resisting our teachers, the French excellence. Because he was its incarnation.

Q.: How so?

E.L.: First of all, a sort of nobility: clearly saying and thinking something deep, presented in such a way that it seems simple. And then not snubbing that which seemed commonplace, ordinary. Nobility in human relationships too. No condescension! And with that a simplicity toward man, the other man, without concern for his origin or his social rank. It always surprises me when someone proclaims to be from Burgundy or the Auvergne. It seems so unnecessary to me when one is French. For me it is a blessing, a quality which I associate with light, with Paris, with Versailles.

Q.: What are you thinking of when you invoke its clarity? The Cartesian model?

E.L.: Not that famous clarity, nor its distinctness either. Rather I was alluding, I insist, to the simplicity with which Blanchot stated the essential. And his talent for paradoxes! Did you know that he who harbored sympathies—very intellectual, it is true—for the Action Française before the war was filled with happiness by the May barricades? With regard to '68, my attitude was much more reserved.

Q.: You were then a professor at Nanterre.

E.L.: Indeed. That period is not, however, among my happiest memories. Not that I had any reason to complain. I was not in rags. But the French universities were to me like institutions with a great and sacred, even consecrated steadiness. The students, of course, were jubilant in being able to topple this. The movement itself seemed rather ordinary to me: not much nobility or great ideas.

Q.: What was your reaction when you heard about the desecration of the Jewish cemetery in Carpentras?[2]

E.L.: I was dismayed like everybody else.

Q.: Were you taken off guard by this event?

E.L.: You know, desecrations are practically commonplace. Therefore, the element of astonishment was not there but rather in the dimensions the deed took, the way it was emphasized. What's more, this incident coincided, or nearly so, with Le Pen's "Hour of Truth," which I watched closely. The weakness of his interlocutors dismayed me. I am not saying that this is an easy task, but how could they let themselves be led on in such a way by "jokes" disguised as arguments?

Q.: To what do you think one should attribute this climate, where the expression of racism and of anti-Semitism can flow freely?

E.L.: There is a general context. I will say this, which will surprise you: when Hitler came to power, there were some rival candidates, an opposition which was fighting for a better society and called for a revolution wherever it might take place. Do not be mistaken. I am shedding no tears over the fall of communism. But the result is that this competition no longer exists today. There is nothing more lamentable or which elicits compassion more than this. When the leader of the Communist Party of France speaks now, there is nothing left to say.

Q.: Is that so bad?

E.L.: Assuredly, for him, the Soviet Union was likened to the existence of God for the believers. I was telling you about Grossman earlier. His testimony is terrible to the extent that he had known its generous inception. Whatever one thinks, the recognition of the other exists in Marxism. What must have seemed exalting and represented a hope was the Soviet continent with its mystery, this radically different experiment. And it is in this context, the end of a certain era, that the Carpentras incident appears serious to me. That is all I can say in light of past experience. There was a positive aspect: sincere reactions that did not stop with merely proper or fitting words. On the Christians' side, the reactions confirmed the efforts toward a better Judeo-Christian understanding, which is, after all, a new phenomenon in postwar Europe. If one seeks consolation, this is it. As to predicting what's in store for us, I have no prophetic gift, even if, sometimes, I read the prophets.

Q.: Your way of thinking is, in itself, an act of resistance to pessimism. But Auschwitz did happen. Was not everything from that point on put back into question?

E.L.: I have said that the *shoah* was felt by Jews with a depth that is understood by Christians staggered by the Passion of Jesus. One wonders afterward if it is still possible to uphold something.

Q.: Because of God's absence during the *shoah*?

E.L.: That is indeed the question. What should one do if there is no *happy end*? Is a *happy end* indispensable to human history in order for there to be humanity? I attempt to suggest not. But that is easily said. Are survivors equal to the task of judging? Do they have the right to judge?

Q.: And what if you were asked to define Judaism, much as Hillel was by the pagan who asked, "Teach me the Torah while I stand on one leg?"[3]

E.L.: Hillel responded with the essence of man, and not with the essence of Judaism. The Torah addresses itself not only to Jews but to all men. In that sense, I truly am a Jew.

Q.: What does the state of Israel represent to you?

E.L.: I have personally never leaned toward an active Zionism. However, for me this is not merely a political doctrine. Nor is it a state like the others, rife with conflict and subject to the requirements of the moment. Is not the ultimate finality of Zionism to create upon Israeli soil the concrete conditions for political invention, and to make or remake a state in which prophetic morality shall be incarnate, along with its message of peace? At present, the subsistence of the Jews as such depends heavily on the continuation of this task, and under a particular form. I do not wish to infer that this sums up for me the essence of Judaism, but Israel represents a security in a world where politics count, and where the cultural depends on the political. On this point, they have enough problems without our adding to them.

Q.: In 1979, Sartre requested from you an article on Palestine.

E.L.: Indeed, this was for *Les Temps Modernes*. I called the piece "Politics, After!"[4] This was a year before Sartre's death, our third and last meeting. I had written to him in 1964, telling him that a man who refused the Nobel prize was perhaps the only one entitled to speak, and that if he visited Nasser to propose peace with Israel, he at least would be listened to. I have since learned that, after having read my letter, he purportedly asked, "Who is this Levinas?"

Q.: Does the current visibility of religions signify a real return of faith?

E.L.: As a matter of fact, I do believe that this return exists. But it is not always accompanied by participation in worship and the practice of the precepts. I am inclined to see in religions a source of consolation for adults, a foyer of true human warmth, which is not limited to the sick, the disillusioned, and the old. When one knows that unemployment, for example, is one of the essential contemporary facts of life, the coldness and harshness of reality will no longer be in doubt. What then does one seek? Not a hidden power, but a source of kinship for mature persons. And also the assurance that it is not totally absurd to have suffered.

Q.: What place does religion have in your life?

E.L.: I do not take literally the ensemble of beliefs. The Torah is not a picture book. I take worship seriously, because those venerable gestures maintain and exalt man's humanity, such as it has been passed down over innumerable generations. That, at least, is how I understand the tradition of Judaism. You are aware of the importance of studying biblical texts in their rabbinic interpretations. But I am only a Sunday talmudist.

Q.: Allow us to doubt that. It seems evident that the Talmud provides you with a sort of happiness.

E.L.: What I love is always the unexpected in a problem, the moment of spirit, certain enlightenments on a question, a certain ambiguity in the response. Let me share something with you. There is a famous passage in which one searches how best to study the Torah. An eighteenth-century rabbinical doctor said, "To approach God, to 'attach' oneself to Him, to unite oneself mystically to Him, you only have to read the Psalms. But to study the Torah for itself is a separate matter. Imagine someone who enters a room in which treasures have been heaped, and the light from these treasures show him above all else that there is another door at the back of the room, that this door opens into another room in which treasures can also be found, whose light illuminates another door. . . ." The study of the Torah is this infinity that is never finished, where the light gained illumines above all the insufficiencies of the light acquired.

TRANSLATED BY MAUREEN V. GEDNEY

The Other, Utopia, and Justice

Q.: Your first philosophical works concern phenomenology. Was your reflection formed exclusively through contact with that tradition?

E.L.: I published one of the first books on phenomenology to appear in France, and a bit later, wrote one of the first articles on Heidegger.[1] This is a purely chronological fact, but one I enjoy recalling. I have related elsewhere my encounter with phenomenology during my training in Strasbourg, at the excellent Institute of Philosophy, a sacred place, with professors bearing the names Pradines, Carteron, Charles Blondel, and Maurice Halbwachs, a member of the Resistance, who did not come back from deportation. By contrast, I have hardly emphasized the importance (which was essential for me) of the relation—always present in the background of the teaching of those masters—to Bergson.

Bergson is hardly quoted now. We have forgotten the major philosophical event he was for the French university and which he remains for world philosophy, and the role he played in the constitution of the problematic of modernity. Isn't the ontological thematization by Heidegger of being as distinguished from being*s*, the investigation of being in its verbal sense, already at work in the Bergsonian notion of duration, which is not reducible to the substantiality of being or the substantivity of beings? Can we continue to present Bergson according to the alternative suggested by the banal formula in which the philosophy of becoming is opposed to the philosophies of being? Do we not find, moreover, in Bergson's last works, a critique of technical rationalism, which is so important in Heidegger's work? *Creative Evolution* is a plea for a spirituality

200

freeing itself from a mechanistic humanism. And in the *Two Sources of Morality and Religion*, intuition, that is, life itself or the lived experience of "profound time," consciousness, and knowledge of duration are interpreted as a relation with the other and with God.

Affection and love are concrete in these relations! I feel close to certain Bergsonian themes, especially duration, in which the spiritual is no longer reduced to an event of pure "knowledge," but would be the transcendence of the relation with someone, with an other: love, friendship, sympathy. A proximity that cannot be reduced to spatial categories or to modes of objectification and thematization. There is, in my view, in the refusal to seek the meaning of reality in the persistence of solids, and in Bergson's reversion to the *becoming* of things, something like a statement of *verbal being*, of *event-being*. Bergson is the source of an entire complex of interrelated contemporary philosophical ideas; it is to him, no doubt, that I owe my modest speculative initiatives. We owe a great deal to the mark left by Bergsonism in the teachings and readings of the twenties.

Q.: Let's get back to phenomenology. It was also in the course of your training at Strasbourg that you encountered phenomenology. From Mlle. Peiffer, who was reading the *Logical Investigations*, which had not yet been translated, you learned who Husserl was; subsequently you translated *Cartesian Meditations* with her. Your first article in *Revue Philosophique* in 1929 dealt with Edmund Husserl's *Ideas*. And so it came about that in 1928, in Freiburg, you attended Husserl's last semester of teaching and Heidegger's first. How do you now interpret the passage from the founder of the phenomenological movement to his disciple, who is considered to be the more original?

E.L.: What do you mean by passage? Is it the fact of one or the other speaking on phenomenology, or the fact that Husserl's readers were prepared to read Heidegger? For Husserlians reading *Being and Time* in 1927, when it first came out, there was indeed both an impression of innovation in the questioning and its horizons and a certainty that we were approaching that marvel of analyses and of projects brilliantly prepared by the phenomenological work of Husserl.

Husserl's own criticisms did not come quickly. From the beginning, the master was dazzled by the wealth of the phenomenological analyses in *Being and Time*, which were still reconcilable with the gestures, possibilities, and procedures characteristic of the Husserlian method despite the unexpected perspectives brilliantly opened up, and even though some of Heidegger's inspiration may have come from elsewhere. It is only later, on rereading the book, that Husserl understood or perceived what were in fact distances. We apparently have access to marginal annotations which indicate his critical reading. Husserl remained convinced that Heidegger had been his most gifted disciple, but always remained sensible of the disharmony. Of the one he had deliberately chosen as his successor, he said to Professor Max Müller: "I have always been strongly impressed by Heidegger, but never influenced."

Q.: After Victor Farias's book, a discussion of Heidegger's Nazism took the center of the media stage in France. Whatever one may think of the productivity of that polemic, it is tempting to ask you: could it have been anticipated since the early discovery of Heidegger's work?

E.L.: Almost everything Farias said was known. In France, Heidegger's political positions were known even before 1933. Right after the war, there were discussions in Paris that had become overly subtle or were languishing, and that Farias rekindled. In 1930, it was hard to foresee the temptations National Socialism could represent for a Heidegger! In my very recent remarks at the colloquium organized by the Collège International de Philosophie[2]—but before Farias's book—I recalled this moral problem, despite my admiration for *Being and Time*. After Farias, a few details were specified, but nothing in Farias's book is essentially new.

The essential thing is the work itself or, at least, *Being and Time*, which remains one of the greatest books in the history of philosophy, even for those who reject or dispute it. In its pages there is certainly no formulation specifically traceable to the theses of National Socialism, but the construction includes ambiguous passages in which they might find accommodation. I would mention, for my part, the notion, primordial in this system, of authenticity, of *Eigentlichkeit*—thought in terms of the "mine," of everything proper, in terms of *Jemeinigkeit*, an original contraction of the I in mineness (*Being and Time*, section 9), in terms of a *belonging-to-oneself* and a *for-oneself* in their inalienable self-appurtenance. Despite the anthropology of *Being and Time*—in which all articulations characteristic of human concreteness, beyond the traditional attributes of the "rational animal," are reduced, as *Existentialia*, to an ontological level—it is indeed surprising that there is no philosophy of commercial exchange, in which the desires and cares of men confront one another, and in which money (would it be a simple *Zuhandenheit*?) is a means of measurement making equality, peace, and "a fair price" possible in this confrontation, despite and before its *Verfallen* [fall] into an enslaving capitalism and Mammon. Authenticity, based on the notion of "mineness," must remain pure of all influence, without admixture, without owing anything to anyone, must remain outside of everything that would compromise the non-interchangeability, the uniqueness of that *I* of "mineness." An "I" to preserve above all from the vulgar banality of the impersonal "one" (*das Man*) in which the I risks degradation, even if the vehement contempt inspired by its mediocre banality may quickly extend to the rightful portion of commonality present in the universality of democracy.

I learned quite recently that the philosopher Adorno has already denounced that jargon of authenticity. That jargon, however, expresses a "nobility," that of blood and sword. It therefore presents other dangers in a philosophy without vulgarity. The uniqueness of the human I, which nothing should alienate, is here thought in terms of death: that everyone dies for himself. An inalienable identity in dying! To sacrifice oneself for another does not make the other immortal. The I exists in the world in relation with others, but no one can truly die for anyone else. And in this existing-toward-death, in this *being-toward-death*, the lucidity of anguish accedes to nothingness instead of evading it vainly in fear. An originary authenticity, but nothing more, in which, for Heidegger, all "relations with others" are dissolved or "cancelled," and in which the meaningfulness of *Dasein* is interrupted. Fearsome authenticity! You can see what I would reject.

Would that make me a friend of the inauthentic? But is the authenticity of the I, its uniqueness, contingent upon that unadulterated possessive "mineness," that proud virility "more precious than life," *more* authentic than love or than the concern for another? A uniqueness that is not achieved as the difference manifested by someone or other who is distinct from the other individuals belonging to the extension of the same logical genus, for, as a member of this extension, the individual is precisely not unique in its genus.

Uniqueness seems to me to assume meaning in terms of the irreplaceability that comes to, or returns to, the I in the concreteness of a responsibility for the other: a responsibility that, straightaway, devolves upon the I in the very perception of the other, but as if in that representation, in that presence, it already preceded that perception, as if responsibility were already there, older than the present, and hence undeclinable, of an order alien to knowledge—as if, for all eternity, the I were the first one called to this responsibility. Non-transferable and thus unique, thus *me*, the chosen hostage, the chosen one. An ethics of the encounter—sociality. For all eternity, one man is answerable for another. From unique to unique. Whether he looks at me or not, he "regards me"; I must answer for him. I call *face* that which in the other regards the I—regards me—reminding me, from behind the countenance he puts on in his portrait, of his abandonment, his defenselessness, and his mortality, and his appeal to my ancient responsibility, as if he were unique in the world, beloved. A call from the face of my neighbor, which in its ethical urgency postpones or cancels the obligations the interpellated I has toward itself and in which the concern for the death of the other can be more important to the I than its concern as an I for itself. The authenticity of the I, in my view, is this listening on the part of the first one called, this attention to the other without subrogation, and thus already faithfulness to values despite one's own mortality. The possibility of sacrifice as a meaning of the human adventure! Possibility of the meaningful, despite death, though it be without resurrection! The ultimate meaning of love without concupiscence, and of an I no longer hateful.

The terminology I use sounds religious: I speak of the uniqueness of the I on the basis of a *chosenness* that it would be difficult for it to escape, for chosenness constitutes it out of a debt *in* the I, older than any loan. This way of approaching an idea by asserting the concreteness of a situation in which it originally assumes meaning seems to me essential to phenomenology. It is presupposed in everything I have just said.

In all these reflections, what emerges is the valorization of holiness as the most profound upheaval of being and thought, through the advent of man. Over and against the interestedness of being, a primordial essence which is *conatus essendi*, a perseverance in the face of everything and everyone, a persistence in *Dasein*—the human (love of the other, responsibility for the neighbor, an eventual dying-for-the-other, a sacrifice in which dying for the other can concern me more than my own death)—signifies the beginning of a new rationality beyond being. A rationality of the good higher than all essence. An intelligibility of goodness. This possibility, through sacrifice, of lending a meaning to the other and to the world, which, without me, still counts for me, and for which I am answerable (in spite of the great dissolution, in dying, of the relation with any other, as stated by Heidegger in section 50 of *Being and Time*) is certainly not survival. It is an ecstasis toward a future which *counts* for the I and to which the I is answerable, but a future [*un futur*] without me which is no longer the yet-to-come [*l'à-venir*] of a protended present.

These analyses, reduced to their primordial data, do not exhaust the phenomenology of otherness. I can only mention the problematic I glimpsed forty years ago in a book entitled *Time and the Other*, through reflections on eroticism and paternity, and in which meditation on the ambiguity of sexuality and love (without concupiscence), "holiness," opens up perspectives to be explored.

Q.: This definition of holiness places us in the absolute. Granted, what you have stated here concerns an ethical requirement via your insistence on the notion of gratuitousness, not reward. But in emphasizing that aspect, in yourself singling out the aspect of impossibility, aren't you afraid that your conception will be criticized as utopian, and you yourself, as a philosopher, for neglecting the concomitant political exigencies of this requirement? This is, I take it, where the idea of a "third" intervenes?

E.L.: The I can find the requirement of what I call responsibility for the other, or love without concupiscence, only within itself; it is in the "here I am" of an I, in the non-interchangeable uniqueness of one chosen. It is originally without reciprocity, which would risk compromising its gratuitousness or grace or unconditional charity. But the order of justice of individuals responsible for one another does not arise in order to restore that reciprocity between the I and its other; it arises from the fact of the third who, next to the one who is an other to me, is "another other" to me.

The I, precisely as responsible for the other and the third, cannot remain indifferent to their interactions, and in the charity for the one cannot withdraw its love from the other. The self, the I, cannot limit itself to the incomparable uniqueness of each one, which is expressed in the face of each one. Behind the unique singularities, one must perceive the individuals of a genus, one must compare them, judge them, and condemn them. There is a subtle ambiguity of the individual and the unique, the personal and the absolute, the mask and the face. This is the hour of inevitable justice—required, however, by charity itself.

The hour of justice, of the comparison between incomparables who are grouped by human species and genus. And the hour of institutions empowered to judge, of states within which institutions are consolidated, of universal law which is always a *dura lex*, and of citizens equal before the law.

These chosen ones, above commonality, must, like all things, find a place for themselves in the hierarchy of concepts; there must be a reciprocity of rights and duties. To the Bible—the first to teach the inimitable singularity, the "semelfactive" uniqueness of each soul, there must be added the Greek writings, expert in species and genera. It is the hour of the Western world! The hour of justice—required, however, by charity. To resume what I have said: it is in the name of that responsibility for the other, in the name of that mercy, that goodness to which the face of the other man appeals, that the entire discourse of justice is set in motion, whatever limitations and rigors of the *dura lex* it may bring to the infinite benevolence toward the other. Unforgettable infinity, rigors always to be mitigated. Justice always to be made more knowing in the name, the memory, of the original goodness of man toward the other, in which, in an ethical dis-inter-estedness—word of God!—the inter-ested effort of brute being persevering in being is interrupted. A justice always to be perfected against its own harshness.

That is perhaps the very excellence of democracy, whose fundamental liberalism corresponds to the ceaseless deep remorse of justice: legislation always unfinished, always resumed, a legislation open to the better. It attests to an ethical excellence and its origin in goodness, from which, however, it is distanced—always a bit less perhaps—by the necessary calculations imposed by a multiple sociality, calculations constantly starting over again. Thus, in the empirical life of the good under the freedom of revisions, there would be a progress of reason. Bad conscience of justice! It knows it is not as just as the goodness that instigates it is good. But when it forgets that, it risks sinking into a totalitarian and Stalinist regime, and losing, in ideological deductions, the gift of inventing new forms of human coexistence.

Vassily Grossman, in *Life and Fate*—such an impressive book, coming right after the major crises of our century—goes even further. He thinks that the little act of goodness (*la petite bonté*) from one person to his neighbor is lost and deformed as soon as it seeks organization and universality and system, as soon as it opts for doctrine, a treatise of politics and theology, a party, a state, and even a church. Yet it remains the sole refuge of the good in being. Unbeaten, it undergoes the violence of evil, which, as little goodness, it can neither vanquish nor drive out. The little goodness going only from man to man, not crossing distances to get to the places where events and forces unfold! A remarkable utopia of the good or the secret of its beyond.

Utopia, transcendence. Inspired by love for one's fellow man, reasonable justice is bound by legal strictures and cannot equal the goodness that solicits and inspires it. But goodness, emerging from the infinite resources of the singular self, responding without reasons or reservations to the call of the face, can divine ways to approach that suffering other—without, however, contradicting the verdict. I have always admired the talmudic apologue that, in the tractate Rosh Hashanah 17b, is presented as an attempt to reduce the apparent contradiction between two verses of Scripture: Deuteronomy 1:17 and Numbers 6:25. The first text teaches the rigor and strict impartiality of the justice demanded by God: all regarding of persons is excluded from it, or, more literally, He doesn't favor the face. The second text, where God precisely "turns his face toward you," profers another language and teaches a contrary sense. It foresees the luminous Face of God turned toward the man undergoing judgment, illuminating him, welcoming him. The contradiction is resolved in the wisdom of Rabbi Akiba. According to this eminent rabbinical scholar, the first text concerns justice as it develops before the verdict, and the second specifies the possibilities of the after-verdict. Justice and charity. This after-verdict, with its possibilities of mercy, still fully belongs—with full legitimacy—to the work of justice. On the condition, however, that the death penalty no longer belongs to [the categories of] justice?

The entire life of a nation—beyond the formal sum of individuals standing for themselves, that is to say, living and struggling for their land, their place, their *Da-sein*—carries within itself (concealed, revealed, or at least occasionally caught sight of) men who, before all loans, have debts, owe something to the neighbor, are responsible—chosen and unique—and in this responsibility want peace, justice, reason. Utopia! This way of understanding the meaning of the human—the very dis-inter-estedness of their being—does not begin by thinking of the care men take of the places where they want to be in-order-to-be. I am thinking above all of the for-the-other in them, in which, in the adventure of a possible holiness, the human interrupts the pure obstinacy of being and its wars. I cannot forget Pascal's thought: "My place in the sun. There is the beginning and the image of the usurpation of the whole world."

Q.: "Ethics would be the reminder of that famous debt I have never contracted." You have developed that idea that my responsibility is recalled to me in the face of the other man. But is every man that "other" man? Is there not sometimes a desertion of meaning, faces of brutes?

E.L.: Jean-Toussaint Desanti asked a young Japanese who was commenting on my works during a thesis defense if an SS man has what I mean by a face. A very disturbing question which calls, in my opinion, for an affirmative answer. An affirmative answer which is painful each time! During the Barbie trial, I could say: Honor to the West! Even with regard to those whose "cruelty" has never stood trial, justice continues to be exercised. The defendant, deemed innocent, has the right to a defense, to consideration. It is admirable that justice worked that way, despite the apocalyptic atmosphere.

It must also be said that in my way of expressing myself the word *face* must not be understood in a narrow way. This possibility for the human of signifying in its uniqueness, in the humility of its nakedness and mortality, the Lordship of its reminder—word of God—of my accountability for him, and of my chosenness qua unique to this responsibility, can come from a bare arm sculpted by Rodin.

In *Life and Fate*, Grossman tells how in Lubyanka, in Moscow, before the infamous gate where one could convey letters or packages to friends and relatives arrested for "political crimes" or get news of them, people formed a line, each reading on the nape of the person in front of him the feelings and hopes of his misery.

Q.: And the nape is a face...

E.L.: Grossman isn't saying that the nape is a face, but that all the weakness, all the mortality, all the naked and disarmed mortality of the other can be read from it. He doesn't say it that way, but the face can assume meaning on what is the "opposite" of the face! The face, then, is not the color of the eyes, the shape of the nose, the ruddiness of the cheeks, etc.

Q.: One last question: what is your major preoccupation today in your work?

E.L.: The essential theme of my research is the deformalization of the notion of time. Kant says it is the form of all experience. All human experience does in fact take on a temporal form. The transcendental philosophy descended from Kant filled that form with a sensory content coming from experience or, since Hegel, that form has led dialectically toward a content. These philosophers never required, for the constitution of that form of temporality itself, a condition in a certain conjuncture of "matter" or events, in a meaningful content somehow prior to form. The constitution of time in Husserl is also a constitution of time in terms of an already effective consciousness of presence in its disappearance and in its "retention," its immanence, and its anticipation—disappearance and immanence that already imply what is to be established, without any indication being furnished on the privileged empirical situation to which those modes of disappearance in the past and imminence in the future would be attached.

Hence, what seems remarkable in Heidegger is precisely the fact of posing the question: what are the situations or circumstances characteristic of concrete existence to which the passation of the past, the presentification of the present, and the futurition of the future—called *ecstases*—are essentially and originally attached? The fact of being, without having chosen to do so, of dealing with possibles always already begun without us— an ecstasis of "always already"; the fact of a control over things, near them in representation or knowing—an ecstasis of the present; the fact of existing-toward-death—an ecstasis of the future. This, more or less (for there is a lot more to that philosophy) is the perspective opened up by Heidegger.

Franz Rosenzweig, for his part, and without resorting to the same terminology or referring to the same situations, also sought those "privileged circumstances" of the lived experience in which temporality is constituted. He thought the past in terms of the idea and religious consciousness of creation, the present in terms of listening to and receiving revelation, and the future in terms of the hope of redemption, thus raising those biblical references of thought to the level of the conditions of temporality itself. The biblical references are claimed as modes of original human consciousness, common to an immense part of humanity. Rosenzweig's philosophical audacity consists precisely in referring the past to the creation and not the creation to the past, the present to revelation and not revelation to the present, the future to redemption and not redemption to the future.

Perhaps what I have told you about the obligation toward the other prior to all contract (a reference to a past that has never been present!) and about dying for the other (a reference to a future that will never be my present) will seem to you, after this last evocation of Heidegger and Rosenzweig, like a preface to possible research.

TRANSLATED BY MICHAEL B. SMITH

The Proximity of the Other

Q.: You write in *Totality and Infinity*, "First philosophy is an ethics." Do you mean to say by this that philosophy should address itself to what is most humanly urgent?

E.L.: When I speak of first philosophy, I am referring to a philosophy of dialogue which cannot *not* be an ethics. Even the philosophy that questions the meaning of being does so starting from the encounter with the other. This would amount to a manner of subordinating knowledge and objectivization to the encounter with the other that is presupposed in all language. To address oneself to someone expresses the ethical disturbance that the interruption of the *conatus essendi* (formula for the essence of being in Spinoza) provokes in me, in the tranquillity of the perseverance of my being, of my egoism as a necessary stage.

A coming out of oneself which appeals to the other, to the stranger. As for the encounter, it comes to pass between strangers; otherwise, the encounter would be kinship. All thinking is subordinated to the ethical relation, to that which in the other is infinitely other, the infinitely other for whom I have nostalgia. To think the other depends upon an irreducible anxiety for the other. Love is not conscience. It is because there is a vigilance before any awakening that the *cogito* is possible, in such a way that ethics is before ontology. Prior to the arrival of the human, there is already vigilance with regard to the other. The transcendental I in its nudity comes from our awakening by and for another.

Every encounter begins with a benediction contained in the word *bonjour*. This *bonjour*, already presupposed by every cogito and by all self-reflection, would be the first transcendence. This greeting addressed to the other man is an invocation. I therefore insist upon the primacy of the benevolent relation in regard to the other. Even if there is ill will on the part of the other, the attention to and welcome of the other (like his recognition of me) marks the anteriority of the good over and against evil.

Q.: Your thinking would amount to an attempt to step out of what you call the formless or the "there is" [il y a], the phenomenon of impersonal being without generosity. How does being pass from nonsense to "something that is"?

E.L.: This concept of the "there is" represents the phenomenon of absolutely impersonal being. "There is" posits the simple fact of being without objects, being in complete silence, in utter non-thought, in every manner of retreat from existence.

"Il y a" in the sense of "il pleut," "il fait beau" ("it" is raining, "it" is nice outside). This "it" marks the impersonal character of this stage in which impersonal consciousness experiences something without objects, without substance—a nothing that is not a nothing, for this nothing is full of murmuring, a murmuring which is unnamed. In this horrifying experience of annihilation, the thematic of the "there is" roots the construction of a subject who, from out of the neuter, will affirm and posit himself. Out of the "there is," out of the enveloping presence of anonymity weighing heavily on the human being, subjectivity emerges, in spite of that which annuls it. This first emergence of the self, this eruption of being, starts with the recognition of things, but is also the stage of enjoyment of life and self-sufficiency. This love of self is an egoism which founds a being and constitutes the first ontological experience. That experience calls for the opening of and veritable departure from self. The human will pass by another decisive stage in which the subject, despite its satisfaction, fails to suffice unto itself. Every departure from self represents the fissure that is installed within the same in relation to the other. Desire metamorphosed into an attitude of openness to exteriority, openness that is a call and a response to the other: the proximity of the other is the origin of every putting in question of the self.

Q.: If Martin Buber conceives a relation of I and Thou in all reciprocity, you find this relation surpassed in the relation of the subject to the other, who would be much more than a Thou. The other would be alterity itself, unreachable alterity.

E.L.: Martin Buber was, in effect, the first to conceive the distinction between a thing that is and a thing that is for me, an "it," an object that I can know. He then opposed to the "it" the relation to an other who is not an object, and who is the one to whom I say "thou." Buber consequently opposed the I-Thou relation to the I-It relation. He thought that the I-Thou relation was irreducible to the I-It relation and that the social relation to the other presented a total autonomy in regard to the establishment of things and in regard to knowledge. The social relation could not be a knowledge because the correlative of this social relation is a human being to whom I say "Thou."

I have thus asked myself whether the true relation to the other rests upon this reciprocity that Buber finds in the relation of the I-Thou. Buber says that when I say "Thou," I know that I am saying "Thou" to someone who is an I, and that he says "Thou" to me. Consequently, in the I-Thou relation, we are from the outset in society with each other, but this is a society in which we are equals, the one in regard to the other; I am to the other what the other is to me.

My aim consisted in putting into question this initial reciprocity with the other whom I address. Would it not firstly be him toward whom I have the sort of relation one has in regard to one who is weaker? For example, I am generous toward the other without this generosity being immediately claimed as reciprocal. Although Buber was one of the first thinkers to place the accent on the I-Thou relation relative to that of the I-It, this concept of reciprocity troubled me because, once one is generous in the hope of reciprocity, that relation no longer arises from generosity but from the commercial relation, from the exchange of proper procedures. In the relation to the other, the other appears to me as him to whom I owe something and in regard to whom I have a responsibility. Whence the asymmetry of the I-Thou relation and the radical inequality between the I and the Thou, for every relation with the other is a relation with a being toward whom I have obligations. I therefore insist upon the signification of this gratuitousness of the *for-the-other*, reposing upon the responsibility that already lies dormant. The *for-the-other* arises in the I like a commandment heard by him, as if obedience were a state of listening for the prescription. The intrigue of alterity is born before knowledge.

Yet this apparent simplicity of the I-Thou relation, in its very asymmetry, is again disturbed by the appearance of the third man who places himself beside the other, the Thou. The third is himself a neighbor, a face, an unreachable alterity.

Here, starting from the third, is the proximity of a human plurality. Between the second and third men, there can be relations in which the one is guilty toward the other. I pass from the relation in which I am obligated and responsible to a relation where I ask myself who is the first. I pose the question of justice: within this plurality, which one is the other par excellence? How to judge? How to compare unique and incomparable others? He for whom one is responsible is unique, and he who is responsible cannot delegate his responsibility. In this sense, he is also unique. At the moment of knowledge and objectivity, beyond and within the nudity of the face, Greek wisdom begins.

I pass from the relation without reciprocity to a relation wherein, among the members of society, there is a reciprocity, an equality. My search for justice supposes precisely this new relation in which every excess of generosity that I should have in regard to the other is submitted to justice. In justice there is comparison, and the other has no privilege in relation to me. Between the men who enter into that relation, there must be established a *rapport* that presupposes the comparison among them, that is, that presupposes a justice and a citizenship. A limitation of this initial responsibility, justice nevertheless always marks a subordination of the I to the other.

Starting from the third, the problem of fundamental justice is posed, that of the right which initially is always that of the other. Vladimir Jankélévitch has put it well: "We have no right, it is always the other who has rights." It is indispensable to know what the second [the other] is in relation to the third, and the third in relation to the second. Who passes before whom?

That is the principal idea: I pass from the order of responsibility, from mercy, where even that which should not concern me concerns me, to justice, which limits that initial precedence of the other from which we started.

Q.: To return to my question about the relation to the other, you write that "the relations with alterity cut through those in which the same dominates or absorbs, or encompasses the other." What really is alterity?

E.L.: In this relation to the other there is no fusion; the relation to the other is envisaged as alterity. The other is alterity. The thought of Buber pushed me to engage in a phenomenology of sociality, which is more than the human. Sociality is, for me, the better-than-human. It is the good, not the makeshift of an impossible fusion. Within the alterity of the face, the *for-the-other* commands the I. So it is a matter, finally, of founding justice—which hides the face—upon the obligation to the face, to the extraordinary exteriority of the face.

Sociability is this alterity of the face, of the *for-the-other* which calls me to account; it is the voice that rises in me before any verbal expression, within the mortality of the I, from the depths of my weakness. This voice is an order to respond for the life of the other man. I do not have the right to leave him alone at his death.

Q.: The access to the face is experienced in an ethical mode. The face is, by itself, a meaning. What does it offer to my regard? What does it say?

E.L.: The face is lordship and that which is without defense. What does the face say when I approach it? This face, exposed to my gaze, is disarmed. Whatever the countenance that it then takes on, whether this face belongs to an important person, accompanied by some pedigree, or a person more simple in appearance, the face is the same—exposed in its nudity. From beneath the countenance it gives itself, all its weakness pierces through and at the same time its mortality, to such an extent that I may wish to liquidate it completely. Why not? This face of the other, without recourse, without security, exposed to my gaze in its weakness and its mortality, is also the one that orders, "Thou shalt not kill." There is, in the face, the supreme authority that commands, and I always say, this is the word of God. The face is the site of the word of God, a word not thematized.

The face is this possibility of murder, this impotence of being, and this authority which commands me, "Thou shalt not kill." What thus distinguishes the face in its status from every other known object is tied to its contradictory character. It is there that all the ambiguity of the face arises. The face is wholly weakness and wholly authority. This order which it exposes to the other also concerns the demand for responsibility on my part. This infinite which, in a sense, offers itself to me, marks a non-indifference for me in my relation to the other, wherein I am never through with him. When I say "I do my duty," I lie, for I am never exonerated before the other. And in this "never exonerated" there is the mise-en-scène of the infinite, an inexhaustible, concrete responsibility. The impossibility of saying "no." Anarchy which makes me say to the other, "here I am" or "send me." Responsibility of which one will never be acquitted and always—once again—future; not what is yet to come [à venir] but what comes to pass [advient]. A responsibility which is prior to deliberation to which I have been exposed, to which I am dedicated before being dedicated to myself.

Q.: You write: "I am for myself to the sole degree to which I am responsible," but you go still farther than that since you define the I as being the hostage of the widow, the beggar, and the orphan. Would not this interpellated I be the hostage of every face that offers itself to him?

E.L.: This manner of being for the other, that is, of being responsible for the other is something terrible, for it means that if the other does something, it is I who am responsible. The hostage is the one who is found responsible for what he has not done. The one is responsible for the sin of the other. I am in principle responsible, prior to the justice that makes distributions, before the measurements of justice. This is not fabricated; it is real, you know! When you have encountered a human being, you cannot simply leave him alone. Most of the time one leaves things; one says, "I've done everything!" But that is just it—no, one has done nothing! It is this sentiment, this consciousness that one has done nothing, that gives the I the status of a hostage with the responsibility of one who is not guilty, who is innocent. The innocent one: what a word! It is he who does no harm [from *in-* + *nocere*]. It is he who pays for an other. The other engages you in a situation where you are obligated without culpability, but your obligation is not less for all that. It is at the same time a charge. It is heavy and, if you will, goodness is just that. The trace of the infinite is inscribed in my obligation in regard to an other in that moment which corresponds to the call.

Q.: You just evoked goodness: this is not a philosophical language, and yet... ! I know that you were profoundly troubled by the witness of Vassily Grossman in his book *Life and Fate*. Could you speak to us of this?

E.L.: That book describes the situation in Europe at the time of Stalin and Hitler. Vassily Grossman represents this society as a completely dehumanized one. There is, of course, the life of the camps; it was the same thing under Hitler and under Stalin. Life seems to be premised upon the total contempt of respect for man, for the human person. Nevertheless, as concerns Stalin, that society came out of the search for a liberated humanity. That Marxism could have turned into Stalinism is the greatest offense to the cause of humanity, for Marxism carried a hope for humanity; this was perhaps one of the greatest psychological shocks for the European of the twentieth century. Grossman's eight hundred pages offer a complete spectacle of desolation and dehumanization. This book is absolutely desperate and in it I see no horizon, no salvation for the human race.

Yet within that decomposition of human relations, within that sociological misery, goodness persists. In the relation of one man to an other, goodness is possible. There is a long monologue where Ikonnikov—the character who expresses the ideas of the author—casts doubts upon all social sermonizing, that is, upon all reasonable organization with an ideology, with plans. Impossibility of goodness as a regime, an organized system, a social institution. Every attempt to organize humanity fails. The only thing that remains undying is the goodness of everyday, ongoing life. Ikonnikov calls that "the little act of goodness."

Q.: This passage is indeed very important and if you will allow me, I would like to cite it. Mostovkoi is in prison and he attempts to read the writings of Ikonnikov. He reads these words: "The majority of beings who live on earth do not set as their goal to define the good. Of what does the good consist? The good is not in nature, neither is it in the sermonizing of prophets, the great social doctrines or the ethics of philosophers. Yet simple people carry in their hearts the love for all that is alive; they naturally love life, they protect life." And a little farther on, he adds, "It is thus that there exists, next to that great, that so terrible Good, the human good in everyday life. This is the goodness of an old woman who, by the side of the road, gives a piece of bread to a passing convict; it is the goodness of a soldier who passes his water bottle to an injured enemy, the goodness of youth that feels sympathy for old age, the goodness of a peasant who hides an old Jewish man in his granary, etc. . . . ."

E.L.: The book is terrifying, and of all its pages this "little goodness" is the sole positive thing. He even specifies that this "little goodness" of the one-for-the-other is a goodness without witnesses. This goodness escapes every ideology; Grossman says, "One could qualify it as goodness without thinking." Why without thinking? Because it is goodness outside of every system, every religion, every social organization. Gratuitous, that goodness is eternal.

It is the weak spirits who defend it and who work for its perpetuation from one being to another. It is so fragile before the power of evil. Grossman writes that it would be as if all these simple spirits wanted to extinguish the world conflagration with a wash basin. This book leaves us in perplexity; for despite all the horrors that men have engendered, this poor goodness holds its own. It is that "mad goodness" which is most human in man. It defines man despite his impotence, and Ikonnikov will again have a beautiful image with which to qualify it: "It is beautiful and impotent, like the dew." What freshness within this despair! But it is true that once this goodness is organized it is extinguished. Despite the rottenness, the amplitude of evil realized in the name of this good, the human subsists under this form of the one-for-the-other, in the relation of the one to the other. The other as face, extraordinary witness of my freedom, the alterity of the infinite which commands me and elects me for its service, represents the ethical agitation of being and will lead being to the path of ethical dis-interestedness. The advent of the human to the ethical passes by this ethical suffering, by this agitation that every face brings with it, even in an orderly world.

This holiness of the human cannot be said starting from any category. Are we entering into a moment in history where the good must be loved without promises? That is perhaps the end of all sermonizing. Might we stand at the eve of a new form of faith, a faith without triumph, as though the only incontestable value were holiness, when the sole right to recompense belonged to the one who is not expecting any? The first and the last manifestation of God would be to be without a promise.

TRANSLATED BY BETTINA BERGO

Who Shall Not Prophesy?

Q.: The global significance of your work is that of finding the meaning of being beyond being, relativizing history and system by that which does not belong to history and to the system: the face of the other which stands in the trace of the infinite. Is this interpretative key correct?

E.L.: I would not say the "meaning of being," but "meaning," namely, a rationality, an intelligibility. When I evoke the face of the other, the trace of the infinite, or the word of God, the important idea is that of a significance of meaning which originally is neither theme nor object of a knowledge, nor the being of a being, nor representation. A God who concerns me by the word—expressed in the form of the face of the other man—is a transcendence that never becomes immanence. The face of the other is his manner of signifying. I also use another expression: God never takes form or body; he never becomes, properly speaking, a being. This is his invisibility. This idea is, in effect, essential to the reading of my book *Of God Who Comes to Mind*.

Q.: For what reason does the face I encounter in daily experience not belong to history; why is it not a phenomenon, a simple experience? Why does it tear itself out of its context?

E.L.: I have always described the face of the neighbor as the carrier of an order, imposing upon the I in respect to the other a gratuitous responsibility—and an untransferable one, as though the I were elected and unique—wherein the other is absolutely other, that is, incomparable. Yet the men who surround me form a crowd! Whence the question: *who* is my neighbor? An inevitable question of justice. The necessity of comparing the incomparable, of knowing men; from this comes the fact of their appearing as plastic forms with visible faces and, in a certain way, as "defaced": like a grouping out of which the uniqueness of the face pulls itself as out of a context, this is the source of my obligation toward others. It is a source to which the very search for justice returns, ultimately, and whose forgetting risks transforming the sublime and difficult work of justice into a purely political calculation—to the point of totalitarian abuses.

Q.: Historicism, materialism, structuralism, ontology: would the limit of all these philosophical figures lie precisely in their fundamental inability to push themselves beyond being and history, their restriction of meaning to essence?

E.L.: In a large sense this is true. Yet I am not tempted by a philosophy of history and am not assured of its finality. I do not say that all is for the best, and the idea of progress is not very certain to me. Yet I think that the responsibility for the other or, if you wish, the epiphany of the human face constitutes something like a breaking through the crust of "the being persevering in its being," the being concerned about itself. Responsibility for the other, the dis-interested *for-the-other* of holiness: I am not saying that men are saints or that they go toward holiness, I am only saying that the vocation of holiness is recognized by every human being as a value and that this recognition defines the human. The human has pierced through imperturbable being! Neither social organizations nor institutions can, in the name of purely ontological necessities, assure or even produce holiness; nevertheless, there have been saints.

Q.: Should one then read the nihilist outcome of contemporary philosophy not as the destiny of philosophy as such, but only that of this particular philosophy which, qua ontology, does not accept the risk of the beyond of being and of transcendence?

E.L.: Agreed, but I will add to this that my propositions lay no claim to the exclusivism of the philosophies of history. If, according to my way of seeing it, the very origin of intelligibility and meaning goes back to responsibility for the other, then it turns out that ontology, objective knowledge, and political forms are arranged according to this meaning and are necessary to its signification. We said above that the origin of the meaningful in the face of the other nevertheless calls—before the factical plurality of humans—to justice and knowledge; the exercise of justice demands tribunals and political institutions and even, paradoxically, a certain violence which all justice implies. Violence is originally justified as the defense of the other, of the neighbor (if he be my parent or my people!), but it is violence *for* someone.

Q.: The notion of meaning is fundamental in your work. In your most recent writings, it reappears continually. What is the philosophical status of this notion? Is it really so certain that philosophy must search for meaning?

E.L.: Except that the philosopher, the scholar, and the statesman who reason and judge will not be excluded from the spiritual. Yet philosophy's meaning is originally found in the human, in the initial fact that man is concerned by the other man. This is at the base of the truism according to which few things interest man so much as the other man. I cannot explain further the moment when rationality commences. A primary notion of signification to which reason goes back within the weight of being, and which one cannot reduce to something else. It is phenomenologically irreducible: meaning signifies. To seek the definition of meaning is like attempting to reduce the effect of a poem to its causes and to its transcendental conditions. The definition of poetry is perhaps that poetic vision is truer and, in a certain sense, more "ancient" than the vision of its conditions. In reflecting upon the transcendental conditions of the poem, you have already lost the poem.

Q.: You reject the perspective of the indefinite dissemination of meaning. Is it correct to say that your conclusions are opposed to those of the theoreticians of writing, Derrida and Blanchot?

E.L.: Yes and no, because I have great esteem for the one and the other, and I admire their speculative gifts. On many points I rejoin their analyses. However, it is not starting from writing that problems come to me, and in regard to Scripture—to Holy Scripture—our positions perhaps diverge. I have often asked myself apropos of Derrida whether the *différance* of the present which leads him to the deconstruction of notions does not attest to the very prestige that, in his view, eternity, the "great presence," and being conserve, and which corresponds to the uncontested priority of the theoretical and the truth of the theoretical, relative to which temporality would be a failure? I wonder whether time, in its very diachrony, is not *better* than eternity and the very order of the Good?

Is not diachrony, beyond the synchrony of every eternal presence, the nodal point of the irreversible (or disinterested) relation of me to the neighbor, to the other? Is not diachrony the impossibility of synchrony and yet a nonindifference, a movement toward God, an *à-Dieu*, and so already love?

Q.: Is it truly possible to exclude all analogical mediations from the use of human language relating to God?

E.L.: In no way do I exclude that language, but I am perhaps concerned not to forget its metaphoric signification; yet what I seek is what Husserl called an *originäre Gegebenheit* ("originary givenness"), the "concrete circumstances" where a meaning can alone come to mind. That is not a gratuitous or vain search for a chronological priority of some sort. I believe that the most fecund contribution of phenomenology has been the insistence upon the fact that the gaze absorbed by the given has already *forgotten* to refer the given back to the entirety of the spiritual procedure which conditioned the upsurge of the given, and thus to its concrete signification. The given, when separated from everything that has been forgotten, is only an abstraction whose mise-en-scène phenomenology reconstitutes. Husserl always speaks of the "blinders" which deform naive vision. It is not only a matter of the narrowness of its objective field, but of the obnubilation of its psychic horizons, as if the object, naively given, already veiled the eyes that see it. To see philosophically, that is, without a naive blindness, is to reconstitute for the naive gaze (which is still that of positive science) the concrete situation of appearing; it is to do one's phenomenology, to return to the neglected concreteness of its mise-en-scène, which delivers the *meaning* of the given and, behind its *quiddity*, its mode of being.

To search for the "origin" of the word *God* and the concrete circumstances of its significance is absolutely necessary. One begins by accepting His word in the name of the social authority of religion. How to be sure that the word thus accepted is indeed that which God speaks? One must search for the original experience. Philosophy—or phenomenology—is necessary in order to recognize His voice. I have written that it is in the face of the other person that God speaks to me for the first time. It is in the encounter with the other man that God "comes to mind" or "comes into sense."

Q.: One has the impression that you have wanted in some fashion to reverse the relation of exclusion between reason and violence, such as Eric Weil proposed when he argued, on the contrary, for the strict solidarity between the two within the totalitarian discourse.

E.L.: I have a great deal of admiration for the work, and much devotion to the memory of Eric Weil. At no time have I wanted to exclude justice (that would be stupid) from the human order. But I have attempted to rejoin justice starting from what one might call charity, which appeared to me as an unlimited obligation in regard to the other and in that sense an accession to his uniqueness as a person, which is love, disinterested love, without concupiscence. I already told you how this initial obligation, before the multiplicity of humans, becomes justice. But it is very important in my view that justice flow or issue from the preeminence of the other. It is necessary that the institutions required by justice be overseen by charity, from which justice itself issues. The justice that is inseparable from institutions, and thus from politics, risks causing us to misrecognize the face of the other man. The pure rationality of justice in Eric Weil, as in Hegel, comes to make us think of human particularity as negligible and as if it were not that of a uniqueness but rather that of an anonymous individuality. The determinism of the rational totality runs the risk of the totalitarianism that certainly never abandons ethical language and has always spoken—and still speaks—of the *good* and the *better*, the famous language "of great boasts" of Psalm 12:4. Fascism itself never admitted that it glorified crime. I therefore say that Eric Weil, the philosopher and infinitely respectable man, had thoughts more utopian than my own, precisely because it is very difficult to vouchsafe oneself against totalitarianism through a politics of the pure concept that treats the attachment to the uniqueness of the other and the radical *for-the-other* of the I as subjectivism. It seems to me that rational justice is compromised when the relation with the other is visibly profaned. And there, between purely rational justice and injustice, there is an appeal to the "wisdom" of the I whose possibilities perhaps comprise no principle formulable a priori.

Q.: You assert that your way of naming God belongs strictly to philosophical discourse, and not to religion. To religion would belong the task of consolation, not that of demonstration. What does this mean precisely? Is religion perhaps something superfluous?

E.L.: The question is more complex than that. Both are necessary; they are not on the same level. What I want to show is transcendence within natural thinking, in the approach to the other. Natural theology is necessary in order thereafter to recognize the voice and the accent of God in Scripture. A necessity which is perhaps the motif of religious philosophy itself. The seducer knows all the guiles of language and all its ambiguities; he knows all the terms of the dialectic. He exists precisely qua moment of human freedom, and the most dangerous of seducers is the one who leads you on through pious words to violence, to contempt for the other.

Q.: What is the exact position of the relation between Judaism and Hellenism that you propose?

E.L.: I'm all for the Greek tradition! It is not at the beginning of things, but everything must be able to be "translated" into Greek. The Septuagint translation of the Scriptures symbolizes this necessity. It is the theme of a talmudic text, which I had to comment upon last year.[1] There is, as you know, a legend concerning the translation of the Bible into Greek: it is said that Ptolemy sent seventy Jewish scholars to Alexandria, that he locked them up in seventy separate chambers to translate the Hebrew Bible into Greek. All of them translated in the same manner, and even the corrections that they judged necessary were the same.[2] Father Barthélemy, Professor at the Catholic University of Freiburg, has called this "a jolly good story for the tourists!" Nevertheless, this legend is taken up in the Talmud. For rabbinic thought, it is evidently an apologetic text, a midrash. The Talmud wanted to approve both the translation of the Bible into Greek and the principle of correction. There are ideas which have their original meaning in biblical thought, and which we must recount otherwise in Greek. But Greek is the language of a thinking which is not forewarned, of the universality of a pure knowing. All signification, all intelligibility, all spirit is not knowledge, but everything may be translated into Greek. With circumlocutions one can construct the narrative of a spirituality rebellious to forms of knowledge.

What I call "Greek" is the manner or mode of our university language as the heir of Greece. At the university—even in the Catholic and the Hebrew University—one speaks Greek, even when, and if, one does not know the difference between alpha and beta.

Q.: The transformation of ontological categories into ethical categories goes all the way to posing the new fundamental question: Do I have a right to be? Does this question belong to the consciousness of original sin?

E.L.: I think that philosophical discourse is independent of this guilt and that the question "Have I the right to be?" expresses above all the human in its concern for the other. I have written much on this theme, it is now my principal theme: is not my place in being, the *Da* of my *Dasein*, already a usurpation, already a violence in respect to the other? A preoccupation that has nothing ethereal about it, nothing abstract: the press speaks to us of the Third World, and we are well off here, our daily meal is assured. At the cost of whom? One can ask oneself this.

Pascal said the I is detestable. In the sovereign affirmation of the I, the perseverance of beings in their being is repeated, but also the consciousness of the horror that egoism inspires in myself. Pascal also says that my place in the sun is the image and the beginning of the usurpation of the whole earth.

If scruples are always already remorse, I wonder if the human itself is not sufficient. Certainly one cannot say that Pascal was unaware of original sin.

Q.: Someone has written that the ethical responsibility of which you speak is abstract and devoid of concrete content. Does that seem to you to be a valid critique?

E.L.: I never claimed to describe human reality in its immediate appearance, but rather that which human depravity itself could not efface: the human vocation for holiness. I do not argue for human holiness; I only say that man cannot contest its supreme value. In 1968, the year of contestation in the universities and around the universities, all values were "up in the air" except that of the other man to which one had to devote oneself. The young people who for hours devoted themselves to all sorts of amusements and disorders went at the end of the day to visit the striking workers at Renault as though they were going to prayer. Man is a being who recognizes holiness and the forgetting of self. The "for-oneself" always lends itself to suspicion. We live in a State in which the idea of justice is superimposed upon that initial charity, but in this initial charity resides the human. Man is not only a being who understands what being signifies, as Heidegger would have it, but also a being who has already understood and grasped the commandment of holiness in the face of the other man. When one says that there are altruistic instincts at the origin, one has already recognized that God has spoken. He began to speak very early. Anthropological meaning of instinct! In the daily Jewish liturgy, the first prayer of the morning says, "Blessed be God, Master of the world, who taught the rooster to distinguish the day from the night." In the rooster's song, the first revelation: the awakening to the light.

Q.: Is there a future for peace? What is the contribution of Christianity to the construction of peace?

E.L.: Ah, you are requesting a prophecy from me! It is true that all men are prophets. Does not Moses say in the words of Numbers 11:29, "That all the people of God be prophets," and does not Amos go still further, to all of humanity: "The Eternal God has spoken, who shall not prophesy?" (Amos 3:8). And yet it is difficult for me to make predictions, unless the verses I just cited are themselves favorable prophecies.

I also believe that the trials undergone by humanity over the course of the twentieth century are, in their horror, not only a measure of human depravity, but also a renewed reminder of our vocation. I have the impression that they have modified something in us. I am thinking notably that the Passion of Israel at Auschwitz has profoundly marked Christianity itself, and that Judeo-Christian friendship is an element of peace in which the person of John Paul II represents a hope.

Q.: What is the value of liturgy and prayer?

E.L.: One does not pray for oneself. Nevertheless the Jewish prayer, the daily prayer, replaces the sacrifices in the Temple according to Jewish theology. Yet consequently, like the sacrifice in the Temple, which was burnt offering, prayer is wholly offering. There is an exception when one prays for persecuted Israel. In that case one is praying for the community, but this is a prayer for the people who are called to reveal the glory of God. In praying to God, one prays *for* God.

When one has true pain, one can mention it in prayer. But shall we thus suppress a suffering that precisely erases sins by expiating them? If one wants to escape one's own suffering, how will one expiate one's faults? The question is more complex. In our suffering God suffers with us. Does not the Psalmist say, in the words of Psalm 91:15: "I am with him in pain"? God is the one who suffers the most in human suffering. The I who suffers prays for the suffering of God, who suffers by the sins of man and by the painful expiation of the sin. The kenosis of God! Prayer, in its entirety, is not for oneself.

There are not many souls who pray this prayer of the just. There are certainly many levels. I have presented to you one of the most rigorous theological conceptions. I believe that the less elevated forms of prayer preserve much of its piety.

TRANSLATED BY BETTINA BERGO

Responsibility and Substitution

Q.: Central to your concept of the relationship with the other is the notion of substitution. That notion allows us to conceive an identity posited straightaway in the accusative, as you say, and thus to understand our relationship with the other in the form of the one-for-the-other, and finally to reach an "untimely consideration" of humanism, that is to say, a "humanism of the other man." Would you please explain the importance of the notion of substitution in relation to the critique of the privileges granted in the Western tradition to the theoretical, to representation, to knowledge, and to the subject?

E.L.: For me, the notion of substitution is tied to the notion of responsibility. To substitute oneself does not amount to putting oneself in the place of the other man in order to feel what he feels; it does not involve becoming the other nor, if he be destitute and desperate, the courage of such a trial. Rather, substitution entails bringing comfort by associating ourselves with the essential weakness and finitude of the other; it is to bear his weight while sacrificing one's interestedness and complacency-in-being, which then turn into responsibility for the other.

In human existence, there is, as it were, interrupting or surpassing the vocation of being, another vocation: that of the other, his existing, his destiny. Here, the existential adventure of the neighbor would matter more to the I than does its own, and would thus posit the I straightaway as responsible for this alterity in its trials, as if the upsurge of the human within the economy of being overturned ontology's meaning and plot. All of the culture of the human seems to me to be oriented by this new "plot," in which the in-itself of a being persisting in its being is surpassed in the gratuity of being outside-of-oneself, for the other, in the act of sacrifice or the possibility of sacrifice, in holiness.

Q.: You often speak of the relationship with the other as a face-to-face relationship. This expression has caused some misunderstandings because it has led some (Blanchot, for example) to believe there is an opposition between spoken and written language. It is my understanding that this is erroneous, because you do not accept Plato's suspicion of writing.

E.L.: The face-to-face is neither a declaration of war against the other, nor is it one arrogance facing another arrogance. Let me remind you of what I say about the face. It is language even before becoming fixed in representation, a call to the devotion that I owe the other. The dis-interestedness of which I am speaking is precisely what is concrete in the encounter with the other person's face. The I suspends its persistence in being, its *conatus essendi*, in its subjugation to the other, as if the I were "guilty" with respect to the neighbor. This is a new style of accusative: guilt without fault, "indebtedness" without loan. An obligation of responsibility for which no one else can be substituted, a debt that no one can pay in the place of me and thus, for that me, the very concreteness of its uniqueness as an I. Correlative with this uniqueness of the I founded in responsibility is the neighbor, "unique in the world"—as in the intimacy of love—through his face. Love does not begin in the erotic. In love without concupiscence, in the disinterested love of responsibility, the beloved one is "unique in the world" for the one who loves. The I and the other, in their uniqueness, are no longer simple individuals within a genus; they are not anonymous points within the logical extension of a concept.
"We are each of us guilty with respect to all, and I more so than all the others," says a character in Dostoevsky's *The Brothers Karamazov*, thereby expressing this "originary constitution" of the I or the unique, in a responsibility for the neighbor or the other, and the impossibility of escaping responsibility or of being replaced. This impossibility of escaping is not a servitude, but rather a being chosen. Religions that have recourse to this term, *chosenness*, see in it the supreme dignity of the human.

Q.: What is the connection between responsibility and justice? Does responsibility toward the other man depend upon a society organized into a State? Or, on the contrary, can we say that institutions and juridical procedures not only are founded on the notion of responsibility for the other, but also, in some way, give it limits?

E.L.: Anonymity settles by necessity into the social reality, interrupting the responsibility between the I and the other, and bringing the uniqueness of the I and the other back to the individuality of the individual within the extension of a species. Reification of the human within the social multiplicity!

The exceptional position of the I as the only one having to respond for the other thus finds itself understood starting from the generality of a code of laws, relevant to all of us. For indeed, in this social multiplicity we are not paired off with the neighbor for whom I am responsible, but are linked also with the third and fourth parties, etc. Each person is, to the I, an other! The exclusive relation of the I to the neighbor is modified. How, in effect, can one be answerable for all? Who comes first among all? This is the essential ambiguity of the relation between the ethical order of the responsibility for the other and the juridical order, to which the ethical nevertheless appeals. This is because in approaching in charity the first one to come along, the I runs the risk of being uncharitable toward the third party, who is also his neighbor. Judgment, comparison, are necessary. One must consent to comparing incomparable beings: the I's, all of them unique. One must be able to classify their uniqueness as a type without chaining them to it! The State, general laws, are necessary. Institutions are necessary to carry out decisions. Every work of politics and justice is necessary. This order negates mercy, yet is called into being by this very mercy with a concern to recognize all the others who form the human multiplicity. This is the order that, perhaps, will be able to reveal its charitable roots in democracy. Justice and the just State constitute the forum enabling the existence of charity within the human multiplicity. This differs from Hobbes's concept of man being "a wolf to man," wherein the State only signifies the limitation of natural cruelty. For us, quite the opposite is true. As the issue of a certain limitation of charity, yet still grounded in love, the State can always review its laws and its justice. Is this concern for reconsideration—for amelioration—not in effect the essence of democracy and of the liberal State, the sign of a mercy and charity that breathe there? An effort in view of an always better law. Is this not a striving to find an ever-improving law? Amelioration and renewal which are not obtained by simple logical deduction of a doctrine that is more and more precise. Rather, they demand a moral effort from the human. When the State lays claim to an unvarying justice that is logically deduced, one must suspect Stalinism and fascism.

The State in which justice is not separate from mercy is a society where there remains the possibility, upon the return of the verdict, for the manifestation in public opinion and in the elite of a consideration in favor of the person judged guilty. To turn toward the face of the condemned! "You shall not be partial in judgment," states Deuteronomy 1:17. In Hebrew, this translates thus: "Do not look at an individual's face when judging."[1] Yet the Bible also says, "May the Eternal One bestow his favor on you [lit., make his face to shine upon thee]" (Num. 6:26). Do those sayings contradict each other? The Talmud responds, "The first before the verdict, the second afterward." And perhaps, across this surplus of charity over justice—but a charity coming in its proper time, after justice has been administered—God comes to mind in Western humanity. Judaism—in the guise of a parable—goes so far as to invent for God a prayer that the Eternal One addresses, in some fashion, to Himself: "May my mercy suppress my anger, that is, the strictness of my justice" (Berakhot 7a). Charity or mercy makes it possible for man, created in God's image, to be "otherwise than being." This means that man is capable of putting the other's existence before his own. This gives meaning to my expression, *a humanism of the other man*. This is not the affirmation of human nature as a matter of rights, but rather as a matter of obligations. This is closer to Kant than to Hegel and is, as a result, the challenge that Kant brings to Hegel.

Q.: In *Beyond the Verse*, you speak about a "writing before the letter." This is because there is no literal sense, on account of the essential metaphoricity of language and because words refer "laterally to other words," as you say in your 1972 *Humanisme de l'autre homme*. What are the theoretical consequences with respect to the conception of reality which derives from this infinite referral, by means of which signification and even experience become reading, exegesis, hermeneutics? Does not this vision of reality give the value of truth—at the methodological and exegetical level—to literature, which demonstrates that we are wrong to perceive as primordial the significations we habitually assign to words, as if they served to express our immediate and sensible experiences?

E.L.: To the extent that writing is not limited in our culture of the book to the information deriving from the pragmatism of our daily actions, our technical ambitions, and our scientific calculations—exegesis enhances and ceaselessly renews the textual meaning of the written and "raises it up to truth." As if writing, in its concern to expose in the form of invariable signs the ideas suggested by an interior voice, found itself, in what is written, inspired and overwhelmed by the spirit bringing forth a message, a "poem," whose obvious meaning is ceaselessly raised to the level of truth by exegesis. This is the marvel of writing, in which Husserl's famous noetico-noematic parallelism is contested, and where the infinite Cartesian God finds enough room in the notion of the finite! As if the writer, the poet, could perceive from outside himself and thus already read within himself that which he thought he was merely inventing. Or, in other words, as if, poetic in its essence, writing were the result of a dictation. Holy Scriptures? Yet the national literatures of our civilization rest just as much within the infinite possibilities of hermeneutics: Goethe's *Faust*, Shakespeare's tragedies, *The Divine Comedy*, Racine, Corneille, and Molière. But today I do not intend to touch upon the many problems of the spirit that in my view solicit, from beyond the light of knowing, a reflection originating in the inter-human, in the relation to the face, where God first comes to mind.

Q.: You yourself take into account the "philosophical teachings" of the literary writers. Take Rimbaud, for example. You say that he is well aware that the sonorous contents devoid of meaning, like the vowels, have a "latent birth" in signification. Baudelaire, you claim, "attests" in his "Correspondences" "that the sensible givens overflow, by their meanings, the element in which they were thought to be locked." These references to profane writing, and thus not only to sacred writing, attest that literary writing (whether sacred or profane) makes possible the surpassing of knowledge. Why this surpassing?

E.L.: You are coming back to the ultimate problems that I had postponed in the last sentence of my previous response. Please do not hold it against me, therefore, if at this time I hold myself to a few brief and very general considerations. These considerations often have the ring of questions. Up until now in our conversation, you may have been aware of a certain distrust on my part of knowledge when it is taken for the ultimate meaning of human spirituality. A conviction which may appear all the more uncertain in that this hesitation with regard to knowledge is always expressed in the form of theoretical propositions. I have no intention of laying claim to ignorance as the foundation of philosophy. But I continue to ask myself whether all knowledge, in the search for the truth that is its meaning, might not be held to the suspension of the ipseity of the interested living being concerned straightaway with the being that carries this ipseity, in order to end up with the dis-interestedness of proximity, or of peace with the other, which is where this dis-interestedness can concretely be possible? A dis-interestedness that, in my phenomenology, is explained as a responsibility for the other, as a holiness in which the self is constituted as the uniqueness of an irreducible I, in the impossibility—ethical or holy—of seeking a replacement for oneself.

I shall not return to the phenomenology of the face, which seems important to me within the itinerary I evoked; I shall not return to the relation with the other, which is not a thematization of knowledge, but being outside-of-oneself before the face; this being outside-of-oneself is found anew in language. And language is not only linked to sonorous or visible signs, but already belongs to knowledge in the tension of being outside-of-oneself; it already belongs to the thought which is straightaway on the tip of our tongues, and, there too, language is already facing the other.

The very first Cartesian truth, the cogito, contains the possibility of bringing us back, one day, to God, but I have often wondered whether this beginning of truth is not already a prayer cried out from the depths of a solitude of doubt.

TRANSLATED BY MAUREEN GEDNEY

On the Usefulness of Insomnia

Q.: Let us imagine, Emmanuel Levinas, that a student who is about to graduate were to ask your definition of philosophy. What would you tell him?

E.L.: I would say to him that philosophy permits man to interrogate himself about what he says and about what one says to oneself in thinking. No longer to let oneself be swayed or intoxicated by the rhythm of words and the generality that they designate, but to open oneself to the uniqueness of the unique in the real, that is to say, to the uniqueness of the other. That is to say, in the final analysis, to love. To speak truly, not as one sings; to awaken; to sober up; to undo one's refrain. Already the philosopher Alain taught us to be on guard against everything that in our purportedly lucid civilization comes to us from the "merchants of sleep." Philosophy as insomnia, as a new awakening at the heart of the self-evidence which already marks the awakening, but which is still or always a dream.

Q.: Is it important to have insomnia?

E.L.: Awakening is, I believe, that which is proper to man. The search, on the part of the one who has been awakened, for a new sobering, more profound, philosophical. The encounter with texts which result from the conversations between Socrates and his interlocutors calls us to wake up, but so too does the encounter with the other man.

Q.: Is it the other who renders one a philosopher?

E.L.: In a certain sense. The encounter with the other is the great experience, the grand event. The encounter with the other is not reducible to the acquisition of a supplementary knowledge. Certainly I can never totally grasp the other, but the responsibility on his behalf—in which language originates—and the sociality with him goes beyond knowledge, even if our Greek ancestors were circumspect on this point.

Q.: We live in a society of the image, of sound, of the spectacle, in which there is little place for a step back, for reflection. If this were to accelerate, would not our society lose humanity?

E.L.: Absolutely. I have no nostalgia for the primitive. Whatever be the human possibilities that appear there—they must be stated. Though there is a danger of verbalism, language, which is a call to the other, is also the essential modality of the "self-distrust" that is proper to philosophy. I don't wish to denounce the image. But I contend that in the audiovisual domain there is considerable distraction. It is a form of dreaming which plunges us into and maintains the sleep of which we were just speaking.

Q.: Your work is altogether imbued with a moral preoccupation. Curiously, after a period of liberation in which it had been rejected, science and, notably, biological discoveries have led men to pose ethical questions. What is your view about this evolution?

E.L.: Morality has, in effect, a bad reputation. One confuses it with moralism. What is essential in the ethical is often lost in the moralism which has been reduced to an ensemble of particular obligations.

Q.: What is the ethical?

E.L.: It is the recognition of holiness. To explain: the fundamental trait of being is the preoccupation that each particular being has with his being. Plants, animals, all living things strive to exist. For each one it is the struggle for life. And is not matter, in its essential hardness, closure and shock? In the human, lo and behold, the possible apparition of an ontological absurdity. The concern for the other breaches concern for the self. This is what I call holiness. Our humanity consists in being able to recognize this priority of the other. Now you can better understand the first formulations of our conversation and why I have been so interested in language. Language is always addressed to the other, as if one could not think without already being concerned for the other. Always already my thinking is a saying. In the profundity of thinking, the *for-the-other* is articulated, or, said otherwise, goodness is articulated, love for the other, which is more spiritual than any science.

Q.: This attention to the other, can it be taught?

E.L.: In my view it is awakened in the face of the other.

Q.: Is the other about whom you speak the wholly Other, God?

E.L.: It is there in this priority of the other man over me that, before my admiration for creation, well before my search for the first cause of the universe, God comes to mind. When I speak of the other I use the term *face*. The face is that which is behind the facade and underneath "the face one puts on things." To see or to know the face is already to deface the other. The face in its nudity is the weakness of a unique being exposed to death, but at the same time the enunciation of an imperative which obliges me not to let it alone. This obligation is the first word of God. For me, theology begins in the face of the neighbor. The divinity of God is played out in the human. God descends in the "face" of the other. To recognize God is to hear his commandment "thou shalt not kill," which is not only a prohibition against murder, but a call to an incessant responsibility with regard to the other. It is to be unique, as if I were elected to this responsibility, which gives me as well the possibility of recognizing myself as unique and irreplaceable, of saying "I." Conscious that in each of my human endeavors—from which the other is never absent—I respond to his existence as a unique being.

Q.: How does a Jewish philosopher like yourself view the Barbie trial?

E.L.: For me it is of the order of the horrible. Horror that could neither be repaired nor forgotten. By no sanction, that is certain. These aren't empty words. In this certainty there is an overwhelming of many of our eschatological meditations, Jewish and non-Jewish. The limit of responsibility? This trial, more horrible than any sanction, should not happen as it is happening. Across the inevitable formalism and juridical artifices, it would be necessary to go to the sentencing without banalizing the horror in its apocalyptic dimensions.

Q.: Does this man remain "other" for you?

E.L.: If someone in his soul and his conscience can pardon him, let him do it. I cannot.

TRANSLATED BY JILL ROBBINS

PART III

A-Dieu

On Jewish Philosophy

Q.: Professor Levinas, regarding the theme of this special issue of *Revue de Métaphysique et de Morale*, you are among those who have contributed most, not only in framing the question of Jewish philosophy, but also in demonstrating its fecundity, in a sense, by the momentum and the example you give. You have written on the subject explicitly in several instances: in *Difficult Freedom*, in your foreword to *Nine Talmudic Readings*, in *Proper Names*, in *Of God Who Comes to Mind*, and in your preface to Stéphane Mosès's study of Franz Rosenzweig's philosophy. You expressed yourself again on this recently in a radio interview, published as *Ethics and Infinity*. One might think, then, that all has been said, and that the reader need only read. But if you will allow me, I would like to ask you a few questions.

E.L.: A dialogue generally includes questions. I expected to be questioned, and was attentive and curious in advance. Your first words appear to direct the conversation more particularly toward myself. Judaism and philosophy: I was thinking of their manifestation in history. But you seem to want to lead me to speak of myself.

Q.: You are right. When you state, in the interview I just mentioned, that the tradition of biblical theology and that of philosophy were for you immediately in harmony, without your ever having explicitly undertaken to reconcile them, I'm a bit surprised.

E.L.: I don't think we ever start out by explicitly setting ourselves a problem of reconciliation. Does the distinction between Judaism and philosophical reflection immediately emerge as a major conflict? We may

239

start out (and this was the case with me, since you wish to speak of me) in a world in which Judaism was lived, and in a very natural way: not at all, or not only, in what is called piety or rigorous ritualism, but above all with the sense that belonging to humanity means belonging to an order of supreme responsibility. An order in which non-Jewish books also are perceived as being concerned with the meaning of life—which is contiguous with the meaning of human existence and already, perhaps, with the meaning of being. I am thinking, for example, of the Russian novels of my very youthful years, or of "to be or not to be" in *Hamlet*, or *Macbeth*, *King Lear*, *The Miser*, *The Misanthrope*, and *Tartuffe*, which I experienced as dramas of the human condition. Philosophy speaks of this also, but in another language, that always strives to be explicit, adjusting its terms to one another and formulating problems where there are breaks in coherence. But has the handing down of the Scriptures ever taken place without transmission through a language of interpretation, which, already disengaged from the verses that sustain it, is always to be found in the gaps between utterances?

Q.: I too was not thinking of contrasting two different theses, nor two theories about the world, but two languages.

E.L.: Perhaps Jewish texts have always been understood as constantly accompanied by a layer of symbolic meaning, apologues, new interpretations to be discovered: in short, always lined with midrash. And the language of philosophy does not mean that an intellectual wind has torn the reader loose from all literalness, all particularity, all features that are "just so," and as such reduced to insignificance. What may have been wished for as holiness of life in the Judaism of my native Lithuania was not separated from the holiness of Scripture itself. That is why there was mistrust with respect to what remained obstinately mythological in a deciphered passage. There was a demythologizing of the text, but also the search for a pretext for thought, down to the very letter of the text. That was the essential aspect of that way of reading. There was also a demythologizing of what was already demythologized, a quest for meaning to be renewed. It is as if the verse were saying over and over: "Interpret me." No doubt you know Rashi's expression: "These verses cry out *darshenu* [interpret us]!" This is not yet a philosophical reading, but it is probably the acquisition of one of philosophy's virtues. Philosophical discourse will appear as a way of speaking addressed to minds which are *not* forewarned and which require totally explicit ideas, a discourse in which all that is normally taken for granted is said. A discourse addressed to Greeks! A way of speaking that is added to and animates that more confidential, closed, and firm way of speaking which is more closely linked to the bearers of meaning, signifiers which will never be released from their duties by the signified. In this, Scripture is holy. Such are the biblical verses, and even the terms used in their first, ancient deciphering by the sages of the Talmud. Tireless signifiers! But one day it is discovered that philosophy is also multiple, and that its truth is hidden, has levels, and goes progressively deeper, that its texts contradict one another, and that the systems are fraught with internal contradictions. Thus, it seems to me essential to consider the fact that the Jewish reading of Scripture is carried out in the anxiety, but also the hopeful expectation, of midrash. The Pentateuch—*Chumash*—never comes to light without Rashi.

Q.: As you say in *Nine Talmudic Readings*, the parchment is never approached "empty-handed."

E.L.: So that is my answer to your first question, and I wonder whether the great reconcilers of civilizations experienced and lived out their undertaking any differently. I do not commit the error of denying the radical difference in spirit between Scripture and philosophy. But, having emphasized their agreement *in fact* at a certain moment in time—perhaps in the maturity or modernity of Greco-biblical civilization—I am now ready to speak (if your questions lead me in that direction) of their *essential* connection in human civilization *tout court*, which is measured or hoped for as peace among men.

Q.: It just so happens I wanted to ask you, in connection with the "great reconcilers," about the traditional opposition made between Maimonides and Judah Halevi. What do you think about it?

E.L.: I do not know whether that division into two is definitive. I do not know whether all varieties of Jewish thought, even during the brief medieval period, enter into that dichotomy. It is an extremely important division, however. On one side there is the great philosophical tradition that finds intelligibility, rationality, and meaning in knowledge. In Maimonides, spirituality is essentially knowledge: knowledge in which being is present to the mind, in which that *presence* of being to the mind is the truth of being, that is, the exposure of being. It is as if *being* meant presence, even if designated as eternity: exposure of being to thought and exposition on the scale of thought; assimilation by thought and immanence, in which the transcendence of God can signify only negatively. This still leaves open the question of how that transcendence per se was ever able to let thought know of its very separation. The link between Maimonides (or that spiritual primacy of knowledge) and Greek thought is obvious; and the undeniable mastery of Maimonides in Jewish thought is a fact, despite all the attacks launched by certain medieval figures and a few young men of today. This indicates that there is communication between faith and philosophy and not the notorious conflict. Communication in both directions.

Judah Halevi is considered a mystic, but he recognized philosophical knowledge to a great extent and never developed the theme of pure and simple union with God, the disappearance of the thinker in the thought. What we can retain of his *Kuzari* is his description of the relation with what he calls "the order of God": *Inyan Elohi*. This relation is not expressed in terms of an indeterminate coinciding with transcendence and the infinite, but in terms like *association* (*hithavrut*) and *proximity* (*hitqarvut*). It is as if these social meanings of the "relation" with the order of God did not indicate a privation of knowledge, some least bad approximation of knowledge, but were rather possessed of a proper and sovereign positivity. What matters to me in that work, in which many significant traits are only hinted at—and in which many others are unacceptable to me—is the possibility of an original thinking and intelligibility other than the immanence of knowledge (and there is no question here of dispensing with knowledge just for the sake of opposing Maimonides). The proximity and sociality that the philosophers seek in knowledge will appear in Judah Halevi as irreducible possibilities of the meaningful. Sociality together with transcendence!

It is, in fact, my opinion that the relation to God called faith does not primordially mean adhesion to certain statements that constitute a knowledge for which there is no demonstration—a knowledge that would from time to time be troubled by the anxiety of a certainty lacking proof. To me, religion means transcendence, which, as proximity of the absolutely other (that is, uniqueness of the unique), is not a failed coincidence and would not have ended in some sublime projected goal, nor in the incomprehension of what should have been grasped and understood as an object, as "my thing." Religion is the excellence proper to sociality with the absolute, or, if you will, in the positive sense of the expression, peace with the other. But since proximity as peace does not entail knowledge, wouldn't it then be reducible to the negative notion of distance—of separation from a *beyond* that would neither concern the thought of any subject nor come down to a simple tolerant neutrality—a non-aggression—within the world? Unless the positive way of being concerned with God (yet otherwise than by a representation, which would make him immanent) comes precisely from the alterity of man, that is, from man's nonconformity to any genus, from his uniqueness, which I call face. Unless proximity itself originally means responsibility for the neighbor. A face beyond the visible that offers itself to our gaze, or to the power of representation that already defaces the other, leaving us looking at the mere plasticity of form. The signifying of the face, defenseless nakedness, the very uprightness of exposure to death. Mortality, and at the same time the signifying of an order, a commandment: "Thou shalt not kill!" The obligation of responding to the unique, and thus of loving. Love beyond all sensitivity, a thinking of the unique. The love of God in the love of one's neighbor. This original ethical signifying of the face would thus signify—without any metaphor or figure of speech, but in its rigorously proper meaning—the transcendence of a God not objectified in the face in which he speaks; a God who does not "take on body," but who approaches precisely through this relay through the neighbor—obligating men one to the other, each one answering for the life of the other.[1]

This seems to me fundamental to the Judaic faith, in which the relation to God is inseparable from the Torah; that is, inseparable from the recognition of the other. The relation to God is already ethics; or, as Isaiah 58 would have it, the proximity to God, devotion itself, is devotion to the other man.

The Jewish Bible I quote is not the originality of an ethnic particularism, no more so than is the Hellenic rationality of knowledge. The Bible means something for all authentically human thought, for civilization *tout court*, whose authenticity can be recognized in peace, in *shalom*, and in the responsibility of one man for another. "Peace, peace, to him who is far off and to him who is near" (Isaiah 57:19). This represents a spiritual event that transcends the anthropological: a questioning through the human of a certain *conatus essendi*, of a being which is preoccupied with itself and reposes in itself. Is the I a substance, the subject of perception, and thus master of what is not itself, the one who originally knows, grasps and owns, and is hard and already cruel? Or is not the I precisely as I already hateful to itself, that is, already obliged to the neighbor, the first person to come along, the stranger? To the neighbor who, somehow, is not merely of the world!

Q.: To take up this word *proximity* in its everyday sense, may I ask if you feel a greater proximity to Maimonides or to Judah Halevi?

E.L.: Who in their right mind would question the existence of Mont Blanc? Maimonides is one of the towering peaks of Judaism, and he has left his mark on it in the way he understood Judaism in the discussions of the talmudic sages, and the way in which, as a disciple of the Greeks, he understood reason. Maimonides is not an accident of holy history. In *The Guide of the Perplexed* he has definitely disengaged Scripture and the tradition from what their metaphors, taken literally, risked concealing (to the great delight of pious obscurantism). And in Maimonides himself, to whom rational knowledge of God, metaphysical knowledge, is the supreme good of the human being (and, precisely, an inalienable good, elevating the self in rational knowledge's own felicity, a good that "profits you alone," in such a way that "no other shares the benefit with you" [*Guide*, book III, chapter 54]), everything culminates in the formulation of the negative attributes. But the possibility of this knowledge is maintained as the ethical comportment of loving-kindness (*hesed*), judgment (*mishpath*), and charity (*tzedakah*), as "for the other." Imitation of God! The love of one's neighbor is at the summit of a life devoted to supreme knowledge. This is a remarkable reversal, unless we are to question the sincerity of this teacher, suggesting that he may have spoken otherwise than he thought to avoid unsettling pious minds.

I will have occasion to return to the theme of how knowledge, its intelligibility and its judgment, are necessary to the signifying of transcendence as sociality or proximity to the other, which precede the discourse of knowledge. There is also the impressive fact that the signifying of transcendence and proximity is itself exposited in a discourse that communicates knowledge—is exposited in Greek and is subsequently clothed there in the logical forms of knowledge, even though this communicating discourse presupposes the intelligibility of the interlocutor as other, and the forms of knowledge do not absorb the articulations of the dialogue they make it possible to relate.

Q.: "Exposited in Greek." This is a quasi-emblematic expression, a kind of motto you use often, it seems to me, for saying Jewish things in Greek. How would you explain this?

E.L.: We will speak of wisdom presently, and come back later to the problem of the relationship between the two spiritual traditions. And be assured that there is not, in that formulation, a Hellenizing snobbery. What I mean by "saying in Greek" is the way of expressing ideas in accordance with our customary mode of presentation and interpretation in the universities. It owes much to the Greeks.

Q.: We will return to the theme of wisdom in a moment, if you don't mind. First, I would like to ask you about something you said in 1975. You said: "To me, philosophy is derived [*dérive*] from religion. It is called forth by religion adrift [*en dérive*], and religion is probably always adrift."[2] This proposition has an enigmatic resonance. Is philosophy simply an offshoot or a debased version, a secularized product of religion, a purely human way of treating the same questions religion does? Or should your assertion be given a stronger meaning, bringing it closer, mutatis mutandis, to St. Anselm's *fides quaerens intellectum*, faith seeking understanding?

E.L.: The proposition you are asking me to elucidate was probably inspired by the contemporary religious crisis and the remedies that have been suggested for it. And one might also wonder whether, despite the bedazzlement of Western science engendered by philosophy, philosophy's primordial curiosity for the hidden presuppositions of the various fields of knowledge was not a transposition of the cult of the sacred into which the proximity of the absolutely other precipitated thought before revealing itself in the face of the neighbor. But the remark in question has a less banal and less approximate meaning. Religion's recourse to philosophy need indicate neither servility nor lack of understanding on the part of religion. It is rather a case of two distinct but linked moments in this unique spiritual process that constitutes the *approach* to transcendence: an approach, but not an objectification, which would already deny transcendence. Objectification, on the other hand, is necessary to the approach, without being able to take its place.

Indeed, the intelligibility of knowledge, truth, and objectivity is called to play its role in the ethical signifying of proximity, peace, and God.

"Peace, peace, to the one who is far off and to the one who is near," says
the Eternal (Isaiah 57:19). Beyond the one who is near, or before him, the
one who is far off compels recognition. Beyond the other there is the third
party. He is also an other, also a neighbor. But which is the closest proximity? Is it not always exclusive? Who then is the first one to whom I
must respond, the first to be loved? There must be knowledge of such
things! It is the hour of justice, inquiry, and knowledge. It is the moment
of objectivity motivated by justice. The unique incomparables must be
compared. We must, out of respect for the categorical imperative or the
other's right as expressed by his face, de-face humans, sternly reducing
each one's uniqueness to his individuality in the unity of the genus, and
let universality rule. Thus we need laws and, yes, courts of law, institutions and the State, to render justice. And thus no doubt an entire political determinism becomes inevitable. But do responsibility, concern for
the other or love without concupiscence, answering to the word of God,
abandon peace and remain without wisdom when faced with the "violence" or rigors of the universal and justice, when the rights of the unique
are no more than a particular case of judgment?

Q.: We will get to wisdom in a moment. But I would like to know
what you call "the philosophical implications of the Jewish vision of
Scripture." In speaking of Rabbi Haïm of Volozin's book *Nefesh Hahaïm*
(*The Soul of Life*), you say you see it as an attempt to "make explicit the
implicit philosophy of rabbinic study." Elsewhere, you say that "all philosophical thought rests upon pre-philosophical experience."[3]
One can well imagine that there is a difference between the pre-philosophical and the philosophically implicit. Would you care to clarify that
difference and the philosophical role of these two orders?

E.L.: I don't make a radical distinction between the philosophically implicit and pre-philosophical experiences. I believe that the philosophically
implicit is "enveloped" in "ways of being," in "comportments," in "customs" (which may clash with other customs), and can thus bring about
wars and persecution before enunciating itself. We must also take into account the institutional life of philosophy in the university, and a language
in which explication is pushed very far, and from which so-called pre-
philosophical experiences that have not been rendered explicit may be
quite remote. I am rather inclined to believe that in all meaningful
thought transcendence is manifested or has been reduced.

Q.: You have often expressed the reasons behind your mistrust of ontology; but your mistrust of knowledge and science in general may cause surprise. No doubt the former calls to mind Kierkegaard's protest against the system, as well as Rosenzweig's challenging of the totality. You have explained your views on that score. The latter had a Bergsonian, or even a Nietzschean accent—but it was to art, and not ethics, that Nietzsche in his suspicion of the "will to truth" appealed, in order to "master knowledge."

To what degree can a philosophy such as yours, which is not after all an irrationalism, relinquish taking the relation to science into account in a more positive manner?

E.L.: I have mainly tried to place due emphasis on an "intelligibility" or a signifying, differing from that of knowledge, and that tends to be construed as a simple privation. But in our conversation I have been sufficiently insistent upon the inevitable recourse of all meaningfulness to knowledge, and on the role incumbent upon knowledge in the ethically meaningful, to avoid the reproach of having underrated knowledge. Its derivative nature is not an indignity.

Q.: Derivative, or dangerous?

E.L.: Dangerous when it is taken to be the only kind of meaning. Dangerous when we forget, in speaking, that we are speaking to the other, that the rationality of discourse is already borne by the previous signifying of dialogue or proximity. Dangerous when we think that the logical forms of knowledge in which all philosophy is indeed expressed are the ultimate structures of the meaningful.

Q.: There is something that is not knowledge and that is different from both religion and philosophy, though close to them. It is called wisdom. We have come to it at last. I have in mind your statement, in the preface to your second volume of talmudic lectures, *Du sacré au saint*: "We wished in these readings to bring out the catharsis or demythicization of the religious that Jewish wisdom performs." How is wisdom to be understood in this instance?

E.L.: What I call wisdom (and I am glad that we have come, or come back, to this question) implies precisely a whole culture of knowledge of things and men. It is a thought guided by the care for objectivity and truth, but a thought in which, in this care, the memory of the justice that gave rise to them is not lost. Justice that relates back to the infinite original right of the neighbor and to responsibility for the other. Truth and objectivity do indeed limit this right of the other man, and the original *for-the-other* of the human, through respect for the rights of the one to whom I referred earlier as the third. Thus I wrote: "Upon the extravagant generosity of the for-the-other there is superimposed a reasonable, ancillary, or angelic order of justice through knowledge and philosophy; here is a *measure* applied to the infinity of the being-for-the-other of peace and proximity and, as it were, the wisdom of love."[4] But it is still a matter, in that wisdom, of preserving the face of the other man and his commandment amid the harshness of justice based on a complete and sincere knowledge and behind the forms of knowledge taken to be ontologically ultimate in Western thought. A matter of revindicating the face of the other man, within an order always to be created anew. A human order, always to be created anew in order to respond to the extraordinary event of the for-the-other; a "becoming" which manifests itself to the naked eye in the living duality between politics and religions, between science and philosophy, in the inevitable exteriority protected by the famous defense of the rights of man vis-à-vis the structure proper to the legitimacy of states. Behind reason with its universal logic, wisdom is always there listening, disquieting, and sometimes renewing it. Behind reason with its universal logic there is the wisdom that has neither method nor fixed categories. It is not serenity: the wise man is never wise enough. Wisdom as the freedom of reason, if not freed from reason. This wisdom is incumbent precisely upon the *uniqueness* of the one who thinks—as if, beyond all contingency, his identity as a monad, logically unjustifiable, indiscernible, were chosen. Wisdom as understanding of the unique and the chosen. This is in keeping with Israel's ancient belief in the positive function of the uniqueness of the I in the infinite discovery of the truths of the Torah, to the point of thinking that one person less in the world means one less truth in the Torah, lost for all eternity. This is a belief expressed in the Jewish liturgy by the prayer: "Give us our portion in Thy Torah." The portion requested is the one for which I am the condition, by virtue of my uniqueness, and not just the one assigned to me. Wisdom as intelligence of the unique and the chosen, and yet wisdom that joins the wisdom of the others without constituting the species in a genus; rather, according to a new type of unity that is the wisdom or the inspiration of a people.

Q.: When you use the word *wisdom* in this way, do you have the sense that you are precisely translating the word *hokhmah*?

E.L.: *Hokhmah* certainly includes what I have attempted to describe as wisdom. A *hakham* of the Talmud is an erudite scholar, but one who remains within his personal uniqueness. When he is quoted, an effort is made to respect jealously that uniqueness. When he transmits the saying of someone else, it is meticulously noted, and often a few lines of the text are devoted to going back to the one who said it first, mentioning all the intermediaries.

Q.: What you have just said also clarifies this passage from your preface to *Proper Names*: "The proper names in the middle of all those common names and commonplaces—do they not resist the disillusion of sense and help us speak?" But let us come back, if you will, from wisdom to philosophy. Perhaps philosophy is not one. Its historical deployment, at any rate, justifies our hesitating between at least two different projects. There is one according to which, as you say, philosophy "is not only the knowledge of immanence but immanence itself." That is the philosophy that exhausts itself in the assimilating knowledge of ontology: the philosophy of the system, or of the totality. And then there is a philosophy that is other; the one that is—appropriately no doubt—called metaphysics. It is, to borrow an expression dear to you, a "philosophizing otherwise." This is an act of escape outside being, which you invoke, I believe, in speaking of Jeanne Delhomme and her unraveling the "weave of the ontologies" and her attaining in the end "an increasingly fertile multiplicity of meanings arising within meaning." But do you not also say that "all philosophy is Platonic"?

E.L.: That is a quotation from an early text, I believe. I do not reject it, to the extent that the link between philosophy and transcendent alterity is affirmed in the Platonic theory of ideas, where the problem or the anxiety of that radical alterity—even though there is an attempt to reduce it—seems to me to authenticate philosophy. I have already said that. I do not reject my attachment to Platonism, because to owe the daring formulation *beyond-being* to Plato is good luck.

But beyond being is not a matter of rejoicing in a precious world-behind-the-scenes in which it would be convenient to install the God of religion comfortably. My entire effort consists in separating myself, so to speak, from ontology, where the meaning of the intelligible is attached to the event of being, because it would be "in itself" like *presence*, culminating in its repose and perseverance in itself, sufficing unto itself, perfection that, in Spinoza's view, is its divinity. It is the human self, master and possessor of the world, all powerful and all knowing, who would thus be divinized. To understand the for-the-other in a radical and original way as first philosophy—this involves asking oneself whether the intelligibility of the intelligible is not *prior* to the possession of the self by itself, prior to the "hateful self," and (without having previously evaluated what one is and has, before having made that assessment) involves solicitude for the other, whose being and death are more important than my own. It means asking oneself whether that responsibility for the other, which is madness in a way, is not the human vocation in being? (Being would thus be put in question.) Whether the imperative of that obligation is not the very Word of God—his very coming into the idea, so to speak, where He is thought, as Descartes would have it, beyond what that idea can contain.

Q.: Your text on Plato is from 1955. In 1967, in connection with Mme. Delhomme, you bring up a different responsibility.

E.L.: In the late (and much lamented) Jeanne Delhomme (to whom it is a pleasure for me to do homage, as she was one of the most subtle speculative minds of the philosophers of my generation), there was no ethical problem underlying the attempt to free thought from allegiance to being. This form of thought, which is qualified as modal or interrogative, was to be understood as the spontaneity of an intelligence that is not set in an ontology, and that, on the contrary, unravels the ontological fabric. Philosophy—or philosophies—as absolute freedom. Pyrotechnics of meaning. A linguistic modality like a poetic language, without my responsibility ensuing from that freedom assumed in relation to being. Intelligence as a difficult game. As a de-ontologizing of philosophy, that daring enterprise seemed to me suggestive (though absolutely opposed to responsibility-for-the-other) of the otherwise-than-being that constitutes the human as such, dispensing with the prior freedom that is invoked to justify obligation. There is also, in Mme. Delhomme's mistrust of the *datum*—present, heavy, and ready-made—a point in common with the phenomenology to which I am attached. You know that in Husserl's methodology there is at once a denouncing of the confusion between the object and the psychism intending it—which is the well-known critique of psychologism—and a return to the noetic concreteness of the noemata, as if the object, looked at exclusively, obstructed the gaze... But perhaps Jeanne Delhomme would not like my making her, if ever so slightly, a phenomenologist!

Q.: Many of those who have written commentary on your work are aware of the highly paradoxical nature of your approach, and they emphasize it in their studies on you. Françoise Wybrands speaks of how "Levinas's thought . . . finds support in the philosophical tradition opened by Parmenides, a tradition from which it constitutes itself as an exception." Catherine Chalier speaks of your "daring intent of choosing the Greek logos only to surprise it utterly." And Jacques Rolland, just as strongly: "It is by the resources of philosophy that it is appropriate to seek a way out of that with which philosophy is closely linked." Is the paradox thus described mandatory or optional for you?

E.L.: I believe I have indicated, apropos of the idea of wisdom, both the exclusion and the inclusion of the paths "opened by Parmenides" in what I call the "opening by the human" in being, which later would suffice unto itself in the *conatus essendi*—an opening that I take to be biblical. The paradox here is neither mandatory nor optional. It corresponds exactly to that advent of the human overturning "the order of things," that *for-the-other*, shattering the "in-itself," that "peace to the one who is far off and to the one who is near." One might indeed ask why, in Isaiah's phrase, is the one who is close not the only one mentioned (in which case his uniqueness would correspond to pure love)? And again, one might ask: why, in the same phrase, does the far-off one—the third party—precede the other? One might thus speak of a structure of fact that is mandatory. I think it would not be impossible to elucidate this factical structure, but I will not attempt to do so here. In any case, the three friends you quote saw clearly and accurately. And Jacques Rolland, in his study published in *Cahiers de la nuit surveillée*, which he edits, has posed the problem of this paradox correctly and forcefully.

Q.: While some, like Jacques Colette, seem simply to note that you are relatively far away from phenomenology, without having given up the "phrasing of phenomenological research," others wonder whether you have sufficiently "escaped" the premises of Husserl's phenomenology. So argued Roland Blum in his 1971 conference in Montreal.

E.L.: Colette, who is a scholar and a keen philosopher, does indeed show that my texts are not always in agreement with Husserl's phenomenological "rules of method." It is true that I do not begin with the transcendental reduction. But the search for the concrete status of the given, setting out from the "I think," the search for concreteness in a "phenomenon," that is, in the noetic-noematic correlation revealing itself in reflection upon the "I think" (and in which the datum, having become purely abstract, no longer obstructs the gaze to which it gives itself), seems to me to constitute phenomenology's fundamental teaching. This privileged "intelligibility" of the concrete is developed as early as in the Third Logical Investigation, and the term "concrete" keeps recurring in Husserl's phenomenological descriptions. I have even taken the liberty of characterizing these descriptions as the reconstitution, for any object or notion thematized in the "natural attitude" of man, of its mise-en-scène. From this perspective, my philosophy would consist in constating, first, that the identity of the I and of this "I think" is not equal to the task of encompassing the "other man," precisely because of the alterity and irreducible transcendence of the other; and second, that the reduction to powerlessness is not negative in the "appresentation" in which representation fails, but it is rather a thought that is other, in a conversion (or return) of the egological "for-oneself" into its original "for-the-other." It is a responsibility responding to a call from beyond being, signified through the face of the neighbor. An I of the *for-the-other*, infinitely obligated, who identifies himself as unique, chosen, in this vocation. The framework of Husserlian phenomenology may have been broken open in the course of the transcendental analysis, but the "destruction" of the dominant I in which the analysis was anchored is not some kind of step toward the insignificance of the person; it is his election to responsibilities, responding to the word of God in the face of the other, God who never "appears," who is not a "phenomenon," who never "becomes flesh," in any thematization or objectivization. That is probably the meaning of the indetermination held to by Judah Halevi's expression *Inyan Elohi* in speaking of God. A subversion in the I that is not its extinction. I have in mind Pascal's "the I is detestable," which is not a lesson in good style or courtesy but the rejection of him who would be master of the world and who, self-sufficient, posits himself a substance or subject. A "usurpation of the world" that already begins, according to another of Pascal's *pensées*, with the I that posits itself in the name of that "place in the sun," even if it seems in appearance, or in worldly wisdom, so "legitimate."

Q.: And that is the opposite of what you call "dis-inter-estedness"?

E.L.: Yes. And I am very pleased that the abstract and negative notion of disinterestedness has received, at the heart of my phenomenology, all its concreteness and all its positivity in the intimate responsibility for others.

Q.: To return to the point of view of methodology, Francis Jacques does, nevertheless, seem to me to ask a pertinent question when, in the course of the elaboration of his "Anthropology from a Relational Point of View," he says: "Either Levinas's discovery of the person of the other as an irreducible datum subverts the phenomenological approach with incomparable depth, or Levinas's method, marked by Husserl and unquestionably associated by him with egological premises, does not fail to reintroduce a paradoxical primacy of the myself." How would you respond to the alternative formulated by Francis Jacques?

E.L.: That is a constant in Francis Jacques's critique of me. I think I have already answered, above. The "discovery" of others (precisely not as a datum, but as a face!) subverts the transcendental approach of the I, but retains the egological primacy of the I that remains unique and chosen in its incontestable responsibility.

In Francis Jacques, there remains a priority of knowing. To me it is important to recognize that all thought is not knowledge, nor is it founded (directly or indirectly) on presence or representation; that the meaningful is not exhausted by science or by the experience that takes place in consciousness, nor in the secrecy of the hiding-place or the modesty of the unconscious. The face of the other is not straightaway representation or the presence of a figure; it is neither a given nor something to be taken. Before the countenance the face adopts or assumes (and through which it enters the system of the world and is perceived, grasped and possessed, comprehended and apprehended within that system as a means of identification), it is surprised as the nakedness, destitution, and uprightness of a defenseless exposure to death. It signifies mortality but, at the same time, an interdiction: "Thou shalt not kill." Before appearing to the I, the face signifies mortality and an ethical commandment. Before appearing, it appeals to responsibility. Thus there is a falling back of the "I think"—of the knowledge that includes and engulfs the world—into that original obedience that is perhaps also the severe name of a love without concupiscence. There, uniqueness without genus, that is, alterity itself, succeeds in signifying in the occurrence of peace.

Q.: Just as, a moment ago, in connection with Jeanne Delhomme, we touched on the possibility of a different way of philosophizing; similarly I could at this point bring up a conception of knowledge no longer based on presence or representation, but on the interlocutionary relation and the alterity of relation. We do not have time. As for that "occurrence of peace" you mention, is it not also a real relation?

E.L.: Before arriving at wisdom—at the level at which we are speaking, I would avoid the word "relation," which always indicates a simultaneity among its terms in a system, and which is the synchrony of the representation of the world, society, and its institutions, its freedom, equality, and justice. If what I just said about wisdom has any meaning, it would be wise to return to all that. But one cannot begin there, if wisdom is the wisdom of love.

I avoid the synchrony of the relation and of the system, because the responsibility for the other that reaches the meaning of the other in his uniqueness does not have a "synchronic" structure. In its devotion—in its devoutness—it is gratuitous or full of grace; it is not concerned with reciprocity. It is younger than the order of the world. Strange irreversibility! It brings to mind the diachrony of time, that is, the ultimate secret of its very order. It is probably the very articulation, the very concreteness of the temporality of a time that signifies through the other.

But for today let us leave off further ascent toward the ethical knots of temporality.

TRANSLATED BY MICHAEL B. SMITH

Judaism and Christianity after Franz Rosenzweig

E.L.: I would like to recount straightforwardly how a transformation occurred in my personal relationship to Christianity in the past few years through the reading of Franz Rosenzweig. I'm going to say this candidly, hoping to offend no one. I discussed our theme for the first time rather by chance one evening with a friend, the poet Claude Vigée, in the corner of a bar. It was, as it were, the first confession he received.[1] You know, of course, that a confession is always made by one who is speaking. A Jew is free, as we have no synagogue giving an official line. Each person is, in a certain sense, free to make clear what comes to him. In this sense, I'd like to recount today what I conveyed to my friend for the first time.

Christianity was a completely closed-off world some eighty years ago while I was still in my childhood. It was a world from which one could, as a Jew, expect nothing good. The first history of Christianity I read was a history of the Inquisition. By the age of eight or nine I had already read of the suffering of the Marrano Jews in Spain. Not long thereafter came a critical study of the history of the Crusades. I was born in Lithuania, a land lacking any contact at all between Jews and Christians. Lithuania is a beautiful country with good people—yet there was still no contact between the two groups. Coming only later to a reading of the Gospels, I found that those readings which did not attack me actually did just the opposite. The teaching in them, and the representation of human beings in them, appeared always familiar to me. As a result, I was led to Matthew 25, where the people are astonished to hear that they have abandoned and persecuted God. They eventually find out that while they were sending the poor away, they were actually sending God himself away. I always said

later on, after I became acquainted with the concept of the Eucharist, that
the authentic Eucharist is actually in the moment when the other comes
to face me. The personality of the divine is *there*, more so than in the
bread and wine. But I have read this in the Old Testament. In Isaiah 58,
the people are said to seek "to know God's ways," "to draw near to him"
(v. 2). God, though, will only approach when the people help the poor,
feed the hungry (v. 7). This is just the opposite, then, of a closed-off
world, and if I may, this is a personal understanding of Christ. What remains unintelligible is not the man, but rather the entire Mystery. The entire theological theme—that remains closed off. But the concept of kenosis, of the descent of God to earth, is actually quite familiar to Jews.

That's not all, though. The terrible thing was that the dangerous matter of the Inquisition and the Crusades were bound to the sign of Christ
and the Cross. I cannot understand these things; they must be explained
to me. Moreover, what attends these concerns is that the world has not
been altered—this is my main concern. "Christian" Europe did not find
it in itself to accomplish this, not by way of what Christians have done *as*
Christians. Above all else, Christianity has not thwarted people from
doing the things they have done—from the Holocaust. It is the primary
thing I have to say, and it is still vital. The message of the Gospels has
been forever compromised for us by history.

When what you call the Holocaust and we call the *shoah* came to pass,
two things occurred. In the first place, all of the perpetrators at Auschwitz
were—as children—baptized Protestants or Catholics; this still did not
prevent them from doing what they did. Secondly, though, and this is important—very important—something you call *caritas, charité, misericordia*
appeared to me. If one saw a black cassock, then there was sanctuary. A
discussion is still possible here. A world in which you have no refuge is a
despair. I often tell the story: I had just moved to Paris. We had an office
from the "Action Pacifique." It happened that a Jewish friend of mine
whose wife was Christian had lost his child. It was in the Christian
Church of Saint Augustine that the service was to be held. It was still
some time before May 1940, and yet already everything was in question.
During the funeral service in the church, I happened to see a small picture, a fresco of Hannah bringing the small Samuel into the temple. It
was my world! Especially Hannah! A completely extraordinary figure of a
woman, with her prayer, the misunderstanding with Eli ["Are you
drunk?"], and her answer: "No, my Lord, I am a woman of sorrowful

spirit. I have drunk neither wine nor strong drink, but have poured out my soul before the Lord" (1 Samuel 1:15). She speaks the authentic prayer of the heart, the prayer of the soul. It is a concrete relation, the mise-en-scène of a soul. Hannah *is* this prayer. This proximity, then, is what I saw in the church. And this proximity has remained with me. And I think I am obligated to this *charité*. My small family owes their life to a cloister, in which my wife and my daughter were saved. My wife's mother was deported, but she and my daughter were themselves saved. This goes beyond gratefulness. And appreciation goes far beyond this, isn't it true? The most important thing is the possibility of speaking together. But this is all a matter of feeling.

Before the war I'd already read Rosenzweig and had read of the philosophical possibility of seeing the truth in both forms, Judaism and Christianity. This possibility was extraordinary. The culmination of the truth is not in one; metaphysical truth remains essentially possible in two forms, in Christianity and in Judaism. Rosenzweig claimed a perfect equivalence of the two forms. This was the first time something like this was said. I am not loyal to Rosenzweig, nor to everything in his entire system. I don't agree that, in Rosenzweig's work, everything has been said in the end. Yet the claim itself—made without compromise, and without a secret betrayal—of thinking precisely in the two forms, of thinking in the form of Christianity and the Christian *miséricordia*, and in the form of Judaism—made it possible for me to think this relation as a positive one, and also to speak of it. Not a mere "speaking about," but rather the possibility of addressing the most crucial matters. This is, approximately, what Rosenzweig built and felt. He could even believe this in his illness, without abandoning the slightest element of Judaism. That imparted to me faith and trust in concrete relations to other human beings.

My response to the Second Vatican Council's Declaration "Nostra Aetate" has been very positive. The Declaration is a logical step forward and offers proof that an attempt is being made to overcome certain things in the past. I welcome the parallel drawn, today, between the two religions in the doctrine of kenosis: the universality of the common element in all human beings, and the universality of what is *for* human beings. This is how I understand Christianity: to live and die for everyone. Do not be shocked by this, but what is genuinely human is that part of being which is being-a-Jew, an echoing in the particular.

Christians place an enormous value on what is called faith, Mystery, sacrament. And now I would like to tell a small story: Hannah Arendt reported in a radio program in Paris not long before her death that as a young girl in Königsberg she told a rabbi in the middle of a religious instruction, "You know, I do not believe." And the rabbi answered her, "Who is asking you about *that*?" This answer is quite interesting. What is important with us is not belief, but doing (*Tun*). Doing certainly means behaving morally, but it also means doing ritual. As if that were two different things! What does it mean to believe? By what means does one believe? As the Psalms say—with your whole body![2] The rabbi wanted to say, obviously, that doing is the most important element. In conclusion, doing is an act of faith.

BISHOP HEMMERLE: It is extremely difficult to reply to a testimony which reaches such depth. I have the impression as well that the mark would be completely missed if I offered mere arguments. As you spoke, I could only be deeply frightened and distressed in the face of what can happen in the name and sign of Jesus. From this I will dare to say in all honesty that I believe to experience Him in such a way I can do nothing but believe in Him, and indeed believe in Him as Christ. I would be unfaithful otherwise, because I am met by Him; I would be as unfaithful as *you* would be if you abandoned your faith. Please allow me, then, to attempt two responses.

To begin with: Is it not basically a sign of the very defenselessness of God, of the defenselessness Jesus accepted, that He comes to me in the innermost element of His message defenselessly? What actually drives me to Him is precisely the defenselessness of kenosis, into which He has entered. For me—and I do not mean by this a dialectical apology—for me, the extreme element of kenosis is that Jesus became incarnate in *Agape*, in *Caritas*, and in God's love and grace, to the point where He can only ask for my love, a point at which He can only bid me to imitate. He is, of course, able to send a spirit capable of directing my faith and deeds, but He will only protect me when I open my heart and my very bones to Him and do not revile Him by doing the opposite of what He is and what He says. For me, this is the most extreme kenosis of God.

I must admit that I am again and again frightened by many things that, as a bishop, I must do, and I ask myself often: am I not perverting Him, even if it now appears "right" to do what I am doing? And I would not stake my life on the fact that I do not pervert Him again and again. Yet is it not perhaps good that I cannot stake my life? If *I* could, then I would have a guarantee. And this guarantee wouldn't be like Him at all... He is the head full of blood and wounds.

Secondly, I can only give witness to what Rosenzweig means to me in this context. I have been able to open a way—a way to faith for people who could not believe—most readily through Rosenzweig's messianic theory of knowledge. (When it is a matter of the soul, I only know through the bones; when it is a matter of the soul, I am only able to believe with my bones.) This conception of Rosenzweig's moved me so much I felt empowered to open the way to Christian faith on its basis, even if I risk fleeing into the aporias of thought. Curiously, what led Rosenzweig on the path of Judaism allows me to understand the Eucharistic Christ: the love which Jesus has for me is love with the heart, blood, and bones. Hence in the end I can only believe with the bones.

Rosenzweig frees me as well from a merely metaphysical activity of "packing stale concepts" into the encounter with the Gospels. And right inside the mystery of the trinity—which to Jews is completely foreign—his work enabled me to deepen my understanding of my own situation on the basis of what I discovered in his work on the relationality, temporality, and the non-substitutability of time and relation to the other. I owe Rosenzweig thanks for a part of my ability to understand and to answer for my Christianity. And I hope that out of his thinking a deep solidarity is able to grow in the shared fact of being exposed to suffering. A path of knowledge has been opened to me by him. On this path I am called to sensibility and responsibility by the horror of what has happened to the neighbor.

HENRIX: From these contributions, we heard of what is signified in a Rosenzweigian language as the "and" of "Judaism and Christianity." Professor Levinas has said that the entire christological theme of kenosis remains closed to him. And Bishop Hemmerle called for a reevaluation of the history between Christians and Jews. This very history is to be understood as an extreme kenosis of God. Bishop Hemmerle chose the term "defenselessness" for this.

E.L.: Defenselessness has cost the lives of many suffering people. Ought this not be pointed out? We are not in the middle of a *disputatio* concerning God's compassionate nature. But you know, I do not understand this defenselessness—today—after Auschwitz. Sometimes it seems to me that what happened in Auschwitz has a meaning if God demands a love which is completely without promise. That is how I imagine it. The meaning of Auschwitz is a suffering, a faith completely without promise. This means gratuitous. And then I say to myself: but this costs really too much—not for God, but for humanity. This is my critique, my lack of understanding concerning "defenselessness." This powerless kenosis costs people much too much.

The defenseless Christ on the cross was carried at the front of the crusaders' army. And Christ didn't climb down from the cross to demand an end to the murder.

HEMMERLE: That was his defenselessness.

E.L.: Defenselessness which was not, however, that of a suffering God, but rather, that of the victims.

HEMMERLE: I don't want to have defenselessness understood as an apology, but rather as a living command which costs everything and demands a complete transformation in our action.

E.L.: But that appears theological to me.

HEMMERLE: As long as I merely say it, it is only theological. I believe that a concrete change in actions must lie behind it; otherwise this change, I admit, remains mere verbiage.

CASPER: I would like to go into the problem of the "and" [in the name of our roundtable discussion of Judaism and Christianity] since I think that will lead us to a deeper level—even at the risk that the discussion will be led for a moment away from existential structures. Professor Levinas, you have always stressed—for example, in the preface to *Totality and Infinity*—that you received the impetus for the shattering of totality from Rosenzweig, as well as the liberation from the compulsion to have to think everything in One. This compulsion includes, to put it in Rosenzweig's own words, all of Western thought "from Ionia to Jena," and this means from the Greek philosophy of nature to Hegel. You say that you learned from Rosenzweig that precisely in plurality lies truth and that the plurality of "being"—if one wants to let this word stand here—signifies the possibility of thinking freedom and being-called by the other as the ground for understanding all truly human thought. Because of this, ethics—as it has been said—becomes *prima philosophia*, first philosophy.

I wonder whether that is not also a decisive ground on which to think the relationship of Judaism and Christianity otherwise. Otherwise than it has been thought since the first Christian century, in which Christianity was received immediately into the Hellenistic world and therefore received directly into the thought of totality and unity. Does not the possibility of understanding anew the relationship between Judaism and Christianity depend on very fundamental notions? For example, how is one able to do justice to the other as other? Do not these notions provide the condition for the possibility of understanding in a new way—to use the words of John Paul II—the relationship between the younger and the older brother?

I'd like to add a small biographical note here. I think I see that the necessity for Rosenzweig to reflect on philosophy from Ionia to Jena arose just as much from personal conflicts. The question of how reality is to be understood was for Rosenzweig certainly a question for thought. But it was for him simultaneously a highly personal, existential question—namely in the encounter with Eugen Rosenstock. Implied in Rosenzweig's much considered decision to remain a Jew is his remark to Rosenstock: "Recognize that there is the other."

We have, therefore, before us two different strands as it were, one intellectual and one biographical. An intellectual strand—by this I mean abandoning the thought of totality and unity. Thought is able to bring everything into one formula and has thereby the right to struggle against what doesn't fit as either dumb or merely refractory and force it into a unitary formula. This problem, which Rosenzweig was convinced was offered when idealism collided with the problem of historicism, he gathered into the name of "new thinking," whose fundamental position was "I require the other and time."

Beside the intellectual strand, though, runs a parallel biographical strand. It leads right to understanding a new relationship, which is the "and" between Judaism and Christianity. The other is called as I am called, offering me the possibility of seeing and recognizing, by way of the other, the splendor of God, without thereby placing in question the obligation I have to my own path.

Here I have woven two things together. I would like to limit my question to Emmanuel Levinas, though, to the sphere of Rosenzweig's "new thinking." Wouldn't you agree that what became so important for you—the shattering of totality and the experience of truth in plurality—places us on completely new ground, one which in the history of Judaism and

Christianity has not until now existed? And is this not because we both have, as long as there have been Christians on earth, a shared history interwoven in Greek history? Wouldn't you agree that this new fundament—the shattering of totality and the perception of truth in plurality—offers completely new possibilities for understanding the "and" between Judaism and Christianity?

E.L.: Shattering of totality was never a reason for me to introduce the truth. The shattering of totality signifies for me a way toward the singularity of the human being. The way toward the singularity of the neighbor amounts to more than the attempt to think diverse truths as belonging together. Perhaps the latter would be a consequence of the former. The most important thing, however, is that the person has no genus. The thinking of justice does not permit the singularity of the human being to disappear. Justice is itself demanded by the singularity of the human being. The human being, the other, is singular. And the third is singular as well. The question is: why does Rosenzweig come to a truth which has two forms and not more than two? He completely excludes Islam just as he excludes Buddhism. That is quite unusual in a world where Islam and Buddhism were taught in the universities. How is this possible? To this, I only say that I find only Rosenzweig's sincerity consequential. In his sincerity, dualism is tenable. Should the shattering of totality be thought to its end? Should each person have a particular religion? A particular way? I have not thought about this.

CASPER: I would still like to insist: in asking why Judaism was attacked by Christianity, was thought to be a deficient figure of truth and hence subject to Christianity's putative right to *compelle intrare* [sic], "to compel entrance [into the Church]," then I also problematize a Hegelian thinking which says, "truth is a system of the same," namely, that there is only the one truth, a truth which is empowered by the actually "rational," and that consequently I must compel the other to enter into this truth for the sake of his redemption. But if, like Rosenzweig, I see that the truth must prove itself and that this proving itself in the end always occurs between myself and the other (this perhaps constitutes the "messianic theory of knowledge" mentioned by Bishop Hemmerle), then I am freed from the compulsion of the *compelle intrare*. I believe this to be Rosenzweig's essential contribution toward a new relationship between Judaism and Christianity. But I do not want just to banter back and forth. One must ask after the truth with passion. One has seen that truth proves itself in what happens between the other and me. Yet it must be asked whether there are not deficient forms of confirming oneself and truth, as we see in Rosenzweig, phenotypically, for example, as I would say in the figure of Islam.

What seems to me a fundamental insight is: every human being is singular. And the way of humanity takes place always between the other and me. There alone truth proves itself. The proving-itself of truth in the last instance stands "with God." In Rosenzweig's words, only "before Him is the truth one." This fundamental insight appears to me to be exceedingly helpful in finding a new relationship between Judaism and Christianity.

E.L.: It confuses me a bit when you place so much weight on the theme of truth. I always thought that Rosenzweig taught the priority of love over the domination of the theoretical, of the theoretical which presents the horizon of meaning and point of departure for the concept of truth in the history of Western thinking. But isn't what we really call the truth determined by the "for-the-other," which means goodness? And not in the first place by the "in-itself" and "for-itself" of the truth?

I am often quite put off by the systematic in Rosenzweig. I derive the importance of a new relationship between Christianity and Judaism from an event in history, from the Holocaust. What is new does not arrive by way of some kind of construction. Rosenzweig only gave the *possibility*.

But you speak of the passion of Israel as the kenosis of God. This defenselessness has cost too much. . . .

GÖRTZ: For me, the significance of Rosenzweig and his view of Judaism and Christianity's relationship lies in the suggestion that being a Jew is what is genuinely human—a suggestion worthy of further thought. The risk that Christianity will become Hegelianism exists. Bishop Hemmerle spoke just now of his experience of Rosenzweig, that Rosenzweig was for him the liberation of Christianity from a mere metaphysical pack of ideas, and from a modern form of Gnosis. Here lies Rosenzweig's significance. Franz Rosenzweig himself said at one point: Judaism saves Christianity from becoming Gnosis. For me, this is Rosenzweig's significance in terms of the question of the relationship of Jews and Christians. I hear again and again in his discussions with friends what he so insisted upon: "Be careful, dear Christians, of what you make of your Christendom, lest you make it a *Weltanschauung* and think only in the dimension of truth."

So what is this truth he mentioned here? One not yet mediated by the same actuality as the floor on which we stand? I recall the questions he put to Hans Ehrenberg: "For what do you really live and die? What is the floor on which you are standing? Can you live and die for the truth?" One cannot live and die for the truth, but rather only for actuality! This means: I cannot live for the truth which is not mediated by actuality, by the fact of my existence which I experience myself. It rests on the singularity that I am. And this is so without the truth being at all mediated. Such mediation doesn't work as merely intellectual. Everything you have said of faith, Professor Levinas, is indeed so. Faith is a mediation that happens along with all of existence and with the bones. I do not live in the truth without it being mediated by this fact. And truth which is not mediated by this is, at bottom, truth of a Hegelian sort.

HEERING: We are discussing Franz Rosenzweig and his *Star of Redemption*. It occurs to me that we are, then, discussing in detail a book which would never have been written without Christian provocation. The provocation was Eugen Rosenstock. Yet the Christian provocation had in fact a Jewish source, because Eugen Rosenstock was originally Jewish. I understand our histories as from time immemorial interlaced with each other. Jesus and Paul were Jews, a fact which must be kept clearly in mind. How will this interlaced history go on from here? If I may say something personal: Buber helped me to survive the occupation of Holland, the war, and the Holocaust. Buber's books were always close by. 1935 was just beginning when a friend gave me a book of Buber's in which there was an article with the title, "What Should One Do?" Buber answered: Who? *One* should do nothing, but *you* should! He went on to end his very short article, written to Jewish youth in Germany, with the exhortation: you should not hold yourself back! And that always stayed with me, giving me courage as well through all the subsequent years of preaching the Bible. And I must say again personally: Judaism and Christianity are infinitely interwoven. It is no accident that I later came to read Rosenzweig and that in the end I had the great joy and honor to become acquainted with Emmanuel Levinas and to read him and to hear him. I will not go into the difficulties that have existed between Jews and Christians for centuries and right up to our own demonic twentieth century, because it has always been—to put this in a Yiddish way— *Nebensachen* standing between us. These "minor matters" were never the major issues. I would risk putting it this way.

Could it be possible that we Jews and Christians reconcile ourselves in

Isaiah 53, to that which, in this chapter, is constantly alluded to in great Jewish works: the Lamb of God who carries the sins of the world? Whenever we write and speak about messianic existence, it is done in the tone of this chapter. Messianic existence is to take on oneself the sins of the world, or the sins or needs of the neighbor, to permit oneself to become exemplary. Christians say Jesus is the exemplary one. If I believe in Jesus, in the Messiah, then I must follow on his path. Messianic existence from a Christian vantage point is, through Jesus, bound up with Isaiah 53. When Jews speak of messianic existence, they are saying the Messiah lives among us, and in manifold ways we are called to messianic existence or to "being-Messiah." Christians say that the world is saved, and Jews say that the world is not saved. I believe that there are not many Christians who relish the implications of all this. If redemption still happens today, it comes in the form of a secret that changes our lives. And if redemption remains still to come, then we stand as Jews and Christians together, and Jews—at least Rosenzweig (but Professor Levinas said this as well)—will say: we already experience in his example something of the approach and therefore the splendor of redemption.

Would it then be possible to find ourselves in Isaiah 53, to find our point of departure, and to move forward from there? We are seeing in our own times that Christians are becoming a minority in many Western countries. In this situation, we glance at Judaism: how do they do it? To be a minority in the world and yet still to bear a responsibility for the neighbor? How does one do this? To stand as the Lamb of God and still live?

E.L.: Isaiah is full of chapters in which one can find oneself. But it seems to me especially that the thought of human responsibility is essentially for all others. I think the redemption of humanity concerns everyone and is for everyone. Each person is completely different. One expects a resolution of humanity through a chosen people. To be the Son of God... Jews have always asked this of the Jew. As Christians, you know this as well, and name it *imitatio Christi*, the imitation of Christ.

CASPER: Professor Heering proposed that a commonality of Judaism and Christianity is given in the thought of the exemplary one which Isaiah 53 articulates. This is a path which we could walk together, the way of the servant of God, of the Lamb of God. "Yes, but..." Emmanuel Levinas replied. And this "but" says, you Christians see redemption definitively accomplished once and for all by the One. I think that a demand has been placed before us Christians to formulate our "Christology" more completely than it appears in the theses of Emmanuel Levinas. First of all, he himself added: there is, still, something like *imitatio Christi*. One could recall here the exhortation of Paul "to sacrifice our lives" (Romans 12:1).

Secondly, I would like to draw attention to the fact that the development in Christology in the last two centuries forces us to reformulate, within the context of a doctrine of redemption, what the great councils of the fourth and fifth centuries said of Jesus. It is, so to speak, the leading theme of contemporary Christology: one cannot use Christology anymore to make statements on the two natures of Christ or the Hypostatic Union. Or only insofar as one sees these statements in the light of the way of redemption brought by Jesus into the world. When one reflects carefully, there remain, indeed, decisive differences. We mustn't overlook this. We differ in the *eph hapax*, in the "once and for all," in the Christian belief that the unsurpassable Word of God has come to pass in Jesus Christ. In the Christian understanding of redemption there remains something which is not rendered in Judaism. We must let differences stand. But I think that we Christians have long ago seen that just staring at what came to pass in Jesus is not giving full witness to how Jesus encounters us in the Gospels. For a Jewish-Christian discussion, it would be important to carry the great proximity, which allows for many common paths, through the reformulation of Christology into the greater context of soteriology.

HENRIX: Can the attempt to formulate more completely Christology be at the same time the attempt to designate the proximity of Christianity to Judaism, Bishop Hemmerle?

BISHOP HEMMERLE: I am able only to give hints and tentative suggestions in directions capable of being thought further. I am referring to the Protestant-Catholic dialogue, one place that I believe can lead us closer together: we find God alone more purely through "God *and...*" than through God alone. God acts alone precisely because love is his innermost secret, the way in which He says the "and." Because He is love, He is even more himself, He includes us in the saying of the "and." This principle—which I do not want to understand abstractly but rather as something capable of bursting merely systematic thinking—appears to me to dominate the relation between Christology (a view of Jesus' act alone) and the actions asked of every single person. Jesus alone as savior, His *consummatum* and His completion, cannot be a substitute for our action. If I believe that the kenosis of God takes place in Him, and He is as one of us and with us as the lamb and the servant of God, then I understand that we are intended and called up to bear with Him now the whole, and "with Him" means each in his position in his uniqueness.

The present pope has expressly underlined the connections between anthropology and Christology. He cited this already in his first encyclical, *Redemptor Hominis*, the pastoral constitution *Glaudium et Spes*: "Because he, the Son of God, united himself (to us) in his becoming-human. . . ." In my opinion, there is a necessary corollary: every human being has to carry and join with the destiny of God's servant, Jesus Christ. The pope goes so far as to say something quite daring about the *misericordia*: God asks for our mercy. God needs, as it were, the human being—not because of an ontological need, but rather because of His covenant—as the one who bears-along-with.

I think that there remains a difference between us which indeed aims us toward the "and." The human being, hoping for God's salvation and placing his hope in God, is called in the name of this hope to act exemplarily. The human being is called by the common ground of his deeds, because acting and believing are not to be separated. Rather, faith approaches us in our bones. The exemplary action of each of us for the whole is, in its inexcusable uniqueness, simultaneously the starting point for acting *with each other*. Precisely the inexcusable uniqueness of this necessity-to-act is what does not lead us away from each other but rather binds us together, and exactly at this point in the world leads to corresponding action.

E.L.: I think everything that you have said occurs to the Jew without Christ. That is the Jew's stubbornness: "For thou art our father, though Abraham does not know us and Israel does not acknowledge us" (Isa. 63:16). Not all Jews get to this spiritual height, just as (to say the least) not all Christians imitate Christ. But it comes absolutely to the fore in Jewish spirituality. I mean a Jesus without Incarnation, without the drama of the cross. Yet, there is still a moment in which what we share is still quite different. I mean that you begin with "God is love." The Jew begins with obligation. And the *happy end* is uncertain.

TRANSLATED BY ANDREW SCHMITZ

Discussion Following "Transcendence and Intelligibility"

JEAN HALPÉRIN: In your lecture yesterday evening, you spoke of presence as exposition in the absolute frankness of a being, as a faultless assemblage and synchrony and, as another way of saying this, you added: the past and the future are the lapses of presence.

E.L.: They are interpreted and even experienced thus in the preference accorded to knowledge, its manner of recuperating that which, at a certain moment, slips away. It is always a matter of reestablishing coexistence in a system of unity. By no means did I qualify these modalities of temporality as inferior—on the contrary!—or as expressing the quality of a lapse. I was saying that in this preference accorded to knowledge the past and the future are always *of* a present, which one recuperates by imagination, by anticipation, and by reminiscence. Reminiscence remains one of the essential functions of thought, but for me it is not the truth of time. What I would like to substitute for this stranglehold of presence is, on the contrary, temporal diachrony. In exactly this way I have tried to maintain that immanence is not the supreme gift of the spirit, just as I think that the future [*le futur*] is not simply what is yet-to-come [*un à-venir*]. On the contrary, what I admire in Bergson is that his work announces a rupture with this interpretation of time: duration itself would be the access to "novelty," without it being necessary to presuppose a "supplement" to the coming into consciousness of duration in which presence, in one manner or another, would absorb or embrace temporality. Certainly Bergson does not always employ this paradoxical language. It is clear, however, that for him novelty would be given *in* the intuition of duration. But is not intuition vision, and thus presence of... already acceding to a "novelty" dispossessed of its novelty, an alterity which is no longer other? We are so habituated to the language of knowledge that we even state that which breaches presence in terms of knowledge. In order to understand correctly the Bergsonian teaching, wouldn't it be necessary to insist on a novelty signifying by force of the very diachrony of duration, without any recourse to some experience of which one would become conscious—to insist on a novelty signifying by force of the concordance in the very discordance of time? Or, if one wishes to speak of an *experience* of novelty, wouldn't it be necessary to say that duration itself is this experience, this acceding to novelty, without there being, moreover, contemplation of some kind of appearing? Cannot the signifying of such a novelty and of such a future, which is not exhausted by what is yet-to-come, be called the pro-phecy of time? A time whose flow—retained by reminiscence and anticipated by waiting or imagination—would not be the ultimate or living metaphor? Prophecy as the very duration of time, which is not identical to the vision of the visionaries and the diviners; prophecy that must be understand as the very *à-Dieu* of time, as its inspiration, with all the ethical conjunctures of a theological "intrigue." My research is there, and these reflections are the attempt—or at least the temptation—to say that prophecy is the concreteness of the future, which, inseparable from the ethical, has been "instructed" by God more than has the present. A theme to be developed. It is a contestation of that which was so clear in Husserl, where the past and the future are designated with reference to a present that has been retained or protained, and consequently, like something thinkable which, in the present, is substituted for something no longer present, although in the mystery of this substitution the whole temporalization of time is precisely dissimulated.

But let us stop there! Reference to an argument not yet published, nor even yet researched, is always convenient... even if its purpose was to suggest an orientation. In fact, it is in Bergson, in his notion of duration, that there is not only this idea of "novelty," but also this idea of intelligibility through time. Time is the very intelligibility of the meaningful.

DAVID BANON: But in the notion of prophecy as you develop it in *Otherwise than Being* you reject the side of vision or oracle in order to insist on its aspect as an "idea placed in us," that is to say, an aspect without relation to time, something that enters clandestinely.

E.L.: If I said that prophecy is also oracle, I would turn it into a vision of what is yet-to-come. It's not like that at all. Within the notion of prophecy, this reference to a future is not convertible into a line of time where what is yet-to-come already "waits" for presence. I am always troubled when one speaks of "the presence of God"—a terminology current in our religious language, in all our religions. I do not think that "presence" is the original intelligibility of God.

MARC FAESSLER: In what sense then would there be revelation? I was struck by the title of your latest work, *De Dieu qui vient à l'idée* [*Of God Who Comes to Mind*], in which the word "mind" [*idée*] is central. I have had the impression that your philosophical reflection is not anchored solely in the resources of rationality, but that you also draw from the talmudic sources' originary manner of apprehending the empirical. Whence the question: Is there a root of revelation or transcendence, within the modality that you describe, which is given as enigma, as fundamental intrigue?

E.L.: What do you mean by "resources of rationality"? There, precisely, you presuppose presence as that which gives itself.

MARC FAESSLER: What I meant was rather the effort of thought.

E.L.: I don't take my point of departure from rationality as a notion taking in a system of categories of our very logic of knowledge, but I would like to enlarge the notion. My point of departure is the meaningful, in which the human is held before all system. I have neither the impression that the meaningful is originally or exclusively articulated in knowledge, nor that the very place of the meaningful would be knowledge. In the obligation toward the other there is a meaning. That subsequently, upon reflection, evidently, the meaning can become a knowledge—that philosophy itself would be this knowledge—does not signify that the status of the meaningful in knowledge would be its proper and original modality. Applying a code or a rational regimentation to it is certainly not rational. But I say, on the contrary, that it is possible, beginning with meaning, to think the rational otherwise. And my attempt consists in saying that the relation with the other, with the face (if the word relation is appropriate here), is the very place where "God comes to mind," that this coming to mind—this descent—belonging to the interpellation of the I by the face, distinguishes it from *appearing* and from experience.

It is there that, for the first time, I employ the word *God* as if I were naming a being. If you object that this is imposed in conformity to certain logical or psychological codes, I concede, absolutely. But does not the meaningful begin here? This was the whole object of my lecture last evening. Perhaps it is not convincing, but it is all that I wanted to say. At the close of my lecture, I asked myself if it would not be possible to affirm what I am formulating now by saying that the psyche is originally theological. In order to say this, I have recourse to words like *insomnia, wakefulness,* or *vigilance.* The knowledge in which the hegemonic I appears is one of the possibilities of the human psychism, but in order for there to be knowledge, there must already have been an awakening of the psychism. And to say the awakening, I have recourse—for there is no further recourse—to Descartes, where *infinity* lodges itself in the finite. I discussed this once in an essay, "From Consciousness to Wakefulness."[1]

MARC FAESSLER: There you take Husserl as your point of departure.

E.L.: I almost always begin with Husserl or in Husserl, but what I say is no longer in Husserl. It is not that I am cleverer than he, but it is because I am embarrassed by Husserl's fifth Cartesian meditation. It does not seem to work by itself; inexplicit presuppositions subsist. When he constructs the alter ego by deducing it through analogy with my corporeal presence, gestures of association already intervene. These are treated as "associations by resemblance," in particular insofar as the other and I appear in what Husserl calls a "transcendental coupling." This association remains ambiguous enough. For among all possibilities, is the manner in which I am associated with another face the resemblance of two images? Would this not already be the fact of my being referred to the other socially, to the face of the other? In any case, there is the fault in the meaning of simple resemblance. With the time of the "awakening of the psychism," one touches on something very old and theological. Is then the animal psychism not already part of theology? Wouldn't that be scandalous? But in the Bible man is not a rational animal; he resembles God... this is not Aristotelian at all. And do you know that the morning prayer of Jews begins by a series of benedictions of which the first consists in rendering thanks that God conferred on the rooster the discernment between day and night?

MARC FAESSLER: Then to what extent is the Bible revelation?

E.L.: Positive religions think of themselves as knowledge. But the faithful do not always profess them as such. The law of God is revelation because it enunciates: "Thou shalt not kill." All the rest is perhaps an attempt to think this—a necessary mise-en-scène, a culture in which this can be heard. At least, that is how I try to say it to myself. "Thou shalt not kill" signifies, and this is understood, "thou shalt do everything in order that the other may live." Certainly I am embarrassed by your question, but I will perhaps also have the chance to formulate revelation as a manner of reading a text, always from the vantage point of a prior text.

In the *Nefesh Hahaïm* [*The Soul of Life*, 1824] of Rabbi Haïm of Volozin, an admirable book, as is its author, but one that is little known outside traditional Judaism, the author affirms: to study the Torah is to be united with God. He completes this by recalling that, according to rabbinic tradition (and this is no doubt an apologetic text), the Torah as a whole—Scripture and its commentary—given at Sinai contains even the naive questions of a student learning the Hebrew alphabet and questioning his teacher about it. These questions, too, would already be an indispensable articulation of revelation. The study of Torah would already belong to the articulations of the Torah, as they would belong to the *haggadah*, the *midrashim* which, at first glance, do not concern ethical laws. The tradition says here, in the guise of an apologetic, what I am reformulating in insisting on the priority of ethics in revelation. All these communicated knowledges have the same "savor," the same "odor," as the Decalogue, and they lead to the same goal. Even if they are narratives which, for example, tell how beautiful Sarah, the wife of Abraham, was. I am going to tell you this story. A *haggadah* relates the story of Abraham, who wishes to bring Sarah into Egypt without the Egyptians seeing her, for she is too beautiful. He hides her in a casket. "At the Egyptian frontier, the tax collectors ask him about the contents of the casket, and Abraham tells them he has barley in it. 'No,' they say, 'it contains wheat.' 'Very well,' Abraham replies, 'I am prepared to pay the tax on wheat.' The officers then hazard the guess, 'It contains pepper!' Abraham agrees to pay the tax on pepper, and when they charge him with concealing gold in the casket, he does not refuse to pay the tax on gold, or on precious stones. Seeing that he demurs to no charge, however high, the tax collectors, made thoroughly suspicious, insist upon his unfastening the casket and letting them examine the contents. When it is forced open, the whole of

Egypt was resplendent with the beauty of Sarah."² A marvellous story, and very distantiated from thou shalt not kill, is it not?

DAVID BANON: I have discerned a double movement in your work. In one, you propose to transcribe the meaning of the biblical message into the Greek language. (In *Beyond the Verse* you say that the Septuagint remains unfinished.) In the other, you attempt to subvert philosophical language by introducing biblical notions into it, for example, the notion of holiness, or that of election. Is there not a conflict between these two movements? In *Otherwise than Being*, you say that in order to render explicit an "otherwise than being," a "speaking otherwise" is required. Must this "speaking otherwise" unfold itself in a Greek language?

E.L.: The Greek language—beyond vocabulary and grammar—is our university language. But one talmudic text, which I commented upon at the last Colloquium of French Jewish Intellectuals, asserts a difference between Greek *language* and Greek *wisdom*.³ One must certainly know the Greek *wisdom*, insofar as one is mixed up in affairs of the State. It is as if this *wisdom* were fundamentally political. But it is not necessary to teach it to children. Children must learn the Greek *language*, namely, a manner of speaking which is not, however, that of the Gemara itself, although the rabbinic authorities had a direct knowledge of it.

Now, about the introduction of biblical notions in philosophical language. Certainly I do not utilize uniquely the categories which from Aristotle to Kant and to Hegel have been classical in philosophy. But a notion such as election is neither popular nor magical. In my work, election substitutes for the notion of individuation. I say, for example, that there is in responsibility an individuation of the I in election. I attempt a rehabilitation of heteronomy, insofar as it is conceived only in terms of slavery. It is a matter of knowing first of all who is the *other* of heteronomy. I think, in effect, that the content of terms which are thought can break up certain formal necessities. Many notions suggested by the Bible allow us to disengage an intelligibility "stronger" than that which the contradictions of formal logic delimit. The "otherwise said" also means, as it were, that all language is still insinuation and that it always comports a reduction of what it comes to affirm: not solely because of some lack of firmness on the part of the speaker, but on account of that which in the said is ineffable, and which, in a language twisted over itself, is communicated just the same.

The talmudic text to which I am alluding states that in the Greek language the Hebrew Bible conserves the plenitude of its religious intentions.[4] But it constates at the same time the existence of an untranslatable, an essential remainder of sense. The historical fact of the translation of the Pentateuch into Greek, namely the Septuagint, and its legend, recounted in the guise of a midrash to pages 9a and b of the talmudic treatise Megillah, include the modification of fifteen verses of the original text by the translators (who were inspired and miraculously concordant). This would signify the approval given by the rabbis both to the Greek translation and also to the precautions in the translation. According to them, certain things cannot be said in Greek without soliciting misunderstandings. Many would prefer to translate with a benign inexactitude lest they compromise the general meaning of a Scripture which nevertheless conserves its authenticity in Greek. There, too, is an "otherwise said." But the occasion is ripe to tell you about one of these corrections. Genesis 2:2 reads in Hebrew, "God concluded his work on the seventh day." According to the Talmud, the Septuagint translates "on the sixth day." The translators were distrustful; they did not wish to let themselves believe in the profanation of the Sabbath within the very work of creation! Whoever is not forewarned risks understanding the literal translation of the Hebrew in this way. And Greek is perhaps the very language which is addressed to minds without forewarnings. The reader who approaches this verse in Hebrew is already forewarned by the midrash. A world without leisure, a world without free time, a world without the Sabbath—doubtless this is still what philosophers call *being*, but this is not yet the *creature* of whom the Bible speaks. It is the seventh day without activity that achieves the creature as creature. It is no longer a peripety of being, a hazard of ontology. The Sabbath comes from elsewhere. It is not a simple fracture of time or of history. Whatever be the dignity of the natural rhythm of repose and work which spans historical duration, the Sabbath is older than nature. Whence the remarkable midrash that a reader of Scripture who has been "forewarned by the oral law" will also have understood in reading Genesis 2:2. "In giving the Sabbath to Israel, the Eternal gave her a treasure of his Treasury." Does not the Treasury of God hold values which are prior to the creation of the world and which are already missing from the notion of being?!

All the modifications which have been brought to the Hebrew text by the translators, according to the page of the Talmud about which I speak, do not justify themselves in the same way. A detailed study of the fifteen examples of "correction" given by the Talmud should be attempted. They are all the more significant in that only three among them can be found in the Pentateuch of the Septuagint. But perhaps also, between Hebrew and Greek, the problem of the "otherwise said" is not the simple effect of a discordance of vocabulary and semantics, but the very test of the spirit unfolding itself in two adventures the Scriptures run in their reading, two adventures which are equally necessary. Within the Jewish reading, that which is intelligible is sketched out on the basis of a spiritual experience or of a word always already past, on the basis of a tradition in which transmission and renewal go hand in hand. A reading on the part of a spirit which is never not forewarned. Without this essential forewarning being confused with the sterile partiality of dogmatism. It remains the secret of a creativity and of an eternal beginning again of newness which is probably the ineffaceable trace of a thought marked by revelation. And on the other hand, the Greek reading—of books and of things—intelligence of a mind marvellously not forewarned, thanks to which symbols are an attempt to be decoded, to be said in clarity, which has become our university language. Two inseparable adventures!

DAVID BANON: Is it in this sense that it would be necessary to go beyond the universal notions that one finds in Judaism and to go toward a Jewish singularity? Is this what you would call Jewish singularity?

E.L.: No, I wouldn't say it that way. In my book *Beyond the Verse*, I wished above all to say that hermeneutics is part of revelation and that it is necessary to go through revelation toward the inescapable meaning of the verse, and also that, at every moment, it is necessary to attempt translation into Greek, into its universal signification.

DAVID BANON: I was thinking more particularly of your text entitled "Assimilation and New Culture," which concludes *Beyond the Verse*.

E.L.: Oh yes. It is there that I speak for the first time about Greek and I say that the Septuagint is not yet finished! But there it is a matter of the content of the very history of humanity as Genesis says it. Until a certain moment, sacred history is universal, up until Abraham. Starting from there, everything is structured differently. The last episode of universality is Babel. Since then the human is found starting from the singularity of Abraham, a singularity open to all men who wish to join themselves to it.

ESTHER STAROBINSKI: You have distinguished between Greek wisdom and Greek language. But can they be disassociated? In a certain manner, wisdom comes with language.

E.L.: The distinction is made in a talmudic text. It is to Rabbi Judah ha-Nasi—who presided over committing the Mishnah into written form—that this distinction is attributed. Greek language would not necessarily be corrupted by the ruses of the politics which guide philosophy. An apologue—rather than a historical fact—teaches us the origin of the saying "cursed is he who teaches his son Greek wisdom" (Sota 49b): the Jews under siege in Jerusalem used to let down money in a basket to the besieger and would haul up an animal destined for a sacrifice, which would protect the city. Someone who "was learned in Greek wisdom" advised the besiegers to substitute a pig for a ram. Then the city was taken by the enemy, after the very ramparts of Jerusalem were shaken by the raising up of an impure animal. One then curses him who "teaches Greek wisdom to his children." Apologue which causes forgotten presuppositions to intervene. But where the essential is perhaps in "political wisdom," of an intervention, minimal in appearance—the substitution of one animal for the other—which makes a system and a State totter; or in the lucidity of him who teaches the efficacy of preferring ritual, all the while making use of belief in ritual. Political wisdom. Wisdom of ruse and of betrayal.

ESTHER STAROBINSKI: Political only?

E.L.: Isn't it possible to discern this wisdom behind art, too, behind a certain mythology, and even behind a certain morality?

ESTHER STAROBINSKI: A certain rationalization.

E.L.: It seems to be accorded to the language. But even if the condemnation of wisdom is not objectively justified, it comes out of talmudic texts, just as the connivance of this wisdom does in politics. This wisdom is, in effect, authorized for those who have to deal with the political authorities and who are used to diplomacy, to ruse, to the ambiguity within a concern for efficacy. It is the Greek vision of the world, in which everything possible will someday be permitted, that is denounced. The germ of a certain "modernity" and of an efficacy at any cost.

MARC FAESSLER: But would you reject Christianity as being on the side of Greek wisdom?

E.L.: Listen, that almost opens up a question about my religious credo! I am not Christian... For me certainly there are in Christianity many elements which have come from "Greek wisdom" or from Greece, notably the accord, across the very facts of Western history, between evangelical values and the cruelty of political action. History of the righteous and of saints, certainly; but the history of Christianity is not illustrated only by holiness.

MARC FAESSLER: Do you think, if I am not being indiscreet, that what Christians call the "New" Testament can in fact be read as a christological midrash on the Hebrew Bible? For at the interior of Christianity there exist currents of different thoughts, of which the Protestant current is perhaps closer to Jewish thought than the others.

E.L.: It is not for me to chose between Protestantism and Catholicism. Catholic Christianity has a grandeur that I have never failed to recognize, no less than the primordial importance attached to purity on the part of the majority of my Protestant friends. There is in the history of the church something which seems very important to me: the continuity, the idea of the Master (of whom I have no fear), etc. I don't make any distinction... With reference to the essence of your question, there are certainly today Jews who read Christian Scripture according to the model that you envision! Perhaps André Chouraqui, for example. To me personally, this is a foreign reading. But one cannot contest the fact that with the Christianity of today there is, I don't say a dialogue—everybody abuses this term—but a possible contact within a consciousness of shared ancestry, notably in the face of the entirety of the world, all this immense humanity which has not known our common Scriptures. Ecumenicalism certainly has, among its inspirations, the appearance of a billion human beings of the Third World who perceive, between Judaism and Christianity, but a single discussion that opposes two sects of the same spiritual family. Your question is not an indiscreet question; it is a question shared by people who know each other, as is my response. But I have never experienced the reading of the New Testament, since I live the reading of the Old Testament, in which I am not missing anything.

GABRIELLE DUFOUR: I have a Spanish friend who calls himself a Judeo-Christian. He is a Marrano, the son of converted Jews of Spain who camouflaged their Judaism for centuries. He has rediscovered his roots and reads the New Testament in "Judeo-Christian."

E.L.: Among Christians there are certain ones who are shocked by the very word "Judeo-Christian": what could such a contradiction in terms mean? Of course, such shock is not without a little taint of anti-Semitism. But the Judeo-Christian is a reality just the same.

JEAN HALPÉRIN: I want to come back to the dialectic between the universal and the specific. We Jews claim a certain form of specificity comprised by revelation itself. In *Ethics and Infinity* you say that there are very great literary works which are perhaps also of the essence of revelation. How would the passage be situated between this specificity to which we adhere and this universal that we bear?

E.L.: It is difficult. But perhaps the consciousness of the universal does not, in Judaism, begin with the agreement of everybody concerning a truth, but with the responsibility for everybody. Perhaps, thus, universal history is reflected in Jewish history. Hardly an easy destiny, difficult to speak about it.

JEAN HALPÉRIN: At the beginning of your lecture you define knowledge as a relationship of the same to the other in which the other is dispossessed of his strangeness. Could you say more about this phrase "dispossesed of his strangeness"?

E.L.: It's a metaphor. In reality, what appears to me, appears in my world, is absolutely open to me and, in this sense, is no longer strange to me. It is immanent. Immanence, that is the world, our world, the world which is given to us and in which the other is no more than the same. That does not correspond to my relationship to God. My relationship to the transcendence of God is the relation to transcendence as such, without God entering into the world. Within what one could call the phenomenological tradition of the history of philosophy, immanence is thought as a supreme grace of the spirit: the hidden God is but God, incompletely. I asked yesterday if the rapport with the transcendent as such is simply something imperfectly arrived at, if religion as relation with what reason has not equaled does not have its own excellence. My thesis consists in affirming that sociality is a rapport entirely other than that which is established in knowledge and that sociality itself is commanded by the word of God, which is the face of the other. Consequently, sociality, and this is very important, would not be a degradation of unity and would not arise from the Neoplatonic tradition. Did not Plotinus teach that even the One conscious of itself is already multiple, already degraded? Society would be at the limit, a degraded unity.

JEAN BOREL: But Damascius already refused this aspect of Plotinianism.

E.L.: Exactly. But we continue to speak of sociality as if it were an incomplete confusion or incomplete concreteness of unity between terms. One continues to deplore the fact that the lovers are two, while in my opinion it is this duality which counts the most. That is its excellence, irreducible to fusion. It is necessary that there be relation to transcendence as such. It is not necessary that the rapport cause transcendence to lose the strangeness that belongs to its majesty.

GABRIELLE DUFOUR: Today one valorizes difference... another kind of uniformity.

E.L.: My assertion concerns the relation itself. I contest the application of the term *relation* to time. Because relation still supposes the absolute ideal simultaneity of terms. They are together in the relation. That is why I try to formulate time as diachrony. It is time precisely which separates the terms of the relation.

But our discussion around Christianity is very important, and I would not wish it to be forgotten, and I would not wish it to be misunderstood. It is certainly a domain where we are brought into proximity. We can here understand each other or at least speak, but—I would like to come back to what I have said to you—Jews cannot experience or read the Gospels in the same atmosphere as they do the Old Testament and its secular commentaries, through which they have formed their sensibilities. Doubtless when one wishes to formulate the differences, one says things which are utterly impoverished (for instance, "You lack this..."; "Well, you lack that..."). There is also and above all the personality of Jesus, with whom the Christian tradition has a unique relation which is notably missing from rabbinic sensibility. Perhaps from the fact that Jesus has been associated, in the course of history, with persecutions. The Crusades were carried forward by the figure of the cross. These memories are very alive, almost as alive as those of the *shoah*. In my opinion, that is the veritable difference, more profound than the ideological oppositions to which one tries to reduce them.

JEAN BOREL: I ask myself if there is not in the Christian message itself something that we Christians do not tolerate. In your article "God and

Philosophy," you write: "As responsible, I do not leave off emptying my-self of myself. There is infinite increase in this exhausting of oneself, in which the subject is not simply an awareness of this expenditure but its locus and event and, so to speak, goodness." Reading this, I cannot not think in Christian terms.

E.L.: … of Jesus Christ…

JEAN BOREL: … of kenosis, of all that has been said in our tradition about kenosis.

E.L.: I accept kenosis, absolutely.

JEAN BOREL: I cannot go further into the universality of kenosis than when I read this passage of yours. We Christians have objectified all this in the person of Christ to such an extent that his universalizing function in his project of effectuation in each believer has been occulted.

E.L.: That is why I was saying: in seeking out differences I say only ba-nalities, but in finding resemblances I say things which are valuable for everyone.

JEAN BOREL: It seems that here we are touching on a capital issue of your thinking, where one rejoins, beyond confessions and our traditions, a center that is one of the achievements of the Bible as such.

E.L.: Absolutely, you know, within a Jewish context my reference to kenosis has provoked objections. Recently, I was supposed to translate the Hebrew word *anav*, a very important term which characterizes Moses in Numbers 12:3. I translated it as "humility." That gave rise to an objection. Someone said to me: "Call it 'modesty.'" He caught a whiff of kenosis… We took out the dictionary, an altogether elementary procedure. *'Anavah* was translated by "modesty," but looking up the word *humility*, we found *'anavah*.[5] The term *tsiny'ut* which can signify modesty, should rather have been translated by "decency," but in Tractacte Megillah 13b it signifies the justice of the just. But this is in reality a separate discussion. I get accused of defending kenosis.

DAVID BANON: It is associated with the epiphany of the other.

E.L.: One says: the face of the other. But what I say about the face of the neighbor, the Christian probably says about the face of Christ.

I have already told you about my admiration for the person and the

work of a nineteenth-century Lithuanian rabbi, the student of the celebrated Gaon of Vilna, Rabbi Haïm of Volozin. His posthumous publication, *Nefesh Hahaïm* [*The Soul of Life*], which appeared in 1824, is one of
the most astonishing syntheses of traditional Judaism, and it is, moreover,
the work of an eminent talmudist and Kabbalist whose vision of Judaism
could never be confused with the subjectivizing so frequent in our era,
impressions which, however brilliant on the surface, should inspire but
mistrust. It is not my intention to resume for you this synthesis, in which
the man who says "I" is interpreted as assuming in this conduct a responsibility for other persons. Permit me to say a few words solely about
the conception of prayer that this text proposes. True prayer would never
be prayer *for oneself*. In truth, one prays always for the others, or for Israel,
whose trials and persecutions signify the attainment of the glory of God
as manifested in revelation. And here is the most striking thing: man in
distress, torn in two by pain, can pray for himself, but only because the
suffering of the particular is always the suffering of God who, in the
words of Psalm 91:15, "is with him in distress." The meaning of true
prayer for oneself is a prayer for a God who suffers. This is kenosis, insofar as Judaism announces it: the humility of God in his association with
the misery of the miserable! And one can no doubt invert the terms of this
theology of suffering and understand God from the starting point of a
suffering that, in my suffering, comes to Him. One can say that He who
suffers in my suffering—be it a suffering I have merited on account of my
sin—is God: an intimacy or correlation which is expressed in another
midrash according to which God himself "puts on tefillin," or phylacter-
ies.[6] These are the little boxes containing biblical verses which are attached
to the cords that are tied around the left arm and that surround the head
of the faithful during morning prayer. That God would be constrained by
the same obligation as man might seem a ridiculous anthropomorphism.
But the midrash knows a lot more about this, since in the tefillin of the
children of Israel the following verse is inscribed: "Hear O Israel, the Lord
is our God, the Lord is one" (Deut. 6:4). In the tefillin of the Eternal, one
will find inscribed the verse from 2 Samuel 7:23, "Who is like unto Israel,
your people, unique on this Earth!" Beyond the primitive anthropomorphism, there is a rigorous correspondence of the unique to the unique. In
all the pain of here and now, the suffering of the Most-High. The
midrash knows this too: "That my head be comforted, that my arm be
comforted"—prayer of God whose head and arm are tied around by the

cords of the tefillin and who carries all the weight of the suffering of
Israel—that is to say, all the suffering of humanity, even that suffering
which it owes to sin. The prayers of men who suffer the torture or Passion
of God. Is this kenosis? It is there, I think, that it comes close to it. My
formulation about "God who comes to mind" expresses the life of God.
Descent of God! In German it is still better: "wenn Gott fällt uns ein"
("when God falls under sense"). This comes back to what we were saying
earlier about proximity. It is perhaps because of this that Vatican II invites
Jews and Christians to instruct each other mutually on their doctrines. As
if this conversation were more fruitful than the struggle of one for the
conversion of the other.

GABRIELLE DUFOUR: Earlier you used the word *kenosis*.

E.L.: Yes, we agree on this Greek word!

JEAN HALPÉRIN : What would be the equivalent in Hebrew?

E.L.: I said it earlier: *'anavah*. A talmudic text, Megillah 31a, says of
God: "Wherever you find grandeur of the Holy One, blessed be He, you
will find his humility (*anvetanuto*)."

GABRIELLE DUFOUR: It is paradoxical, because the word *kenosis* resonates for me in a Hegelian or Marxist content, influenced over the centuries by the Neoplatonic scheme, a descent and a fall...

E.L.: The descent and the fall are its perfection, its elevation. In
Bossuet's sense when he speaks of the "glorious abasements of Christian
charity."

GABRIELLE DUFOUR: But Hegelianism has done a crazy injustice to
the Christian mentality. It has caused us to understand the abasement of
Christ, the abasement of God in the incarnation, in a completely false
fashion.

E.L.: No, listen, abasement has an exalting sense for the readers of
scriptures. Higher than the high, as in Psalm 113, where God is praised
in his height and where the elevation increases to the extent that his regard abases itself, down to the barren woman more miserable than the
miserable.

GABRIELLE DUFOUR: But the descent itself is here a height, whereas in
the dialectical scheme it is a passage. That is completely different.

LAURENT ADERT: You often let the words *responsibility* and *response* play on each other. Is the minimal status of the ethical relation to the other simply to be obliged to respond?

E.L.: To be obliged to respond is no small thing. It is not necessary to approach it in its derivative and banal stage. It is not the formality of some judicial interrogation leaning on public strength. There is here an extraordinary obedience—service without servitude!—to the uprightness of the face of the other man whose irrecusable imperative does not proceed from a threat and whose incomparable authority commands across a suffering precisely as the word of God. It is there that God probably comes to mind. Response demanded in this obligation, though never exhaustive and never annulling responsibility. I would like to step back from the very language of communication to this response demanded, just as I would like to return the psychism of consciousness back to the theo-logy of the idea of infinity. I say, I would like to, but so much research is still necessary.

ESTHER STAROBINSKI: I would like to come back to what you said about prophecy. You describe it in its ethical sense. But there is also in Jewish thought an intellectualist interpretation: prophecy as a perfectly purified intelligence.

E.L.: That is Maimonides!

ESTHER STAROBINSKI: Do you see in such an interpretation something foreign to Judaism or something that is integrated there?

E.L.: I do not have the impertinence to contest Maimonides. Prophecy may precisely signify this perfectly purified intelligence. I think that in its ethical signification this notion of purity and this superlative are less metaphorical.

JEAN HALPÉRIN: What about the talmudic tradition, according to which prophecy has ceased since the destruction of the Second Temple? To the extent that prophecy represents a category of the ethical, one would like to be able to believe that prophecy continues under one form or another.

E.L.: There is first of all the current tradition which affirms the end of the prophetic era with Malachi, the last of the prophets, and the opening of the rabbinic era, the era of the interpreters and the sages, the *ha-*

khamim. But this opening is also that of an alternative. Is the new inspiration, that of the exegete, a degradation or an exaltation of the old one? According to a saying from the tractate Baba Batra 12a, "The *hakham* is superior to the prophet." Would Rabbi Akiba then pass *before* Moses? His spiritual power, which resides, no doubt, in the vigor of his interpreter's dialectic, is described by the metaphor of someone who "makes mountains crumble by rubbing one against the other." Tractate Horayoth 14a designates the alternative between prophecy and rabbinic exegesis by an audacious or picturesque formula: "Some say that Mount Sinai is the strongest, and others that the one who tears up mountains is the strongest." An alternative in which, in the last analysis, neither one of the two terms would be rejected.

In Tractate Megillah 9a–b, the concordance between the seventy-two translators of the Pentateuch into Greek is taken for a sign of heavenly approval because they were working without communicating among themselves. Prior to all exegesis, the inspired origin of the translation of Scripture into Greek. Here is an admission by the "doctors" of the Talmud of a prophetic message which was produced in an epoch well posterior to "the end of prophecy." All this was contradicted in Baba Metsia 59b in the famous discussion between Rabbi Yehoshua and Rabbi Eliezer in which the former invoked the celestial signs to permit him to justify his thesis.

But already the alternative—end or continuation—of prophecy admits a plurality of meanings. You know the passage from Numbers 11:24–29, where seventy elders are attached to Moses to comfort him in his task. These verses are commented on—or oriented or elucidated—by a midrash on page 17a of Tractate Sanhedrin: all the tribes of Israel had to be equally represented among the seventy elders; but this number could not be divided by twelve; Moses thus brought together seventy-two names and, in order to know the divine will, proceeded with a kind of lottery. Two blank ballots permitted the necessary division and subtraction. "Eldad and Medad remained in the camp" (v. 26). And seventy elders met around the Tent of Meeting. But when the seventy received the spirit of God and prophesied (v. 25), the two who were excluded started to prophesy back in the camp, which they had not left. The midrash also suggests that the two found themselves in the camp on account of their extreme humility; they weren't judged worthy of prophecy. Thus, doubtless, the Talmud wished to suggest that the two excluded ones were in truth the two chosen ones. Would humility permit one to merit the spirit of God and of prophecy? Or would it already be this very spirit and these very prophecies? Spirit and prophecy of Eldad and Medad deploying themselves in full view of the camp and scandalizing Joshua (v. 27–28). But is this not the very prophecy that Moses wishes for all Israel (v. 29)? It is as if the spirit of God resulting from humility were the very humanity of man. Here, once again, is kenosis, identical to the spirituality of the spirit. Can such a prophecy have an end in history? Verse 25 of Numbers 11, recounting the prophecy of the seventy elders "grouped by division" that the midrash evokes, has the words "and so they prophesied" followed by two others, *velo yasafu*, translated as "but they did so no more." They were the prophets of a single day or of one time. To them the midrash opposes Eldad and Medad, who prophesied without ever losing the gift of prophecy.

I'll not hide from you an opposing opinion with reference to the meaning of *velo yasafu*. According to the translation of Onkelos these words signify "And they [the seventy elders] did not stop," that is, they did not stop prophesying.

A midrash from Sanhedrin 17a recalls in a significant fashion the formula *lo yasaf*, which is applied in Deuteronomy 5:19 to the eternal voice of God whose echo has never stopped. The excellence of Eldad and Medad would rest, according to this midrash, on the past tense—"they [the elders] prophesi*ed*"—of verse 25 of Numbers 11, to which is opposed the present—"they [Eldad and Medad] prophes*y*"—of Numbers 11:27. They still prophesy. The prophecy endures even today within the oral tradition enveloping the prophetic word, infinitely renewed and signifying in its contemporaneity through the speaking of the *hakhamim*, the sages.

DAVID BANON: Can one put into relation what you say in your work with certain themes of the Reb Soloveitchik as they appear in *The Lonely Man of Faith* and *The Man of the Law*? I am thinking notably of the "He," which could be compared with your notion of illeity, or to formulas like "causing infinity to descend in the finite." Then there is the attraction for Rabbi Haïm of Volozin, of whom he is one of the epigones.

E.L.: I cannot accept being compared to such eminent talmudists. I read mostly *haggadah*, and I came to its utilization beginning from traditional philosophy. I have thought for a long time that this was a culture "on the side." I had a deeper contact with the Talmud later, in the pres-

ence of M. Shoshani. He turned over to me neither his immense knowledge nor certainly his incomparable intelligence, but he did show me how
one should approach these texts—this unattainable level. Next to him,
what I do is nothing, and I am nothing. He was a terrifying dialectician.
He could, when he wished to, defend one day to the same students almost the contrary of what he had taught the day before. With an extraordinary virtuosity but also, each time, with new dimensions of meaning! I conserved from him an unforgettable and incommunicable
recollection of the life of the spirit.

TRANSLATED BY JILL ROBBINS

Glossary

BEFINDLICHKEIT: "State-of-mind," as Macquarrie and Robinson translate it in sections 29–31 of *Being and Time*. In Heidegger's usage, *Befindlichkeit* is connected to *befindlich* and *sich befinden*. State-of-mind is equiprimordial to understanding. "In a state-of-mind *Dasein* is always brought before itself, and has always found itself, not in the sense of coming across itself by perceiving itself [*wahrnehmendes Sich-vorfinden*], but in the sense of finding itself in the mood that it has [*gestimmtes Sichbefinden*]."

BETH MIDRASH: Lit., "house of study." A school for studying the Torah, the Talmud, and the commentaries.

BUND: A broadly based Marxist organization of secular Jews founded in Vilna in 1897 and strongly opposed to Zionism.

CONATUS ESSENDI: Formulation used by Spinoza in his *Ethics*, part III, prop. VI: "Everything, insofar as it is in itself, endeavors to persist in its own being [*unaquaeque res, quantum in se est, in suo esse perseverare conatur*]." Although arguably Spinoza is not thinking being in the way Levinas does, in Levinas's usage this essential tendency, "the perseverance in being," becomes an anti-Heideggerian formula.

GEMARA: A later commentary on the Mishnah. The Mishnah and the Gemara together make up the bulk of the Talmud.

GEVIERT: The "fourfold"—earth, sky, gods, and mortals—as Heidegger articulates it in the 1954 essay, "Building Dwelling Thinking." It can be described a way of thinking finitude in nonsystematic (i.e., non Hegelian) language.

HAGGADAH (also AGGADAH): From *le-haggid*, "to tell." Traditionally defined as everything in talmudic literature which is not *halakhah* (Jewish law). It includes the amplification of biblical narratives, legendary, imaginative, and speculative material.

HALAKHAH: An accepted decision in rabbinic law. Also refers to those parts of the Talmud concerned with legal matters.

HASIDISM: A religious movement founded in the eighteenth century by Israel ben Eliezar, otherwise known as the Baal Shem Tov, and characterized by a mystical-emotional view of Judaism.

HASKALAH: Hebrew term for the Jewish Enlightenment, when Western European Jews embraced the ideals of the eighteenth-century philosophical movement. In the East, its impact on Jews in czarist Russia was felt almost a hundred years later.

HESED: Often translated as "goodness," "kindness," or "loving-kindness," this comprehensive word corresponds fairly closely to the Latin *pietas*. A relational concept with an active, social meaning, Simon the Righteous mentions it in the Talmud as one of the three pillars of Judaism. *Gemilut hasadim* is an act by means of which one demonstrates one's response to someone, in obedience to him or out of loyalty to him. It encompasses a wider range of human kindness than does "charity." Charity can be given only with one's money, *gemilut hasadim* by personal service ("with his body") and with material goods.

KADDISH: A prayer recited by mourners after the death of a parent or child or on the anniversary of their deaths.

KEHRE: Lit., "turn." Term used to describe the turning point of Heidegger's career, in which *Dasein* is displaced in favor of *Gelassenheit*, "openness," and a radical thought of being's own self-lighting.

KENOSIS: Within Catholic theology, the term denotes the condescension or humility of God in the Incarnation. Its first biblical usage is in Phillipians 2:6–11: "His state was divine, yet he did not cling to his equality with God; but *emptied himself* to assume the condition of a slave, and became as men are." Levinas uses it as a primordial description of responsible subjectivity.

MIDRASH: From the Hebrew *darash*, "to seek or search out," the word denotes interpretation or exegesis, a searching out of the text's nonobvious meaning. This genre of biblical exegesis flourished between second and fifth centuries C.E. The term designates both a procedure—or attitude—within rabbinic interpretation and also the actual literary compilations of rabbinic interpretations, in which the original interpretations, many of them first delivered and transmitted orally, were eventually collected.

MISHNAH: "Repetition." An authoritative codification of Jewish law and practice put into its final form around 200 C.E.

MITNAGDIM: Lit., "the opponents." The rabbinic opponents of Hasidism in eighteenth-century Eastern European Judaism.

NOEMA: The object meant as such, in Husserl's understanding. *Noesis* is the act of consciousness correlative to such a *noema*.

NUMERUS CLAUSUS: A discriminatory law passed in 1887 in czarist Russia limiting the number of Jews allowed to attend schools sponsored by the government.

PENTATEUCH: The first five books of the Hebrew Bible.

RAHAMIN: "Mercy." Levinas notes: "The word contains a reference to the word *Rekhem*, 'uterus': it is a mercy that is like an emotion of maternal entrails." *Collected Philosophical Papers*, 147n6.

SEPTUAGINT (from Lat. *septuaginta*, "seventy"; abbreviated LXX): The Old Greek translation of the Hebrew Bible, so called because of a legend that holds that the Pentateuch was first translated into Greek by seventy (or seventy-two) Jewish scholars who, though working in complete isolation, nevertheless produced identical translations. This legend is found in the Letter of Aristeas.

TETRAGRAMMATON: The Divine Names, which consists in Hebrew of the four letters (transliterated) YHWH.

TZEDAKAH: Lit., "righteousness," although the primary sense of the word, as it is used throughout rabbinic literature, is "charity," or helping the needy by gifts.

YESHIVA: Hebrew term for a Jewish religious school of higher learning.

Notes

Introduction

1. Jacques Derrida, "Violence and Metaphysics," in *Writing and Difference*, trans. Alan Bass (Chicago: University of Chicago Press, 1978), 111.

2. Theodore de Boer, *The Rationality of Transcendence* (Amsterdam: J.C. Gieben, 1997), 49.

3. Derrida, "Violence and Metaphysics," 104.

4. Maurice Blanchot, *The Infinite Conversation*, trans. Susan Hanson (Minneapolis: University of Minnesota Press, 1993), 212.

5. Jean-François Lyotard, *Just Gaming*, trans. Wlad Godzich (Minneapolis: University of Minnesota Press, 1985), 22.

6. Martin Heidegger, *Being and Time*, trans. John Macquarrie and Edward Robinson (New York: Harper and Row, 1962).

7. Jacques Derrida, "At This Very Moment in This Work Here I Am," trans. Ruben Berezdivin, in *Re-Reading Levinas*, ed. Robert Bernasconi and Simon Critchley (Bloomington: Indiana University Press, 1991).

8. Roger Burgraevve's *Emmanuel Levinas et la socialité de l'argent* (Louvain: Peeters, 1997) contains Levinas's essay (which first appeared in the *Cahiers de l'Herne* devoted to Levinas) and a detailed commentary on it.

9. Mordechai Altshuler refers to "the rapid chain of events from occupation to obliteration" in *Jews and Jewish Life in Russia and the Soviet Union*, ed. Yaacov Ro'i (Essex: Frank Cass, 1995), 181. See also *The Holocaust in the Soviet Union: Studies and Sources on the Destruction of the Jews in the Nazi-Occupied Territories of the USSR, 1941–1945*, ed. Lucjan Dobroszycki and Jeffrey S. Gurock (London: M.E. Sharpe, 1993); Abraham Tory, *Surviving the Holocaust: The Kovno Ghetto Diary*, ed. Martin Gilbert, trans. Jerzy Michalowicz (Cambridge, Mass.: Harvard University Press, 1990); *Hidden History of the Kovno Ghetto* (Boston:

Little, Brown, & Company, 1997); William W. Mishell, *Kaddish for Kovno: Life and Death in a Lithuanian Ghetto, 1941–1945* (Chicago: Chicago Review Press, 1998).

10. The fact of the concealment of the Holocaust in the Soviet Union is what leads one commentator, Zvi Kolitz, to refer to the extermination of the Jews in Lithuania as not just physical but metaphysical. See Dobroszycki and Gurock, *The Holocaust in the Soviet Union,* and Ro'i, *Jews and Jewish Life.* Ilya Ehrenburg and Vassily Grossman's *The Black Book* was translated into English by John Glad and James S. Levine (New York: Holocaust Library, 1981). A recent French translation, with the missing section on Lithuania restored, was published in 1995 by Editions Actes Sud.

11. Salomon Malka, *Monsieur Chouchani: L'énigme d'un maître du XXe siècle* (Paris: Editions Jean-Claude Lattès, 1994).

12. Elie Wiesel, "The Wandering Jew" in *Legends of Our Time* (New York: Avon Books, 1968), 121–42, and "The Death of My Teacher" in *One Generation After* (New York: Random House, 1970), 120–25.

13. Elie Wiesel, 1994 interview with Salomon Malka in *Monsieur Chouchani.*

Interview with François Poirié

Note: Conducted by François Poirié in 1986, this interview with Emmanuel Levinas—a condensed form of which first appeared in *Art Press* (March 1986)— was published in François Poirié, *Emmanuel Levinas: Qui êtes-vous?* (Lyon: La Manufacture, 1987): 63–136; rpt. Actes Sud, 1996.

1. Under Alexander II, the Jews benefited from the "great reforms" of the 1860s. Alexander II repealed the severe "Cantonist" laws (which ordered the conscription of Jewish youths into the army) and granted the right of residence outside the Pale of Settlement and throughout Russia to selected groups of "useful" Jews, which in 1861 included university graduates.

2. For Husserl's letter, which was to Roman Ingarden, see Ingarden, ed., *Briefe an Roman Ingarden* (The Hague: Nijhoff, 1968), 56.

3. Reprinted in *Discovering Existence with Husserl,* 3–31.

4. Pascal, *Pensées,* no. 295.

5. The phrase "I am responsible for everyone and everything and I more than all the others" is stated by Father Zosima in book six of Dostoevsky's *The Brothers Karamazov,* entitled "Notes in the Life of God of the Elder Zosima" (redacted by his disciple, Alyosha Karamazov), and iterated by each of the characters in the novel.

6. The conversation to which Levinas alludes in which "defenselessness" is at issue is "Judaism and Christianity after Franz Rosenzweig." In that conversation,

conducted in German, Hemmerle and Levinas used the term *Hilflösigkeit*, or "humility."

7. Since the time of Levinas's statement in 1985, the Church has recognized the state of Israel.

8. "Apropos of Buber: Some Notes." See *Outside the Subject*, 40–48.

Interview with Myriam Anissimov

Note: Conducted by Myriam Anissimov, this interview was originally published in *Les Nouveaux Cahiers* 82 (1985): 30–35.

1. The finest and most influential modern Hebrew poet, Bialik (1873–1934) was often hailed as the poet laureate of Jewish nationalism.

2. In October 1961, a certain number of intellectuals, at the behest of *Les Temps Modernes*, Jean-Paul Sartre's journal, signed a manifesto in which one could read: "By remaining passive French citizens would become complicitous in the racist explosion whose theater Paris has now become; we refuse to make any distinction between the Algerians piled up at the Palais des Sports while waiting to be 'dispatched' and the Jews stored at Drancy before their deportation."

Interview with Salomon Malka

Note: Conducted by Salomon Malka, this interview was originally published in *L'Arche*; rpt. in Malka, *Lire Levinas* (Paris: Cerf, 1984): 103–14.

1. Levinas refers to a 1965 debate regarding statutory limitations for Nazi war crimes in which Vladimir Jankelvitch intervened. Concerning Heidegger, Jankélévitch asked: "Why would we pardon those who regret their errors so little and so rarely?" Jankélévitch, "Pardonner?" in *L'Imprescriptible* (Paris: Seuil, 1971); "Shall We Pardon Them?" trans. Ann Hobel, *Critical Inquiry* 22 (1996): 552–72.

2. The "thirty-six righteous ones" (*lamed vav zaddikim*) are, according to a tradition which originated in the Babylonian Talmud and became renowned in fiction and folklore, especially in Kabbalah and Hasidic legends, the minimal number of anonymous righteous men living in the world in every generation.

3. Levinas seems to be referring to *Greph: Qui a peur de la philosophie?* (Paris: Flammarion, 1977).

4. *Guide of the Perplexed*, 1:33 and 1:34.

Vocation of the Other

Note: Conducted by Emmanuel Hirsch, this interview was originally published in *Racismes: L'autre et son visage*, ed. Emmanuel Hirsch (Paris: Cerf, 1988), 89–102, a collection of interviews with diverse authors, including Levinas, a psychiatrist, a geneticist, a legal scholar, a historian, an activist, and several theologians. The editor unifies these responses to the problem of racism under the conceptual figure of face.

1. Elisabeth de Fontenay, a professor of philosophy at the University of Paris I, played a central role in helping to plan the Colloquium of French Jewish Intellectuals.

2. Levinas often writes this word with double hyphens: *des-inter-essement* (disinter-estedness). Its special force in Levinas's later work can be seen at the beginning of the first chapter of *Otherwise than Being*, where he states that *esse* is *interesse* (essence is interest). The particle of separation *dis-* emphasizes what Adriaan Peperzak terms "a movement away from the interested business of being" (*Basic Philosophical Writings*, 185). The term also plays on the etymology of *inter* ("between") and *esse* ("being"), suggesting that if essence is inter-esse ("between being"), that is because it is relation and not a being.

3. The 1987 preface to the German translation of *Totality and Infinity*; rpt. *Entre Nous*, 197–200.

4. The French word *altruisme* comes from *altrui*, variant of *autrui* ("other") in Old French, oblique case of *autre* ("other") from the Latin *alter*.

Being-for-the-Other

Note: Conducted by Jean-Christophe Aeschlimann in 1989, this previously untitled interview was originally published in a collection devoted to Levinas entitled *Répondre d'autrui*, ed. Jean-Christophe Aeschlimann (Neuchâtel, Switzerland: A la Baconnière, 1989), 9–16.

1. This analysis, criticized by Simone de Beauvoir in *The Second Sex*, appears under the subheading "Eros" in part 4 of *Time and the Other*. See especially Levinas's 1979 preface to the reissue of *Time and the Other*, where he first states that he has changed his mind.

2. In "The Anaximander Fragment," published in *Early Greek Thinking* (trans. David Farrell Krell and Frank A. Capuzzi [San Francisco: Harper and Row, 1984], 41), Heidegger asks: "How is what lingers awhile in presence unjust? What is unjust about it? Is it not the right of whatever is present that in each case it linger awhile, endure, and so fulfill its presence?"

The Philosopher and Death

Note: Conducted by Christian Chabanis in 1982, this interview was originally published in Chabanis's *La mort, un terme ou un commencement?* (Paris: Librairie Arthème Fayard, 1982), 341–52.

1. Pascal, *Pensées*, no. 455.

Being-Toward-Death and "Thou Shalt Not Kill"

Note: Conducted, in German, by Florian Rötzer, this interview was originally published in Rötzer, *Französische Philosophen im Gespräch* (Munich: Klaus Boer Verlag, 1987), 89–100.

1. The questioner alludes, almost verbatim, to Hegel's *Phenomenology of Spirit*, the section on lordship and bondage, para. 184. Note that Levinas's answer ignores the allusion altogether.

2. A reference to Heidegger's discussion of the tool and the modality of the ready-to-hand (*Zuhandenheit*) in *Being and Time*, section 15.

Intention, Event, and the Other

Note: Conducted, in German, by Christoph von Wolzogen, this interview was originally published in *Humanismus des anderen Menschen*, trans. Ludwig Wenzler (Hamburg: Felix Meiner Verlag, 1989), 132–50.

1. *Destruktion* (dismantling or destroying), as Heidegger discusses it in section 6 of *Being and Time*, is not equivalent to blowing something up; its positive meaning is a critical philosophical encounter with tradition.

2. *Husserliana*, 6:15.

3. Manuscript fragments from fall 1887, in Friedrich Nietzsche, *Sämtliche Werke* (Munich: de Bruyter, 1980), vol. 12, p. 564.

4. For the expression *worauf es eigenlich hinauswill*, see *Husserliana*, 6:73.

5. Heidegger's 1922 text was not published until 1989 in the *Dilthey Jahrbuch für Philosophie und Geschichte der Geisteswissenschaften* (bd. 6); *Phenomenological Interpretations with Respect to Aristotle: Indication of the Hermeneutical Situation*, trans. Michael Baur, *Man and World* 25 (1992), 355–93.

6. In all likelihood, this is a reference to the 1863–66 *Grundriss der Geschichte der Philosophie von Thales bis auf die Gegenwart*, written by Friedrich Überweg.

Reality Has Weight

Note: Conducted by Christian Descamps, this previously untitled interview was published in *Entretiens avec 'Le Monde'*, ed. Christian Delacampagne (Paris: La Découverte, 1984), 138–47.

Philosophy, Justice, and Love

Note: Conducted by R. Fornet and A. Gomez, this previously untitled interview was originally published in abridged form in *Esprit* 8–9 (1983), 8–17; rpt. *Entre Nous*, 121–39. The English translation appeared in *Entre Nous*, trans. Michael B.

Smith and Barbara Harshav (New York: Columbia University Press, 1994), 103–
21. Reprinted with the permission of the publisher.

1. "Si j'appartiens à un peuple, ce peuple et mes proches sont aussi mes
prochains. Ils ont droit à la défense comme ceux qui ne sont pas mes proches."

2. Maurice Merleau-Ponty, *Le visible et l'invisible* (Paris, Gallimard, 1964), 185,
194–95; *The Visible and the Invisible*, trans. Alphonso Lingis (Evanston, Ill.:
Northwestern University Press, 1968), 141, 147–48.

3. The comment was Derrida's ("Violence and Metaphysics," 145n79).

4. Stéphane Mosès, *Système et révélation* (Paris: Seuil, 1982), preface by
Emmanuel Levinas, 7–16; *System and Revelation*, trans. Catherine Tihanyi
(Detroit: Wayne State University Press, 1992), 13–22.

5. "Apropos de Buber: Quelques notes," originally published in the collection
*Qu'est-ce que l'homme? Philosophie/psychanalyse: Hommage à Alphonse de Waelhens
(1911–1981)* (Brussels: Facultés Universitaires Saint Louis, 1982), 127–33; rpt.
Outside the Subject, 40–48.

6. Jean-Luc Marion, *Dieu sans l'être* (Paris: Fayard, 1982); *God without Being*,
trans. Thomas A. Carlson (Chicago: University of Chicago Press, 1991).

The Awakening of the I

Note: Conducted by Roger Pol-Droit, this previously untitled interview was published in *Les imprévus de l'histoire* (Montpellier: Fata Morgana, 1994), 203–10.

In the Name of the Other

Note: Conducted by Luc Ferry, Raphaël Hadas-Lebel, and Sylvaine Pasquier, this
interview was published in *L'Express* (July 6, 1990).

1. In this 1929 letter, discovered in 1989 in the Baden government archives,
Heidegger complains of "the Jewification of the German spirit" (*Die Verjudung
des deutschen Geistes*).

2. The desecration of Carpentras cemetery took place in May 1990.

3. Shabbath 31a: "Do not do unto others what you do not want to be done to
you. And for the rest, go study!"

4. "Politics After" was reprinted in *Beyond the Verse*, 188–95.

The Other, Utopia, and Justice

Note: Conducted by Jacques Message and Joel Roman, this interview was originally published in *Autrement* 102 (November 1988), 53–60, in a special issue devoted to the history of philosophy, which included essays by Jürgen Habermas,

Jacques Derrida, Francis Jacques, Pierre Macherey, Claude Lefort, Jean-Luc Nancy, and Paul Ricœur. It was reprinted in *Entre Nous*. The English translation appeared in *Entre Nous*, trans. Michael B. Smith and Barbara Harshav, (New York: Columbia University Press, 1994), 223–33. Reprinted with permission of the publisher.

    1. "Martin Heidegger et l'ontologie," *Revue philosophique de la France et de l'étranger* 113 (1932): 395–431; rpt. *En découvrant l'existence avec Husserl et Heidegger*, 53–76.

    2. This 1987 colloquium was published as *Heidegger: Questions ouvertes* (Paris: Osiris, 1988). Levinas's lecture, "Dying For," was reprinted in *Entre Nous*, 207–17.

The Proximity of the Other

Note: Conducted by Anne-Catherine Benchelah, this interview was originally published in *Phreatique* 39 (1986), 121–27.

Who Shall Not Prophesy?

Note: Conducted by Angelo Bianchi, this interview was originally published under the title "Violence du visage" in *Hermeneutica* 5 (1985), 9–18; reprinted in Levinas, *Alterité et transcendance* (Montpellier: Fata Morgana, 1995), 172–83; *Alterity and Transcendence*, trans. Michael B. Smith (New York: Columbia University Press, 1999).

    1. Megillah 8b and 9a–b; "The Translation of Scripture," in *In the Time of the Nations*, 33–54.

    2. Levinas is referring to the *Letter to Aristeas*, a pseudepigraphical document which tells the story of the miraculous origin of the Septuagint and establishes the translation as inspired.

Responsibility and Substitution

Note: Conducted by Augusto Ponzio, this interview appeared in Ponzio, *Sujet et alterité sur Emmanuel Levinas* (Paris: L'Harmatton, 1996), 143–48.

    1. The verse continues, "Do not be afraid of the face of man, for judgment is the Lord's."

On the Usefulness of Insomnia

Note: Conducted by Bertrand Révillon, this interview was published in *Les imprévus de l'histoire* (Montpellier: Fata Morgana, 1994), 199–202.

On Jewish Philosophy

Note: Conducted by Françoise Armengaud, this interview was orginally published in *Revue de métaphysique et de morale* 3 (1985), 296–310, a special issue devoted to the question of Jewish philosophies; rpt. *In the Time of the Nations*, 167–83.

1. [E.L.'s note] This is in keeping with an admirable midrash in Rabbi Ishmael's *Mekilta* which does not hesitate to emphasize, in the format of the Ten Commandments in two columns of five, the prolongation of "I am the Lord thy God" as "Thou shalt not kill." [Levinas gave the reference as Jethro, ch. 5, but I found it in Tractate Bahodesh, ch. 18—Trans.]

2. "Damages Due to Fire," *Nine Talmudic Readings*, 182.

3. *Ethics and Infinity*, 24.

4. "Peace and Proximity," *Basic Philosophical Writings*, 169.

Judaism and Christianity after Franz Rosenzweig

Note: A roundtable discussion, which included Levinas, Bishop Hemmerle, Hans Hermann Henrix, Bernhard Casper, Heinz-Jürger Görtz, and H. J. Heering, originally conducted in German and published in *Zeitgewinn: Messianisches Denken nach Franz Rosenzweig*, ed. Gotthard Fuchs and Hans Hermann Henrix (Frankfurt am Main: Josef Knecht, 1987), 163–84. It was translated and reprinted in an abridged form in *In the Time of the Nations*, 161–66.

1. Claude Vigée, a poet and one of Levinas's closest friends, noted this conversation in *Une voix dans le défilé: Vivre à Jérusalem: Chronique* 1960–1985 (Paris: Nouvelle Cité, 1985), 60–63.

2. This appears to be a reference to Psalm 35:9–10: "Then shall my soul rejoice in the Lord, exulting in his deliverance; / All my bones shall say, O Lord, who is like unto thee?"

Discussion Following "Transcendence and Intelligibility"

Note: This interfaith discussion with Levinas, organized by Jean Halpérin, which included David Banon, Marc Faessler, Esther Starobinski, Gabrielle Dufour, Jean Borel, and Laurent Adert, took place following Levinas's delivery of the lecture "Transcendence and Intelligibility" at the University of Geneva on June 1, 1983. (*Basic Philosophical Writings* contains a translation of this lecture.) Both the lecture and the discussion were originally published in Levinas, *Transcendance et intelligibilité* (Geneva: Labor et Fides, 1984), 33–68.

1. *Discovering Existence with Husserl*, 153–68.

2. Louis Ginzberg assigns this passage to Tanhuma Lek. Louis Ginzberg, *The*

Legends of the Jews, 1:222 and 5:220, To render Levinas's paraphrase of the story, I have freely adapted Ginzberg's version.

3. Menahoth 99b–100a; "Model of the West," *Beyond the Verse*, 13–33.

4. Megillah 9a–b; "The Translation of Scripture," *In the Time of the Nations*, 33–54.

5. Levinas gives the substantive form and not the adjectival *anav* ("humble") because humility accentuates the sense of relinquishment.

6. Berakhot 7b: "And I will take away My hand, and thou shalt see My back." R. Hama b. Bizana said in the name of R. Simon the Pious: "This teaches us that the Holy One, blessed be He, showed Moses the knot of the tefillin."

Glossary

The following sources were consulted in the preparation of the Glossary: Judith Friedlander, *Vilna on the Seine* (New Haven: Yale University Press, 1990); Geoffrey H. Hartman and Sanford Budick, eds., *Midrash and Literature* (New Haven: Yale University Press, 1986); James Kugel, *In Potiphar's House* (San Francisco: Harper, 1990); Alice Stone Nakhimovsky, *Russian-Jewish Literature and Identity* (Baltimore: Johns Hopkins University Press, 1992); *Encyclopaedia Judaica*.

Select Bibliography of Works by Emmanuel Levinas

Alterity and Transcendence. Trans. Michael B. Smith. New York: Columbia University Press, 1999. Originally published as *Alterité et transcendance.* Montpellier: Fata Morgana, 1995.

Basic Philosophical Writings. Ed. Adriaan T. Peperzak, Simon Critchley, and Robert Bernasconi. Bloomington: Indiana University Press, 1996.

Beyond the Verse. Trans. Gary D. Mole. Bloomington: Indiana University Press, 1994. Originally published as *L'au-delà du verset.* Paris: Minuit, 1982.

Collected Philosophical Papers. Trans. Alphonso Lingis. Dordrecht: Martinus Nijhoff, 1987.

De l'évasion. Ed. Jacques Rolland. Montpellier: Fata Morgana, 1982 [1935–36].

Difficult Freedom. Trans. Séan Hand. Baltimore: Johns Hopkins University Press, 1990. Originally published as *Difficile liberté.* Paris: Albin Michel, 1976 [1963].

En découvrant l'existence avec Husserl et Heidegger. Paris: Vrin, 1974 [1967]. Partial translation in *Discovering Existence with Husserl.* Trans. Richard A. Cohen and Michael B. Smith. Evanston: Northwestern University Press, 1998.

Entre Nous. Trans. Michael B. Smith and Barbara Harshav. New York: Columbia University Press, 1998. Originally published as *Entre Nous.* Paris: Grasset, 1991.

Ethics and Infinity: Conversations with Phillipe Nemo. Trans. Richard A. Cohen. Pittsburgh: Duquesne University Press, 1985. Originally published as *Ethique et infini.* Paris: Librarie Arthème Fayard, 1982.

Existence and Existents. Trans. Alphonso Lingis. The Hague: Martinus Nijhoff, 1978. Originally published as *De l'existence à l'existant.* Paris: Vrin, 1974 [1947].

Humanisme de l'autre homme. Montpellier: Fata Morgana, 1972. Translation (without the preface) in *Collected Philosophical Papers.*

In the Time of the Nations. Trans. Michael B. Smith. Bloomington: Indiana University Press, 1994. Originally published as *A l'heure des nations.* Paris: Minuit, 1988.

Nine Talmudic Readings. Trans. Annette Aronowicz. Bloomington: Indiana University Press, 1990. Contains translations of *Quatre lectures talmudiques* (Paris: Minuit, 1968) and *Du sacré au saint* (Paris: Minuit, 1977).

Of God Who Comes to Mind. Trans. Bettina Bergo. Stanford: Stanford University Press, 1998. Originally published as *De Dieu qui vient à l'idée.* Paris: Vrin, 1982.

Otherwise than Being: or, Beyond Essence. Trans. Alphonso Lingis. The Hague: Martinis Nijhoff, 1981. Originally published as *Autrement qu'être: ou, au-delà de l'essence.* The Hague: Martinus Nijhoff, 1974.

Outside the Subject. Trans. Michael B. Smith. Stanford: Stanford University Press, 1994. Originally published as *Hors sujet.* Montpellier: Fata Morgana, 1987.

Proper Names/On Maurice Blanchot. Trans. Michael Smith. Stanford: Stanford University Press, 1996. Contains translations of *Noms propres* (Montpellier: Fata Morgana, 1975) and *Sur Maurice Blanchot* (Montpellier: Fata Morgana, 1975).

Time and the Other. Trans. Richard A. Cohen. Pittsburgh: Duquesne University Press, 1985. Originally published as *Le temps et l'autre.* Montpellier: Fata Morgana, 1979 [1947].

The Theory of Intuition in Husserl's Phenomenology. Trans. André Orianne. Evanston: Northwestern University Press, 1973. Originally published as *La théorie de l'intuition dans la phénoménologie de Husserl.* Paris: Vrin, 1963 [1930].

"The Trace of the Other," in *Deconstruction in Context.* Trans. Alphonso Lingis. Ed. Mark C. Taylor. Chicago: University of Chicago Press, 1986. Originally published as "La trace de l'autre," 1963; reprinted in *En découvrant l'existence avec Husserl et Heidegger,* 187–202.

Totality and Infinity. Trans. Alphonso Lingis. Pittsburgh: Duquesne University Press, 1969. Originally published as *Totalité et infini.* The Hague: Martinus Nijhoff, 1961.

"Useless Suffering," in *The Provocation of Levinas: Rethinking the Other.* Trans. Richard A. Cohen. Ed. Robert Bernasconi and David Wood. London: Routledge, 1988. Originally published as "La Souffrance inutile," in *Les cahiers de la nuit surveillée,* no. 3. Paris: Verdier, 1984.

Index

M E R I D I A N

Crossing Aesthetics